ALL TOMORROW'S FUTURES

FICTIONS THAT DISRUPT

EDITED BY
BENJAMIN GREENAWAY & STEPHEN ORAM

Print Edition
Hardback ISBN: 978-1-7395939-2-6
Paperback ISBN: 978-1-7395939-3-3
Ebook ISBN: 978-1-7395939-4-0
Published by Cybersalon Press 2024

Cover design by Jessica Bell
Interior design by Amie McCracken
Copyright of original contributions retained by the authors.

Welcome to a journey through speculative fictions, where the possibilities of tomorrow are explored like never before.

In a new collaborative approach, renowned experts, armed with their deep knowledge of justice, energy, digital money, longevity and learning, join forces with talented authors to weave narratives that transcend the future that you may currently believe is inevitable.

Situated in 'real-life' between accelerationism and scepticism, this volume of disruptions serves as a thought-provoking look into the potential consequences of scientific progress, technological development and societal evolution.

Be prepared to immerse yourself in speculative landscapes that spark discussions about the implications for our future human experience.

Contents

Preface

"DECISIONS," AARON SORKIN once quoted, "are made by those who show up."

Founded in 1997, the think-tank Cybersalon exists to process, explore, and in some cases guide, the many and varied transformations of society brought about by the third industrial revolution. The book that you're holding testifies to those transformations underway and those yet to come.

Here, within its pages, you'll meet Arjun and his wearable assistant, Krishna, helping him to manage his autism; migrant caregiver Jacqui as she navigates the boundary systems of her new nationality; menopausal writer Galena Lane weighing the side effects of a proposed breakthrough treatment; and neighbourly Stace reported to the Civil Defence police force by an overly enthusiastic smart fridge, along with many more familiar, yet unique, characters. Characters conjured into place by our authors, so that you may better see the worlds they inhabit.

This is not a book of predictions. Rather, it gives a glimpse into some very real futures that could potentially manifest, depending on which paths we might collectively take in getting there. This is considered to be foresight, not the more familiar forecasts or predictions that look forward along the extrapolated lines of a particular technology. It provides validated ideas about what those futures could be, each born out of a series of detailed discussions and conversations over the course of eighteen months. Firstly, between us, the editors, and our domain experts, to provide each topic with a solid, evidentiary framework. Secondly, between the domain experts and our selected authors, who each provided a story outline to pitch situations, environments, and technologies for their story. And thirdly, over a more extended and iterative period among all three. This all culminated in the stories and commentaries that you now hold, on: Policing and Justice; Power and Energy; Finance and Digital Money; Health and Longevity; and Learning and Education.

We wanted inspiration through imagination, but not so much that we lost sight of the reason to do this in the first place, which was to bring these conversations to the page by walking the fine line between creativity and plausibility. As an author, this does put constraints on your creativity, but in the case of this book that constraint is a good thing. It gives you, the reader, a degree of security in imagining and discussing the futures presented. For example, and not surprisingly, although we didn't set out to focus on climate change, it's there in the background of a lot of the stories.

Making use of this open collaboration and iterative discussion process, rather than simply commissioning stories on given subjects was not itself without risks—editors, authors, and experts did not know exactly what they were getting into and had to be open to iterating the process as well as their ideas. For us, the editors, we selected authors, not stories, so we didn't really know what we were going to end up with. The authors had to step into a largely unknown process that on some level we were iterating as we went, not knowing whether we would like or accept their final story. The experts also took risks, by stepping into that largely unknown process, wondering what these stories and ideas would be and whether they'd be able to comment seriously on them once completed. While it was an extremely intense experience for everyone to co-create a book in this way, it was also extremely rewarding. The risks were in a very real sense what made the whole thing work.

The creation of this book has also affirmed for us with no shadow of a doubt that experts who might seem distant and unattainable are more than willing to show up and to engage in thinking about the wider issues within which their particular expertise lies. As one of our experts, Dr Elizabeth Black, says in her commentary, "There's so much pressure, to publish, to bring in funding, to improve student experience, to increase student numbers—it's really important these pressures don't overwhelm us, that we make time to step back and think about the potential consequences of our work, as this experience has allowed me to do." The opportunity to make links with others and other ideas proves to be as exciting and stimulating for them as much as it is for us. After all, they are people like you with hopes and dreams for their futures and the future of those they love.

As you read these stories you may feel that what you have been presented is a set of possible futures to avoid. Although, if we've done our job correctly, what you will find is a mix of ideas that inspire good futures and ideas that warn against the bad. We also hope that the accompanying commentaries with their contrasting and complementary perspectives will serve as jumping-off points into further discussion with others. Most importantly, in that dynamic, you should remember that, like our authors, you too have expertise on these subjects—not least, it's your life that's being affected.

As we assemble this manuscript to go to print, the social media networks that constitute our electronic free press appear dominated by the personal fiefdoms of just two American multi-billionaires. Two-thirds of the Internet itself is hosted on the servers of just three US companies. Sure, the future looks easy, clean—predictable, even—if you are one of this tiny minority of stakeholders in its digital infrastructure. It's only when you mix in the true range and richness of humanity that it gets 'messy'. But unless that's where we start, there will always be far too few of us contributing opinions, perspectives, and expertise to the decision making, with all the attendant privileging of outcomes that ensues.

All Tomorrow's Futures, then, is not just our take on foresight. It is also our invitation for you to participate in that future, starting today. This invitation to participate we like to call 'Open Futures' to defend its range of potential outcomes from the more usual narratives of any particular, predetermined, or even inevitable future—'Closed Futures'.

However much it is unknown and uncertain, 'the' future is a place you will call home. And, as we hope this book is able to demonstrate, a home that you are able to populate—and make critical decisions about—right now, albeit through the vehicles of near-future-fiction and discussion. All of which, we think, is well worth showing up for.

Stephen and Ben
England, January 2024

Introduction

"They were the children of the ... [19]80s that wasn't; they were Heirs to the Dream. They were white, blond, and they probably had blue eyes. They were American. ... the Future had come to America first, but had finally passed it by. But not here, in the heart of the Dream. Here we'd go on and on, in a dream logic that knew nothing of pollution, the finite bounds of fossil fuel, of foreign wars it was possible to lose. They were smug, happy, and utterly content with themselves and their world. And in the dream, it was *their* world."
— William Gibson, *The Gernsback Continuum*

IN WILLIAM GIBSON'S 1981 story "The Gernsback Continuum", its protagonist is haunted by the 'semiotic phantoms' of Golden Age sci-fi machinery from Hugo Gernsback's 1930s pulp magazines: delta-winged planes, giant airships, aerodynamic cars, and ziggurat skyscrapers. These hallucinations of the industrial future evoked an optimistic attitude towards social and technological progress which was all too obviously no longer credible in post-industrial America. Yet, as Gibson affectionately mocked in his tale, the science fiction genre in the 1980s was still obsessed with the aesthetics of Gernsback's past future. Above all, the invention of awe-inspiring gadgets remained the most efficient remedy for almost all of the problems of humanity. The longevity of this prophetic vision derived from the lived experience of the producers and consumers of sci-fi books, TV series, and films who grew up during the long boom of Fordism. Predictions of flying cars, intelligent robots, and warp drives might not have been fulfilled, but these Americans were enjoying the high standard of living and social mobility which had been promised by the Golden Age writers of the 1930s. Although their details of the future were often incorrect, the concepts promoted by Gernsback's pulp magazines proved to be sound. For a few brief decades, the affluent society in the USA was prophecy made into reality.

Gibson's satire of disappointed utopia was a pioneer of the new style of 1980s science fiction: cyberpunk. A few years after its publication, his novel *Neuromancer* would define the template for this upgrade of the genre. As its iconic trope, cyberpunk predicted that the ascendency of neoliberal globalisation would create a grimy future of social polarisation and malign technologies. With power and wealth monopolised by the superrich and their megacorporations, the impoverished and criminalised masses were confined to decaying slums while the destruction of nature continued unabated. Far from liberating humanity, technological progress had exacerbated the worst features of this oppressive society. Oligarchs could now transcend biological limits and live forever as disembodied AIs. But, for everyone else, new technologies were materialised as either tools of police brutality or forms of escapist media. In this neoliberal future, the only hope for humanity lay in the small band of dissidents who were able to take down the corporate hegemon by repurposing its discarded machinery and hacking its virtual worlds. As Gibson emphasised, cyberpunk was the apotheosis of 'hi-tech and low life'.

Like its Golden Age predecessor, the popularity of this new generation of science fiction derived from its predictive power. Although the details might be exaggerated for effect, the cyberpunk vision of the future anticipated how the rapid improvement and dissemination of digital technologies were radically reshaping the Western world. Abandoning their predecessors' obsession with outer space, its proponents were instead fascinated by the emerging virtual spaces of the Net. Surfing webpages with a 286 PC and its 54k modem was the premonition of navigating fully immersive 3D simulations with wearable computers connected by mobile broadband. Cyberpunk was defined by this quintessential technology: cyberspace. However, its 'semiotic phantom' of the Net wasn't a 1980s iteration of delta-winged planes or aerodynamic cars. In contrast with the boosters of the Californian Ideology of the next decade, cyberpunk contemptuously rejected the techno-utopianism of Silicon Valley. Instead of freeing individuals from unaccountable power, deregulation and privatisation of media, computing, and telecommunications were consolidating the global power of corporate behemoths. Catalysed by the spread of digital technologies, the imposition of austerity on the welfare state and the hollowing out of democratic institutions were responsible for the class inequality, social alienation, and deteriorating infrastructure of the post-industrial city. Unlike Gernsback sci-fi's shiny and safe utopia, the cyberpunk future was a dirty and dangerous dystopia.

In the four decades since its publication, *Neuromancer* has provided the archetype of how Western culture imagines the shape of things to come. Following the decline of European social democracy and the collapse of Russian Stalinism, it was almost universally accepted that there could be no alternative to the unipolar dominance of American neoliberalism over the planet. Cyberpunk's dystopian nightmares expressed deep fears about how this imperial ascendency of free markets and digital technologies was transforming everyday life for the worse. From the 1990s to the 2020s, what once was fiction rapidly became reality: billionaires living in luxury compounds guarded by private security forces, streets filled with tent cities of homeless people, masked protestors clashing with militarised police, ubiquitous computerised surveillance by secretive state and corporate agencies, devastating natural disasters caused by runaway climate change, widespread availability of psychotropic chemicals and bodily modifications, and incessant propaganda from multiple media outlets on screens of all sizes. In its sci-fi novels, films and games, cyberpunk was the mutoid commentary that both mocked and lambasted the digital dominance of neoliberal globalisation. The Golden Age's optimistic future of hi-tech plenty had been superseded by a pessimistic vision of social decay and algorithmic tyranny.

Over the past four decades, cyberpunk has lost almost all of its dissident and deviant edginess. Not surprisingly, as Guy Debord and Pierre Canjuers pointed out in 1960 that the initial cultural and political radicalism of avant-garde art movements is sooner or later dissipated by recuperation into the mainstream of bourgeois society. In doing so, the tropes of cyberpunk's sci-fi style have spawned a plethora of imitators: steampunk, dieselpunk, afropunk, solarpunk, and splatterpunk. Coopted as a marketing term, these hyphen-punk subgenres all too often discarded the subversive ethos of the original version. More worryingly, 1980s cyberpunk's dystopian vision has itself now become the cool aesthetic of a past future. In the same way that the conventions of Golden Age sci-fi appealed to those who grew up during the Fordist boom, cyberpunk's tales of hi-tech megacorporations, inner city deprivation, and hacker heroes resonate with the lived experience of today's denizens of neoliberal societies. Ironically, through repeated retellings, what were once satirical denunciations can now be sold as romanticised affirmations of the unipolar hegemony of US capitalism. Despite its debts to Japanese manga, the stateless and borderless cyberpunk metropolis becomes the celebration of the monolithic Americanisation of global culture. Above all, the protagonists of this sci-fi genre are now another iteration of the Western stereotype of the solitary rebel. When workers are treated as disposable replicants, class solidarity and collective action are supposedly unthinkable. In the 2020s, CEOs and tech moguls are no longer baddies, but goodies who lead the acceleration into the cyberpunk future. Reconciled with the Californian Ideology, this speculative fiction welcomes and praises sentient AIs, cryptocurrency havens, immersive metaverses, and transhuman augmentation.

This recuperation of cyberpunk is a repetition of the assimilation of its Golden Age antecedent. Once again, the future is what it used to be. Instead of delta-winged planes and aerodynamic cars, virtual realities and smart machines are the 'semiotic phantoms' haunting the contemporary imagination. But, as in the early 1980s, these conventions of the dominant sci-fi genre are being challenged by the emergence of a new technological paradigm. Like the convergence of media, computing, and telecommunications into the Net, the Fourth Industrial Revolution promises to be the catalyst of a profound socio-economic metamorphosis. Manufacturing, healthcare, transportation, housing, education, culture, and warfare will be transformed by its innovative mix of new and improved machinery: 6G networks, factory robots, big data, high-speed railways, e-commerce, autonomous vehicles, quantum computing, solar energy, designer drugs, genetic engineering, fusion power, drone swarms, and hypersonic missiles. Even manned space travel is making a comeback. From oligarchs at the World Economic Forum to boosters of Fully Automated Luxury Communism, these inventions of the Fourth Industrial Revolution are lauded as the saviours of humanity. Echoing the optimism of Golden Age sci-fi, there soon will be a technological fix for social inequality, global warming, violent criminality, and political manipulation. With the reemergence of this prophecy of hi-tech plenty, it is now cyberpunk's tropes of urban decay and algorithmic despotism that are a past future: the Gibson Continuum.

In 2015, Liu Cixin's *The Three-Body Problem* won the Hugo Award for Best Novel. For the first time, this prestigious sci-fi prize named in honour of Gernsback had been given to an East Asian author. With its Chinese characters and setting, his intertwined tale of alien invasion and human fallibility reflected a very different sensibility than that of previous Hugo Award winners. No Western writer would have made the People's Liberation Army into heroes of their sci-fi narrative! Crucially, its inclusion of virtual reality as an important part of the plot wasn't accompanied by the dystopian cliches of cyberpunk. Since the 1949 Chinese revolution, every generation has lived much better than its forebears. Even in Liu Cixin's apocalyptic tale, the hi-tech future must be shiny not grimy. As his novel proved, the obsolescence of the Gibson Continuum can be explained by not only the Fourth Industrial Revolution, but also the rise of China to the number one economy in the world. Like its Golden Age ancestor, cyberpunk was a cultural product of the American empire. While the former had fantasised about the ascendency of imperium, the latter fictionalised the brief apogee of global dominance. Despite its founders' anti-capitalist ethos, the credibility of cyberpunk's dark future depends on the perpetuation of this unipolar moment. However, like the Galactic Empire in Isaac Asimov's Golden Age Foundation trilogy, the decline and fall of the American empire now appears inevitable. Political instability and economic decline at home are exacerbated by military defeats and insubordinate vassals abroad. Cutting-edge technology for the few can no longer compensate for crumbling infrastructure for the many. In contrast, China is the pioneer of twenty-first century modernity with its mastery of the key sectors of the Fourth Industrial Revolution, from high-speed railways and mobile telephony to ecommerce and renewable energy. Above all, Socialism with Chinese Characteristics' successful synthesis of state planning and market competition flouts all of the orthodoxies of US-style neoliberalism. Cyberpunk's dystopian future is anachronistic in a country when new cities are being built and living standards are increasing every year. Tellingly, instead of imitating this American template, *The Three-Body Problem* looked to the bitter debates within twentieth-century Chinese politics over how to respond to Western imperialism as its inspiration for a sci-fi novel about humanity deciding whether to resist or collaborate with extraterrestrial intruders. A different history had imagined a different future.

Located in London, Cybersalon is preparing the ground for an upgrade of the science fiction genre that can express the hopes and fears of the inhabitants of its own home on an offshore island of the western peninsula of the Eurasian continent. As the ebbing of the American empire gathers pace, the past future of the Gibson Continuum has lost credibility here as well. It is increasingly understood that cyberpunk sci-fi is now guilty of not only selling reactionary politics, but also making false prophecies. In response, Benjamin Greenaway and Stephen Oram have crafted this Cybersalon book with one overriding goal: opening up new ways of thinking about the shape of things to come. Building on their *22 Ideas About the Future* anthology (Cybersalon Press, 2022), *All Tomorrow's Futures* combines speculative fiction and expert commentaries to imagine how humans and their machines will interact in the decades to come. Under the headings of Police and Justice, Power and Energy, Finance and Digital Money, Health and Longevity, and Learning and Education, this book's authors deliberate on the long-term positive and negative social impacts of AI, network computing, cryptocurrencies, bioengineering, and the other technologies of the Fourth Industrial Revolution. By writing fiction, they are able to create freeform thought experiments about potential futures that can't be found in the mainstream media, academic journals, or think-tank reports. Of course, like their Golden Age and cyberpunk predecessors, the authors of *All Tomorrow's Futures* won't always be correct in the details. However, by projecting forward from lived experience, they are able to construct believable models of the near-future out of premonitions in today's world. From these thought experiments, a new template of science fiction is emerging. Learning from this prognosis, humanity's great task now is ensuring that the hi-tech future is a much improved social reality.

Richard Barbrook,
London, December 2023

PART 1
Police and Justice

All Born Machines

Sophie Sparham

Ex-Prime Minister Michael Pattern famously said that "We're all born machines. It's astonishing how few of us evolve to become human." It seems ironic that he died at the hands of his deputy in a street brawl, after a drunken party joke got out of hand. Even more ironic that Francis Scholar was the first AI in UK government. The rumour goes that the two of them were drinking in Kimmy Scott's backyard after winning another landslide election. If those rumours are to be believed, Kimmy had been pouring his speciality cocktail, 'Grounds for Divorce', when Pattern made a comment about Scholar lacking the ability to get inebriated due to his fine-tuned programming. Desperate, as always, to prove his boss wrong, the AI drank the bar dry. When this didn't seem to satisfy Pattern, Scholar resulted to fisticuffs. Unfortunately, play fighting for a super-computer powered robot is very different from play fighting for a fifty-nine-year old man with an undiagnosed heart condition. Those were different times. Cowboy times, when AI was new to the game, and everything was to play for. I thought we'd moved on. We all thought we'd moved on.

I scratch my head, looking at the case files in front of me, then back to the other eleven members of the jury. Akhlan is sat staring out the window, touching each tip of her finger with her thumbs. She does this often. I have come to believe it's some form of mindfulness, a meditation to keep her calm. Maybe we should all be trying it.

"Akhlan," I say. "It's time to decide."

She moves away from the window and sits around the table with the rest of us.

Kane is tapping his watch. "Let's get this over with," he says, as though we'll be able to come to a decision. As though we've not been sat here for days. "All who think guilty."

Three people raise their hands.

"Innocent?" Kane asks, raising his own hand.

Another three.

I keep my head down, try to avoid eye contact.

"Ray," he turns to me. "You haven't put your hand up for anything."

"It's not that simple," I mumble.

"What?" he barks.

"It's not that simple."

"Don't start." He rolls his eyes.

"It's not," I shrug.

"Just choose a side and we can all go home," he says.

I hear children laughing. Outside, a girl and a boy are running towards the playground across the street, the sun beaming down. Kane is sweating in his thick black leather jacket and leather trousers. He's arrived by motorbike every day, always keeping his kit on even with the heating turned up full blast.

"There aren't enough options," I plead.

The room falls silent. My chair squeaks against the tiles as I stand up. "I'm going to get some air."

"Be quick," he squares up to face me. "Some of us need to get on with our lives."

I walk down the stairs, the paint peeling off the walls, the laminate floor a stark contrast to the opulent front of the courtroom. Outside, the cold November air hits me. The smoking area is small, the silver fence high. I shiver, shake my arms to get the circulation going, then pull a cigarette from the packet in my pocket and light it. A sea of images come back to me. Green and yellow flags. Sirens. Blood. I review the case in my mind.

Two police officers charged for murdering three civilians at a protest. Gunshot wounds to the chest. Dead on the spot. Sounds simple, right? I thought so too. Until I realised the police had taken their orders from an AI. Algorithmic policing, designed to eradicate human error. The incorruptible ones and zeros saving us all from ourselves. In the dock, Officer Matlock had pleaded he'd just been following orders.

"...The machine told us they were known terrorists... What else were we supposed to do, lives were at stake?"

I take a drag on my cigarette. Even if they were terrorists, did that mean that they deserved to die? I think back to Pattern. They'd just turned Scholar off. Why couldn't it be as easy as pressing a button? But it was as easy as pressing a button, programming a machine. That's how we got into this mess.

***

I bite my lip as I rerun the tests. A list of names rolls down the screen as the photo scans. Hart Black's mugshot flashes up as a match.

"Shit, shit, shit." I slam my fist on the table. *Wrong again.*

The kettle boils in the office kitchen.

"Are you aware how much you swear when you're running programs?" Bobby asks, a smile curling on her lips as she reaches for a mug.

"I just don't get it," I shake my head. "We tested this thing."

"It's been decommissioned, Blue, leave it alone." She shakes a mug at me and I nod, narrowing my eyes. Outside, London is grey and bleak, broken up only by the flash of a red bus or yellow cab thirteen floors below us.

"Don't you think you should take some time off?" she asks, handing me the mug.

"And do what?"

"I dunno, visit your family, go on holiday, that sort of thing?"

I stare down at my coffee. *I can't go away. I have to fix this.* Have to work out what went wrong, where the malfunction came from. Secure Cop was meant to be the latest in AI technology. The Major had called it 'Scotland Yard's golden boy' when interviewed by the Guardian last week. It was meant to reduce staff costs, increase productivity, make the streets safer. Not *this*.

There is a pile of newspapers cutouts next to my left hand. Anything I could find out about the protest. They'd made us sign an agreement, of course. No speaking out in public, no comments on social media, no interviews. The list went on. At the time, I'd been happy to sign, knowing I was doing my best for my country. I didn't need the fame or gratitude that the new program would bring, just the knowledge that hundreds would be safe because of me and the team. When the news broke, there had been an emergency briefing by the Met.

"Stick to the contract," the woman had said, her suit as grey as the weather, "and you'll get to keep your jobs. Out yourself and the whole company goes under."

Bobby looks over my shoulder. "Are you trying to look like a serial killer?"

I glare.

"Let it go," she pleads.

"How?"

"Like the rest of us."

"Drink myself to death?" Bobby's been arriving each morning with gin breath and dark circles beneath her eyes. She's not gotten over it, none of us have.

"By working on the new project," she points at the Mother Care brochure.

The idea of letting any of our programs near children makes me sick.

"Do you have any idea the amount of shit you could get yourself into if they find this on your desk?" She points at the articles.

"I can't pretend it didn't happen." I look down into my coffee. The grains that didn't evaporate on top of the milk froth.

"It wasn't our fault," she insists.

"How can you be so sure?"

"It wasn't," she slams her mug on the desk. "Machines malfunction all the time. We ran the tests, we did our jobs, we can't be responsible for every little thing they do, we're not..." she hesitates, "We're not God for fuck's sakes."

"We gave them life," I respond, "so technically, we are."

"Don't go all Wikileaks on me," she points a finger accusingly.

I hold my hands up. "Wouldn't dream of it." And I hadn't, until she'd mentioned it. Maybe that was it. The only way to solve this thing, come clean.

***

There are exactly fifty-seven scratches carved into the wall. They're thin, about the width of a hairline. I think about carving one myself. Hell, I could probably do a whole portrait by the time this trial is done. I look at my grazed knuckles. My name is ruined. *I'm* ruined. Officer Matlock. The man who gave the order. I can't get the image of that boy out of my head. He couldn't be much more than twenty-one. Adidas shirt, cardboard banner raised high. He is standing in front of us, screaming, blood running from his nose... *Breathe, Matlock, breathe.*

I lay on the floor. Make myself do twenty press-ups. Plank. Then another twenty. I downward dog, pressing my palms against the cold, concrete floor. When they told us we'd be taking orders from AI, I must admit, I was dubious. I think about when they closed down the Weetabix factory in my town. Too many dead rodents rehydrated over breakfast. I even found one myself. I feel my face screw up. When they looked at the cause, they found there was no barriers to stop the mice climbing onto the factory line. The factory had recently let go of its hundred and twenty workers to cut costs. No surprise there. Fencing was installed, the factory reopened. The problem kept happening but on a less frequent basis. That's progress for you.

At least they drew the line at the Deputy Prime Minister. Shame tragedy had to ensue for that to happen. It's always tragedy which changes things. They never learn. If it was up to me, I never would have put that bloody thing in power. Machines just can't be trusted. How can people think we're anything like technology? The image of the boy flashes in my head. He's on the floor now, blood pooling from the wound in his head.

"No, no, *no*," I slam my fist against the wall. The pain hits like white noise.

"Keep it down in there," an officer yells, banging on the door.

I think back to first meeting Blue. They had half a shaved head and crooked teeth. I kept staring at a tattoo on their wrist as they talked me through the programme. Was it a bird? A butterfly?

"... see," they said, looking back at me, "pretty easy, huh?"

I frowned. I didn't like the way they were talking about this thing. Like it was a baby, a child they'd born and raised into this world. "Here's my card," Blue said. "If you have any more questions."

I smiled, knowing I wouldn't be ringing that number.

"I don't want to work with them," I'd said to my boss, once we were back in the police station.

"Well tough shit," Officer Amble said. "We need all the eyes we can get."

"They're treating it like it's alive."

"They're computer geeks," she waved a hand. "It's what they're like with everything."

I was not convinced.

I take the longest of my nails and scratch it against the stone. Fifty-eight. There has been no mention of Blue or any of the others at Collasos since the attack. The door to my cell opens.

"They're ready for you," an officer says.

I stand up. This isn't my fault, I'm no murderer. When I get out of here, someone's going to fucking pay.

**

The fire door opens and Akhlan steps outside.

"Jesus, it's heated in there," she says, grabbing the packet of cigarettes from my hand and taking one. "What are you gonna vote?"

"Fuck knows," I reply. "Is there a destroy your ballot option?"

Across the road, a Big Issue seller smiles at us before someone grabs his bag. We watch as he's pulled halfway down the street by a guy on a BMX. He shrieks once as he's pulled into the marketplace and out of sight.

"Shit," I mutter beneath my breath.

"Do you think we should do something?"

"Like what?" I ask, looking at the floor. There's nothing we can do in this cage. Trapped like animals. My cigarette is out now. I think of the officers and their families. Then the protesters, their brothers, partners, lovers. I think of them all. Nobody wins from this situation.

"Did they say who programmed the AI?" I ask, rubbing my temples.

Akhlan shrugs. "It wasn't mentioned," she says.

I raise my eyebrows. "Funny, that."

"They could have handled it in a different way," she says, staring at a police car across the road. "They didn't need to fire."

"They also didn't need a computer to hold office."

"Isn't technology meant to make our lives easier?" She asks.

"Maybe it got too easy," I reply after a moment, sucking in a lungful of chill air. "Maybe we forgot how to make the right choice."

She opens the door for me to step inside. "Do you know what you're going to say?"

I smile at her, nod, then turn to walk up the stairs.

Updated Intelligence
Tehnuka

CONSTABLE LEE

Our badgebots finished updating just in time to scan our packed gear. "Confirm arrangements for police detention legal aid."

"Ah, there aren't any." We'd loaded everything else into our vehicle and sat inside, looking over the news on road conditions. "Can you send a message to all badgebots in the station?"

Within minutes, a colleague ran out to shove a dusty box through the window. "It's an old one, we won't miss it. Fully charged. Good luck!"

James drove. The roads were so dodgy we couldn't trust the automated system. Occasionally I flew the drone ahead for a view of the flooding. I was relieved to see it receding, since the chest waders I'd been issued were huge, practically up to my chin.

Our briefing was about welfare checks and supporting Civil Defence. When they mentioned looting, I'd imagined people raiding hardware stores for fuel. We're out in the wop-wops when my badgebot announces a Mr Neil Archbold reporting a potential burglary in progress. His address appears on the GPS screen, twenty minutes off our route. James stops the car in the middle of the road, as pulling over would tip us into a ditch.

"The homeowner received a supermarket order notification," reports the auto-dispatcher, via my badgebot. "His fridge should not reorder items until stock is depleted, so this suggests an intruder."

"Are you kidding?" says James. "His smartfridge malfunctions so he calls the police? More money than sense."

His badgebot beeps. "Caution, value judgement."

Weird. We exchange a look, but there's this fridge-reported burglary to attend to.

"Is the owner on the property?"

"No, at a second residence," says my badge. "He has the only keys to the property. He suggests the alarm system is storm-damaged or offline. His neighbour across the road stayed behind; he is concerned for her safety. I recommend deploying the drone for a situational overview."

The drone travels ahead of us, being much faster than James' pothole navigation. It also has a much smoother trip to the site. I stop paying attention to the nav screen showing its flight while I hang on to the oh-shit handle. When I look again, we've lost telemetry.

By then, there's enough debris across the road that James insists we walk the last kilometre.

"Yeah, a drone would've been good at this point," he says. I try not to be embarrassed. It wouldn't have changed the fact we'd need to walk on a partly washed-out road and climb over fallen trees.

When we reach the address, the front windows are wide open. Circling the property, I spot the broken drone rotor poking out of the recycling bin, and a glass bottle in the muck of the lawn. The door's ajar. Those could be footprints in the mud around the door, disappearing into standing water nearby.

There! A movement by the rundown bach on the neighbouring section. "Look."

"Probably a vagrant breaking into all the houses," says James, after squinting.

His badgebot beeps. "Caution, implicit bias detected."

"What are you, the thought police? Is this the latest update?" He turns to me. "Did you read the badge updates?"

"When did we have time for that?" No one ever reads the update notes, even when there is time.

STACE

The cops knocked on my door after checking Marni's. I saw them coming, but there's nowhere to go and it was raining again.

When I told them everyone else evacuated, they got more suspicious, asking where I'm from. I explained I live here, that it's just Neil next door on the land my aunt sold off, and Marni trying to turn the old farm across the road into a forest, and the other neighbours were too low-lying to risk staying in their houses. They left last year.

"This is the biggest flood ever, I reckon. I mean, I've only been here a few years, but my aunt says her place is the safest in the valley."

A green light flickered on the first cop's shoulder. She was dressed in ridiculous waders, way too big. They both wore uniform shirts, and a flat rectangular patch with a green LED on the left shoulder.

They wanted proof I own or rent the cottage, but I don't do either. I'm trying to show them texts from my aunt on my phone, then her shoulder patch says, "Confirmed legal tenancy," or something. I hoped that would be it.

A few seconds later, it mentioned prior convictions for underage driving and releasing pest animals.

The driving was true. I was fifteen. The pest animal thing's unfair, it was just a mouse in my kitchen that I let out in a field.

"I don't see how it's legal to force us to kill baby mice," I protested.

Complaining might have been a bad idea. They said I should accompany them on suspicion of damaging police property and burglary, and something about rights and free legal advice. So I said I'd wait for that legal advice.

We had to walk to their car, climbing over logs in the rain. The woman had a little briefcase she said was for the drone. The guy walked behind us talking to his radio, and then to his shoulder patch. I had to empty water from my gumboots before climbing in their 4WD.

At least it was a free lift into town.

We park by a soccer field. It's a terrible place for a marquee—more wet grass to walk through. Turns out my guys aren't even local cops, just backup. This is a temporary post until they sort out flooding in the station.

The drone-cop brings over a cardboard box and opens it.

When they said 'free and immediate legal advice', I wasn't expecting a roomba.

It plays a turning-on chime when she places it on the trestle table, as if it's channelling a doorbell. "Lorebot has a comprehensive database of legislation and past cases," she says, already backing out of the marquee. "I've sent it a brief with your details. I'll leave you two to it."

Mud splashes up her uniform trousers as she rejoins her cronies.

The roomba sits flashing a tiny blue light at me, faster and faster, illuminating the dust motes drifting off its back.

I fold my arms, pushing my wet clothes against my chest. I unfold them again. "I smashed up one of you already today."

It answers after the blue light turns steady. "Yes, I understood that from my briefing."

Lorebot sounds like the voice from every furniture sale ad. I'm not sure it can truly *understand* anything, but it cheerfully tells me it knows why I'm here. "To enable me to assist, could you please begin telling me what happened—including with the drone? I'll have questions."

I look around to make sure there isn't another one buzzing nearby. The police have clustered in the corner of the churned-up field, taking their shoulder robots with them. I want to believe they've moved to give me and my 'free and immediate legal advice' privacy, but I see some upstanding citizen has actually shown up with a coffee urn and a stack of paper cups. Suck-up.

"My scans detect no proximal humans or listening devices. A text interface or headset are available if you'd prefer."

What I'd prefer is to not to ask the cops for anything. Leaving the marquee to ask for gear would no doubt trigger some sensor, so I choose to trust the lorebot.

Most houses down the valley became derelict once the council stopped buying out flood-damaged properties. My aunt's cottage was cut off in previous years—roads wrecked, no fresh supplies, a rough few weeks—so I knew what to expect, but I'd promised to look after the place, and where else could I go?

Neil went down south to one of his other houses. I saw his shiny ute disappear—good riddance, I didn't want to deal with that asshole in a crisis. He's been telling everyone for years this is his off-grid apocalypse hideout, even though he disappears to the city whenever things get sketchy and, as it turns out, only part of the house is off-grid.

Marni decided to evacuate to her girlfriend's after the latest forecast. I helped tetris the kids' suitcases into her car boot.

"So I know you guys don't talk and his dog's always digging up your kūmara or whatever. As a favour, though, if you could keep an eye on things there too…"

What was I meant to do, sandbag Neil's multitude of double doorways if it looked dodgy? Couldn't his self-driving lawnmower do that for him?

Marni could have offered me a lift. She knew my car's broken down because she's the one who took me grocery shopping the last two weeks. Sure, I didn't have anywhere to go if she'd offered, but she didn't.

Even the fancy new forecasting models never get flooding right. My aunt's cottage stayed safe at the back of the section, but I didn't go out during thirty-eight hours of nonstop rain. Later, I waded across the road to check Marni's place as the sun came up. I would've texted that the bottom of her garden was buried in silt, except there was no phone signal. Cell towers down again. Or a substation flooded again. No way I'd pay for satellite trains ruining the darkness just to text neighbours who buggered off before a storm and left me with the mess.

***

I'm careful about which of these details I share with the lorebot, but I do mention that part. "I gather you are not keen on the latest technology," it says. "I can understand that."

***

At least it didn't mention me not being keen on the neighbours.

Neil's the opposite with tech. He has the latest gadgets. His monster of a house sits right near the road, roof covered in solar panels.

***

"I opened Marni's shed to air out, then walked across to Neil's place and saw he'd left the laundry window open."

Lorebot blinks faster when I hesitate at the break-in. "I am processing your data solely for informed provision of legal advice."

"The key was in the laundry door. When I...pulled the window further, I could unlock it."

"They say you broke the window latch, could that have been an accident?"

A robot lawyer should come with a less cheerful voice. "I might have pulled quite hard."

I'd gone in, opened the windows that didn't need keys. The carpets were saturated. No alarms went off, I don't think he'd set them. It didn't occur to me about alarms until later.

"So you went in to air out the house, which was the neighbourly thing to do after flooding."

That is...a nice way of looking at it.

***

Once I checked the bottom floor I'd gone upstairs, kicking off my boots on the second step where the water hadn't reached. I don't know why. I felt wild, I guess. I did open every window. He had a full-on home theatre in one room. The third floor was a huge den with skylights, and a kitchen. I don't know why one guy needs two kitchens, but it had a big fridge, still running, and I'd come out without breakfast. I hadn't even lit my camp stove since power went, saving gas in case it took weeks to sort. Neil has solar panels covering his roof. When the rain started again it was more comfortable to stay, with toast and a coffee machine and cold beer, the heated towel rail in every bathroom to dry my pants...

It's a ten-minute walk between our places when his lawn's underwater. I went home for my meds and pajamas but spent the night on his couch. Next morning, I checked Marni's sections again, came out to drop my pajamas at home, and found the drone hovering by the back door.

***

I'm honest about the drone. "I thought it would tase me! The recycling bin was right there. I didn't think I'd actually hit it."

"You threw a glass bottle at the drone with no expectation this would help you escape?"

The cops are looking in my direction. I wonder what they're saying about me. "Are you on my side or theirs?"

"I'm programmed to provide legal advice. Given case-specific information, I can tailor my responses."

"Well, I wanted a sec to get away. And I...felt a bit wild." A robot can't understand being abandoned by neighbours. It can't care whether it's out of pity or guilt that Marni helps me.

The lorebot says I could be charged with property damage and burglary. "There may be evidence you'd entered—cameras or the drone may have seen you coming out. We shouldn't assume footage was destroyed in the crash. Admitting you broke the latch trying to get in should work in your favour. After all, you were doing a kind thing for your neighbour. You can expect property damage charges for the drone, but that wasn't premeditated. We'll explain you're a technophobe who saw a threat."

Technophobe? Still, that's a relief.

Lorebot falls silent as the drone-cop approaches. She waves to get my attention, comes closer to hand me a paper cup of black coffee and backs off again.

"Exploiting a disaster is an aggravating factor in burglary since the 2026 amendment, but there's unlikely to be evidence of looting. You only consumed a little food. They'll be worried about missing high-value items, not fingerprinting the marmite jar. You must have mitigated property damage to a greater value than a window latch and a few beers."

***

I could have run when the drone whirred into the wall and thumped onto sodden ground, but, again, nowhere to go except home to the cottage. The cops showed up before I'd decided what to do. I'd left gumboot prints everywhere and there was a broken drone in the recycling bin.

***

CONSTABLE LEE

The lawbot must have told our detainee to confess. Stace refused to talk beforehand, and now it's a blithe, "Yeah, I saw it and panicked."

"Just so you know," James says, "a police drone is essential lifesaving equipment. It's closer to being a dog than a camera. This is a serious charge."

Stace frowns, paper cup crumpling in thin fingers. Lawbot's blue light is blinking again.

"The maximum sentence for wilful damage is seven years. However, my case law database indicates property damage out of self-defence is likely to result in a financial penalty."

That's not true. I know this, given the number of people who go after our drones. They changed the laws three years ago to—ah.

"Lawbot, when was your legal database last updated? Do you have the 2048 amendment to the Crimes Act?"

The lawbot blinks faster. "That information is unavailable."

"You don't scan lawbots to check their updates, huh?" I tell my badgebot. "James, a word?"

James is already red-faced. We're meant to be out reassuring the community and we've wasted over an hour on this detour. "Bloody useless! That bot, and whoever gave it to you, and didn't you think to check, either?"

His badge beeps. "Caution—"

"And you'd think someone who's been convicted twice would know what to do with a lawbot!"

His badge beeps again. "Caution. Implicit bias detected."

"And this bloody beeping badge update! If I had that glass bottle—"

"Threat to badgebot detected. A meeting with your supervisor has been scheduled."

I really should read those update notes. But more urgently, "James, between this confession thanks to bad legal advice by an out-of-date lawbot, and being called out for a malfunctioning smartfridge..."

***

STACE

The cops offer a lift home. I'm hesitating when I learn that the phone signal's back because Neil rings to say he's worried his place is flooded. Marni gave him my number. I say it was just his first floor, and I aired it, but I had to break a window and the police caught me.

"Oh! That's my bad. Something went haywire with my electronics. My alarm and cameras aren't working, so I gave them a call."

When I tell him I'm stranded in town thanks to that, he promises to cover a ride home if I can find one. He's really grateful. He's quite nice when he's grateful. That last kilometer walking back will be tough, but I'll stop by the supermarket first anyway for a six-pack and groceries. If I hide the recycling and restock his fridge, he'll never know I raided his beers.

Ego Statistical

Stephen Oram

IT'S BEEN A lot of hard work to be able to afford to live around here, but I've done it. I've taken the risks and they've paid off. I never want to leave and I never want to return to those miserable streets that we grew up in. Charlotte and me, me and Charlotte, meant to be.

Sweet scents from the gardens of the tidily kept houses elevate the afternoon. Long shadows elongate our legs, mine and hers. Litter bots clean, carefully avoiding the relaxed residents out for a stroll. Sunshine streams through the trees with its winter warmth while the wind gently shakes the leaves. "I love this time of day," I tell her for the thousandth time.

"Josh. I know you do sweetie," she replies in that breathy way she has when she's happy.

We form an arch with our arms, and keeping hold of each other as a bot glides between us, we laugh. I squeeze her hand and she squeezes back. Once the bot passes, we swing our arms back and forth like ten-year-olds.

"Will you collect the kids?" she asks.

"I'd love to, really I would, but I can't."

"Can't?"

"Business. You know how it is."

She sucks her lips with her teeth, a habit from her childhood that still draws attention whenever she forgets herself in the polite company that we now keep, reminding me how fragile our future is.

"Honey," I say.

She stops.

Letting go of my hand, she speaks with that annoyed edge to her voice. "Sorry. But, business? Again?"

"No choice if you want them to have the latest headsets."

She clicks her tongue and shakes her head. "You do us proud," she says and squeezes my hand harder than ever. "I'll get them," she says and kisses me on the cheek. "I need some money for food though," she whispers, as if she's almost afraid to mention it.

I'm about to answer when a delivery bot behind us interrupts. "Coming through," it says, but slows down to match our pace, waiting for us to let it past.

"Money?" she says and holds out her card.

In the cipher which is known only to me and my card, I tell it to transfer three hundred pounds, plus the ten percent premium to keep the transaction private. I tap and she smiles. "Enough for fish and chips," I say and blow her a kiss.

She checks her card. "Are you sure?" she asks. "That's enough for a portion each."

"I am totally sure. You deserve it, all of you." I point at the delivery bot. "Quick, catch up and give it your order."

I watch her run after the bot and I'm about to head off to my little bit of business when a car screams up beside me. Why has it decided not to be silent? I turn to look.

Four police bots are gliding towards me. "Come with us," they say in unison.

"What—"

"Now, or face the consequences."

My mouth dries up and my stomach tightens. Suddenly, I feel like I need the toilet, but all I can really do is obey. I slide into the back seat between two of them. I risk a sideways glance at the other two who are on the road, gliding alongside the car. If it wasn't for the profuse tell-tale sweating and the clenched jaw, you could think that this wasn't so serious, laughable even. In this moment of heightened anxiety, a funny thought occurs to me. What if the neighbours think I'm some sort of VIP? Now, that would be interesting. Once this is all over and I'm safely home, maybe that's what I'll tell them.

***

From the moment they arrest Josh, he has no human contact whatsoever. An automated arrest leading directly to an automated cell. The charge is robbery with violence, or mugging to give it its more familiar name. No matter how much he protests his innocence, the machines are not listening.

The cell is comfortable. Cosy but clean is how the rental details would describe it. The walls are soundproofed, or if they aren't then he is the only inhabitant because he hears nothing, no feet on the floor outside and no faint murmuring of guards. It is stone dead silent.

To an empty, sterile cell, he explains there's been a mistake, he asks for proof of his guilt, and he reminds the blank walls of his human rights. He shouts as loud as he can, he begs for someone to listen to him and he punches the door. Nothing does any good. Even the failsafe fact that all four officers spoke together, to prove collective responsibility when charging him, does not provide him with any solace. He was scared when they arrested him, but now he's petrified of what is about to happen.

Fitfully, he dozes. Fitfully, he dreams the nightmares of drowning and being caught in a fire, unable to escape, suffocating in whatever new hell he dreams up. In fits of rage he shouts the filthiest obscenities he can think of over and over again, but nobody comes. He tries to control his breathing, to limit the shock to his body, but fails and teeters on the edge of hyperventilation. The isolation is excruciating. He needs to talk, to someone, to anyone. But all that happens is that the stifled silence of the cell becomes more oppressive with every shout he utters.

After hours of solitude he's ready to welcome a bot with open arms, not caring that it has no feelings or emotions. Seeing something, anything, that resembles life in its basic form would be a relief.

But nothing happens, not until the morning when they open the cell and let the painfully bright light in.

"It is time for your court hearing," says the bot standing in the doorway, preventing him from leaving. "Do not resist. My response could harm you if you do not do as I ask."

Four of them move in unison, guiding him to the seat which has appeared from the wall. "Sit," they say and depart, taking up positions on the outside of each corner.

He shouts in protest, only to be ignored.

The walls become opaque once more, each of them streaming a scene from the court. Or maybe this is the actual court taking place inside his cell, he can't tell.

A glitching judge presides over the courtroom. "Court is in session," it announces.

A jury of diverse avatars sit opposite him. They too are glitching, like cheap deep-fakes.

"Robbery with violence. How do you plead?"

He pleads his innocence. He tells them they've got it all wrong. Displayed on each of the flanking walls is a barrister AI; one prosecuting and one defending. They begin to test the validity of each other's facts, which is a relatively new approach to cross-examination.

The prosecuting AI begins. "He has been located near the scene at the time of the crime and his card has far more money on it than it should, given his income and his previous pattern of spending." The avatar winks at the jury. "Where did all that come from?" it asks in a rhetorical tone.

His defence AI is useless, only able to speculate that he's come into money from selling possessions or doing some work on the side. Neither of which it can provide any factual evidence for. Maybe a loan from his family, it suggests.

"We deal in facts alone," the judge reminds them. "Let the defendant speak," it adds.

***

It seems appropriate to stand up in front of the judge, although I do chuckle at the ridiculousness of showing respect to a room full of machines. Nonetheless, I stand and address the judge formally, as expected of me. "Your honour. I am not that sort of man. As you can see from my data, I do not even watch violent films or aggressive sports. It is not in my nature."

"The prosecution states that you were at the scene and that you cannot account for the amount of money on your card. What do you say?"

"My defence barrister is correct. It was a gift from my parents to help out with the kids. An untraceable transfer, unfortunately."

The judge glitches in its seat and then asks the jury of twelve AIs for their verdict. They run their models and confer before replying that, "There is an eighty-three and a third percent chance that he is guilty."

"Five years," says the judge.

"What about my family, my kids?!" I shout back.

"They will be looked after."

"You have no idea, do you?"

The court is silent.

"Without me, they'll be torn apart. She can't work *and* look after them." I take a few steps towards the judge. "My kids'll grow up without me. You think that's going to help? You think they won't go off the rails? I'm innocent, you fool. Why can't you get it? I want to speak to a real, proper human." I bang my fists on the wall. "Now!"

The court disappears and the walls return to their pure white opacity, but not before I catch a glimpse of the truck that my cell will be hoisted onto for transportation to the prison complex.

A disembodied voice with a soft mechanical tone speaks. "From here your cell will be transferred to the prison and you will be processed. This is nothing to be concerned about. When your transfer is complete you will receive automated care for the duration of your sentence, such as food and exercise routines. You will have five credits per week for virtual visits to your family home."

I collapse, crumpling into the corner of my cell.

Day after day I scream, I shout and I weep, but mostly I cower in silence, moving from one side of my cell to the other. Each time I join my family the pain of seeing them disintegrate is too much and I disconnect. This goes on for two whole months until I skip the weekly visits altogether.

***

Across the distributed police network, data is flowing freely into the seven models that feed the digital twin, the virtual data double of their city. Citizens who are known for their predilections for the relatively new drug, Stim, have been visiting a particular bar more frequently than usual. There are also visitors from outside of the neighbourhood, an unusually high number for a low-key residential area populated by professionals and families, an area that does not attract tourists. Data is digested and tactics decided. Three of the models conclude that drug dealers are likely to be operating out of the bar. This, in combination with the unusually small amount of time that customers are spending there, is enough to tip the twin into action. It dispatches police to investigate.

The bots arrive from every direction, effectively cutting off any escape routes, closing in until the building is surrounded: bots on the ground and a swarm of drones above, poised and ready to raid when given the instruction.

The twin runs diagnostic checks on the surrounding infrastructure to ensure the safety of the local residents. Satisfied that it's safe to proceed, it gives the order. The bots move in unison, steadily shrinking the cordon they've created until they reach the bar and then, one by one, they enter. All speaking together as one voice, they demand that every customer ceases their activity until the twin gives the go ahead to continue. Data that describes a tableau of frozen and fearful humans flows back to the centre. Faces are scanned and will be stored for the statutory twenty-four hours. The twin issues an instruction and the bots ask all occupants of the bar to empty their pockets and place any trace-free cards on the table in front of them. It's only a matter of minutes before the twin confirms that the predictions were correct. There is a lot of drug dealing taking place. Cards are confiscated, drugs are destroyed and those who are deemed to be dealing are forcibly escorted to waiting trucks loaded with portable cells. Finally, the twin enacts its right to access and analyse all data associated with the bar for the past six months, whether that's data belonging to the bar or to individuals. CCTV, transactions, personal location data, photos and videos all go towards building a comprehensive picture of who to keep an eye on. They can't arrest anyone for acts discovered through this method, but they can use it to authorise 'stop and search' in the future.

Curiously, the data shows that a recent conviction for robbery with violence was wrong. Footage and photos from a party of middle-aged men celebrating their friend's birthday show Joshua Cridger, the man who was given five years for the crime, was in fact busy providing Stim all evening. With no ego to get in the way of acknowledging and rectifying the mistake, the twin lodges an appeal with the court for a retrial, reminding them that Joshua cannot be convicted of any crime revealed through the data relating to the raid on the bar.

Immediately and without questioning, the judge and jury consider the appeal and it takes a matter of seconds for them to reach an agreement. They overthrow the conviction and agree to compensate him for the ninety-five days of incorrect incarceration.

***

"Hey kids, why don't you come and listen to it recap the highlights of its day while it recharges?"

Charlotte is standing next to me. "I don't like it," she says. "Josh, it creeps me out."

"All part of the package though." I sigh and repeat the reasoning, again. "A compensation companion for confidence, is how the judge put it. He said that having one as part of the family is perfectly normal in many neighbourhoods."

"I know, but—"

"Please—" I say, interrupting her. "Fetch the kids?"

I glance over at the police bot recharging in the corner of my garage. The idea being, that if it becomes a familiar part of my everyday life, the trauma caused from wrongful arrest and imprisonment will be eradicated. I'll learn to trust the police again. *You can't fear the familiar*, is the slogan for this piece of machine learning insight. What better way is there for the kids to learn to trust the police?

"Dad?"

"Yes?"

"Why does the copbot have to live with us?"

I laugh. "Because, son, we are the trusted guardians of the guardians to be trusted."

"I don't like it. Mum?"

"Yes?"

"Do you like it?"

"Not really. Now you go and play with your sister while I talk to your dad."

My son swaggers out of the room.

"Why did you do it?"

"What? This?"

"No, dealing, of course. Why take the risk?"

"You enjoyed your fish and chips?" I say and grin.

She doesn't even smile. "Are you serious?"

"It's done, and they can't get me for it."

"And you won't do it again?"

"No."

She raises her eyebrows.

"Honestly. An aberration of an otherwise upstanding member of the neighbourhood."

"You'd better be telling the truth," she says and as she's leaving the room, she calls over her shoulder, "That thing will be watching you and your data's every move from now on. Rehabilitation indeed. More like a coercive shadow of control, if you ask me."

I smile at the police bot in the corner, knowing that when it leaves for work, so shall I. Charlotte might be right about the 'at home' surveillance, but maybe I can use it to my advantage. If I can fool it into thinking I'm legit, then it'll vouch for me if I run into trouble. There's no way that my kids are going to grow up where I did, and I'll carry on doing everything to make sure they don't have to.

The Program Never Lies

Ira Nayman

"Do I...KNOW you?" K asked with a friendly smile.

He looked even better than the last time I had seen him: the grey at his temples gave him a distinguished look, and the lines around his eyes gave his smile added warmth. If I had been concerned about such things, I suppose I would have felt bad in comparison, as though my pot belly, pallid skin, and thin white hair should somehow make me feel inferior. But I was at the end of a mission that had lasted over thirty years, and I wasn't about to let myself be distracted by trivialities.

I pulled my gun.

"Whoa!" K held up perfectly manicured black hands, as if they could magically stop what was about to come. "Listen, mister. I don't want any trouble. Tell me what you want, and I'll give it to you, okay? There's no need for violence."

I snorted. No need for violence? Wrong. Wrong wrong wrong wrong wrong. Justice had been thwarted for decades! Wait til I tell Jimmy that one. He'll laugh his—umm...maybe not Jimmy. But I was sure I could find somebody at 52 Division who would appreciate the grim humour.

I first encountered K when he was just a skinny fourteen-year-old with an Afro that was bigger than his head. Auto theft was running rampant in the city, causing much consternation among well-off Mercedes and Ferrari owners. I didn't much care for the rich—it's not like they cared about me. But this was the job, and I always took the job seriously. Always.

My partner Jimmy and I were patrolling the downtown core. When calls of stolen automobiles came in, we would be first on the scene to get information from the owner. The former owner, I guess I should say. Stolen cars were either stripped for parts or shipped overseas; they were rarely recovered. That day, I was grumbling about the fact that our reports were kicked up to the detectives who were responsible for tracking down the ringleaders of the auto theft ring, that they would hog all the glory even though they couldn't do what they do without our legwork.

Jimmy shrugged. He was short but gave the impression of solidity, with his broad shoulders and gruff friendliness. Looking at him, with his almost-trim moustache and unruly brown hair, you wouldn't have guessed that he was a Mormon. "That's the job," he told me as we drove to the site of another car theft. "Always take the job seriously."

Oh. Right. That's where I got that.

When we arrived at the parking lot on Bay, near Queen, a woman in a smart business suit stopped tapping her designer shoe on the concrete near a small pile of shattered glass and said, "About bloody time!" Nearby, a skinny white kid in a blue security guard's uniform was holding on to a squirming Black kid in jeans and a Public Enemy T-shirt. I pointed at Jimmy, then the woman. Jimmy nodded and headed towards her. I headed towards the suspect.

"Let go of me!" the Black kid was shouting. "I didn't do nothing!"

"I didn't do anything," I corrected him.

"Course not," the Black kid retorted. "You're a cop. Cops never do anything."

I'm not a fan of sarcasm. Or bad grammar. I hated the kid instantly.

"Can you hold him?" I asked the security guard.

"Oh, sure, officer," responded the white kid, whose voice couldn't make up its mind if it wanted to be adult or not. The Black kid wiggled and nearly got free. I put a finger up to his nose. "If you aren't here when I come back, I will find you. And you will regret it."

"You got no right to hold me here! I didn't do nothing!" the Black kid loudly insisted. I winced. But I noticed that he wasn't struggling any more, so I returned to the squad car.

My body cam was feeding directly into the computer in the vehicle. I pulled a still of the Black kid from the feed; he wouldn't stand still, so there was a slight blur to the image, but it was clearly identifiable. Then I ran the image through Ferocious Algorithm Leading to Superlative Examinations, software that compares the image of a suspect with the force's database of known perps looking for—oh look: a 93.7% match!

I returned to the kid with a big grin on my face. "Okay, S," I began, "let's try this a—"

"What did you call me?" the Black kid asked.

"S?"

"There you go," the Black kid said, as if he was the adult lecturing a youngster. "You've got the wrong guy. My name is K." He gingerly pulled a wallet out of his back pocket and showed me a couple of cards with the name "K" on them.

I shrugged. "It's not like you'd be the first criminal to use an alias," I told him. Thanking the security guard for his good work, I grabbed K by the arm and led him to the back of the squad car.

"You're making a big mistake, man," K muttered as I jotted some notes down in my pad.

"Was that a threat?" I brightly responded.

K decided that this was a good time to stew quietly.

A couple of minutes later, Jimmy took his shotgun seat in the car. "Can you take the victim next time?" he muttered. "They're so hopeful of getting their cars back—I find letting them down easy heavy lifting!"

"Anything for my partner," I said as I started the engine and began the drive to the station on College.

After the perp was processed, Jimmy and I sat down with him for a lengthy chat. He professed his innocence the whole way through. We offered him a deal for a reduced sentence if he would just admit to his crime and plead guilty. Nothing. We told him we would recommend that his sentence be reduced if he told us who he was working for. We may as well have been talking to the wall behind him.

A few hours later, as Jimmy and I were closing our computers in anticipation of the end of our shift, Sergeant Chenowsky approached the desk we shared.

"John?" he said.

"Yeah," I replied.

"That kid you brought in? K? Drop the charges and let him go."

"What?" I was indignant. "It was a good arrest! The facial recognition software said he was a 93% match!"

Chenowsky looked exasperated. With his chiselled jaw and deep blue eyes, he expressed exasperated really well. "Look, I've told you before," he loudly stated, "93% isn't 100%. If you want any of your collars to stick, you have to find corroborating evidence—and, in this case, I don't see any."

"But—"

"Let the kid go. You know where he lives—if you find any corroborating evidence, you can nab him agin."

"But—"

"Let. Him. Go."

I looked around to see if anybody had heard. Of course, nobody was looking in my direction but everybody had heard. That's when I knew I really hated the kid.

Jimmy and I left K in the plaza just outside 52 Division. "I told you I was innocent," he said with a big smile. No, *that's* when I knew I really hated the kid.

We went on to other cases. I was a little more...circumspect in my use of facial recognition software after that. But I did make it my mission to watch K every so often, just to see if I could catch him in the act. I didn't. Oh, he was good. At first, Jimmy thought I was being thorough and professional. After a few years, he thought I was being obsessive and amateurish. We agreed to disagree, until about a decade after the original event...

Jimmy and I got a call on a drug overdose in The Annex. There was a lot of it going around that year. We parked next to the ambulance and fire truck on Augusta and went into the duplex, ignoring the crowd of gawkers gathered on the other side of the street.

In an apartment with modern art on the walls, comfortable furniture and books piled everywhere you looked—so, typical of the neighbourhood—a man lay sprawled on the kitchen floor. His lips were blue and his eyes had bugged out. Scattered on the table were a variety of coloured pills.

"Fentanyl?" Jimmy asked.

"Looks like," the EMT replied. "Won't know for sure until the coroner does an autopsy."

Jimmy nodded. I told him I would go out to the crowd to see if anybody saw anything.

Can you guess who I found out there? He was taller and had bulked up, but I recognized him immediately. Giddy with anticipation, I rushed back to the cruiser to put his current image into the system. Bingo. K was an 88.7% match with a notorious drug dealer named H.

I returned to the crowd. Fortunately, K was still there. I asked him to come with me to the police cruiser; to my surprise, he agreed.

"How may I help you, officer?" he politely asked. Clearly, somebody had worked on their manners (not to mention their grammar) in the intervening decade.

He denied any knowledge of illegal fentanyl trafficking, of course; he claimed to be a student in pre-law. But the program never lies. When Jimmy came out to the car, he was surprised that I had put K in the back seat, but I assured him, "Don't worry—I know what I'm doing."

Jimmy didn't respond. After K was processed and we had done a preliminary questioning, though, he had a lot to say after we returned to our desk, starting with: "John, do you have any corroborating evidence?"

"I'm working on it," I mumbled.

"The kid says he has nothing to do with drug trafficking," Jimmy said, looking at me hard.

I shuffled a couple of papers on the desk, then returned his glare. "He would say that, wouldn't he?" I replied. "First auto theft, now drug dealing—he's a hard case. And he was in the crowd—criminals often return to the scene of the crime."

"He lives in the neighbourhood," Jimmy argued. "He was shopping in the Annex when he saw the flashing lights of the ambulance and, like everybody else in the crowd, drew close to the building curious to see what was going on. We've got nothing on him other than what the computer program told us."

"The program never lies," I insisted through gritted teeth.

"Maybe not, but its output is imperfect and has to be interpreted," Jimmy pointed out.

I banged a fist on the desk. "Dammit, Jimmy!" I shouted. "Whose side are you on?" He didn't respond. I looked around the room to see if anybody heard my little outburst. Everybody was looking at me. Oh, yeah. They heard.

Just like the first time, we had to let K go. It stuck in my craw, but the powers that be clearly didn't see what I saw. The lump in my craw grew bigger a couple of months later, when Jimmy asked for a new partner. I thought we worked well together, but I now see that he didn't have the stomach to do what needed to be done.

I nearly choked on the lump a few months later, when a class action lawsuit was brought against the police department, claiming that the Ferocious Algorithm Leading to Superlative Examinations computer program contained racial biases that resulted in too many people of colour being arrested, charged, and convicted of crimes they did not commit. I assumed the city was going to fight the lawsuit; imagine my surprise when, a few months later, the cowards quietly settled the lawsuit out of court and discontinued the use of the computer program.

As the years (and partners) passed, I would periodically check on K's progress. He became a lawyer. He married a woman and had three children. He worked in corporate law where he quickly made a lot of money...or used the job as a cover for the vast sums of money he must be making illegally.

Meanwhile, my wife had left me and my career was stalled. Despite doing solid policing, I never made detective. As his criminal enterprise grew, K's influence must have reached into the police department itself. That would explain a lot.

Eventually, nobody wanted to partner with me. So, I was given a dog. A robot dog. "Are you sure you want to do that, John?" quickly became its favourite thing to say. At first, I wasn't thrilled about the assignment, so I named it RoboMutt. But RoboMutt soon proved its worth: it had come with the latest software: Utterly Non-linear Testbed for Regulating Unusual Enemies. That program, which contained all of the crime reports from all of the stations in the city, updating them in real time, built a model of the city that showed the most likely places crime was about to happen. Better: using those crime reports, it could predict who was most likely to commit those crimes. It was Ferocious Algorithm Leading to Superlative Examinations on steroids with a cute voice!

I've never been as impressed with computer programmers as I was the day I discovered that.

RoboMutt (which had become a term of endearment) gave me leads on low-level drug dealers and a couple of extortionists. At this point in my career—I was pushing sixty and looking forward to retirement—I was happy not to get any major cases. That is, until who should pop up on RoboMutt's radar but K? He was about to commit a financial crime at a movie premiere at the Bell Lightbox.

I got a table at a restaurant on King opposite the Lightbox and waited. Around 6:30, a limo drove up to the building and K and an elegant middle-aged Black woman stepped out. Seeing my opportunity, I ran across the street and shouted, "K! I need to talk to you!" He turned and asked if he knew me. When I pulled my gun, he said there was no need for violence.

I snorted. No reason for violence? There were thirty years of criminal behaviour—the man was the mastermind behind all of the criminal gangs in the city, always moving behind the scenes, pulling strings, never getting caught, never even under suspicion by any law enforcement officer. Other than me. I was the only one who saw him for what he was. That made me the only one who could do anything to stop him.

"Sure, you know me," I said, shooting K twice in the chest. "I am your justice..."

ELIJAH

Wendy M Grossman

WHEN THE DOORBELL rang, I wasn't expecting a police pod. I wasn't even expecting the doorbell. It was 2:13 AM (as verified by the case file), and I was brushing my teeth before going to bed.

"You are under arrest," said the male synthesized voice the press called "Arnie" because it sounded so much like Arnold Schwarzenegger in old movies. "Put your hands up and walk forward. Leave the door open."

I had a vague idea of what would happen next. The pod would send tiny drones throughout my house to photograph everything. The images would be sent back in real time to an AI system back at the station that would analyze them and decide if there was anything to mark for further examination. In the morning, the State would submit its case for processing. By lunchtime, my case would be scored, and I would either be convicted or cleared.

I put down the toothbrush and raised my hands, wishing I could rinse. Habit from watching years of old crime shows led me to say, "What am I being charged with?"

"Murder."

"There must be some mistake—" I started to say. It ignored me.

"You are under arrest. Walk forward."

I wished I'd paid more attention to the design of these pods. Did it have weapons? Could it hurt me? I stood for a moment, weighing competing fears.

"You are under arrest. Walk forward into the pod."

I walked forward.

The pod strapped me into a seat and closed its door. A number pad lit up. "Press one to hear your rights. Press two to see destination. Press three to see..." I pressed one.

"I will now read you your rights. You have the right to remain silent. Anything you say..."

"Those are the wrong rights," I yelled. Then I noticed the pod's branding: Tesla. *American.* "They're from the wrong country!"

"Press OK to agree that you have been read your rights or Replay to hear them again."

I was stuck. I had heard rights, but American rights, not Britain's police caution. There was no option for that. I could sit here replaying the American Miranda rules all night, or accept them and move on. I pressed OK.

The drones that had been flying through my house began docking themselves to the outside of the pod. An arm snaked out and pulled the door closed and stretched a line of crime scene tape across it. The pod moved off and began playing an ad for Carceral Response, a private advisory service on adjusting to prison.

Eight hours later I was in court being asked to plead guilty or not guilty to the murder of Martin Stanwell. By then, I'd learned some details of the charge. A little after eleven the previous night, his body had been found lying by the side of Twickenham bridge, straddling the boundary between Surrey County and Greater London. The body had been found by Harry Smith, a cyclist on her way home from a local theatre production, who reported it. From there, the automated criminal justice system of Greater London took over. Drones had been immediately dispatched to record the crime scene, everything from images of the body and the surrounding area to DNA samples, soil samples, fingerprints, and other biometrics. This mass of data had been fed into Greater London's ELIJAH system, which had somehow spat out my name and address.

What I still couldn't understand was why me. I'd only ever been to that area once, years earlier, when an American friend had insisted I take them to see Richmond. I'd never heard of Harry Smith or Martin Stanwell, I had nothing to do with amateur dramatics, even in my own neighbourhood, and, and, and. Unfortunately, my only alibi was that on the night in question I'd been at home. Most people could probably drum up some proof of that—something streaming, the pattern of electric lights, water use—all the data a house generates as you live in it can serve to prove innocence in a situation like that. But my house was cheap because it had never been upgraded to modern data generation, and although it cost more to live in it as a result, I liked it that way. So my house couldn't help. But that's where I was, reading a book.

When my time came to speak, I made these points. Meanwhile, the AI legal aid was advising me to plead guilty because the system would penalize me for resisting. More than pleading guilty would? I couldn't get the legal aid to tell me; apparently the details of the scoring system were secret, so people couldn't try to game it. I pleaded not guilty.

I tried to follow the State's case, which seemed to rest on ancient CCTV images captured on that long-ago foray with my American visitor. Who, it transpired, had in the intervening years been placed on a watch list of potential criminals. It didn't sound to me like the search of my house had turned up anything of interest, but by then even I could see how they might find that suspicious. My legal aid seemed to find little to object to, but it did ask for the details of the watch list. The US refused to supply them.

As for the victim, it appeared he was a local florist, but ELIJAH seemed more focused on scoring potential perpetrators than investigating the circumstances of the crime.

In mid-afternoon, ELIJAH issued my score: 83% probability that I was guilty. That was well above the threshold for conviction. A pod drove me home, and before opening the door to let me out instructed me to place my left hand on the yellow print. When I followed the instruction, I felt a brief burst of pain as the pod injected a chip. The chip, it informed me, would track all my movements and prevent me from leaving the house except with explicit authorization. Essential supplies would be delivered. Visitors were prohibited, unless explicitly authorized. The house itself had been fitted with new surveillance systems. My Internet access had been limited to an authorized list of sites. I would be staying here until a prison place could be found. I should prepare for that.

***

Three years later, the shock had faded, though the sense of injustice had not. Attempts to challenge the conviction had failed. I still awaited the prison place. A few of my neighbours had by and large been surprisingly kind. Some had tried to make trouble with the local council about "having a prisoner in our midst". Most were indifferent. But a few took the trouble to learn the rules and dropped off what they could to make my home imprisonment less intolerable.

It was one of those neighbours who, one Monday evening in April 2048, dropped a printed sheet through my letterbox. "Surrey woman convicted of manslaughter," it read.

All this time later, the Surrey police had finished investigating the death of Martin Stanwell, identified former girlfriend April Grant as the perpetrator, and successfully prosecuted her. She had, the prosecutor had persuaded the court, run him over in a moment of uncontrolled jealousy over a new romance. Neighbours and friends had testified to their volatile relationship, traces of his clothing and DNA were found on her car's tires, and local video footage clearly showed her in the driver's seat as her car, licence plates correctly read, drove into him.

I stared at the story, dumbstruck. It had never occurred to me that anyone else would be investigating this case. I had tried to get the press interested, but no one was famous, and, as one journalist had written back bluntly, "I can't see any miscarriage of justice here. You were scored at 83%."

By this time, I knew a lot more about the automated system that had convicted me. The series of cost-of-living crises that began with Brexit and the covid pandemic had led to a rise in crime throughout the capital, while cuts to every part of the criminal justice system had created lengthy backlogs in the courts. The promise of accurate, speedy justice at a lower cost and without the liability risk of abusive policing had sold the city, now a devolved region, on adopting ELIJAH. I had yet to find an explanation of what ELIJAH stood for. (Electronic Legal Investigation Justice Automated...what?)

But Surrey County was not part of Greater London. Under the Regional Devolution Act of 2043 it operated its own criminal justice system and police force. I had forgotten that crucial detail, that the body was found lying across the boundary. A few feet in either direction...

It seemed that the dispatcher had forwarded the report to the police in both jurisdictions. The Surrey police sent DI Daniel Oliver to the scene, and he had proceeded to lead a traditional police investigation. The body was taken to the coroner's office for a post-mortem examination. The report would of course have been available to police in any jurisdiction, but it seemed clear that it couldn't have arrived before my conviction—the coroner, like the prison system, moved in traditional human time. Unlike ELIJAH, which was designed to analyze whatever data was available and render a speedy decision.

What remained unclear was what to do now. The London courts had clearly become rubber stamps for whatever ELIJAH advised. I had already tried appeals. Both the software provider and the police authority were insistent that the computer could not make errors. The only errors they agreed were possible were in the input data. ELIJAH only operated—with perfect accuracy—on the information it was given.

It didn't help that Greater London had signed a deal with ELIJAH's maker, a specialist in predictive policing, that allowed the company to refuse to disclose its proprietary algorithm. "Commercially sensitive," the company said. "Too easy for criminals to game if the details were known," Greater London said.

So even though I could find out—or at least guess—what information the system had been given, I couldn't find out which parts it weighted most heavily in scoring my case. From something one of the journalists let slip, I got the impression that my lack of footprint was considered suspicious. What was I hiding by rejecting so many of the electronic parts of modern life? Maybe they'd have understood it better if I had remained stuck into the social media of 2025, or watched TV like some of the younger generation who'd decided it was cool again.

Fuelled with the first hope I'd felt in a long time, I began writing again to anyone I thought could help pointing out the new conviction. Didn't that prove my innocence?

Daniel Oliver was quick to respond, saying he would send the file to the Greater London Appeals Board for consideration. I know he did, because they acknowledged getting it. Then I reread the message and saw the note at the bottom. "There is a backlog in processing. Expected wait time is thirty-eight months."

I also tried writing to the newly convicted Ms Grant. I don't know what I thought. Maybe that she'd tell someone who would listen. Maybe that she'd write back in sympathy. Something. But...silence.

Martin Stanwell's mother, who had submitted a victim impact survey in my case, had since died. I had some response from a criminal justice reform campaigner, but he said even in extreme circumstances they were finding it hard to get anyone to take seriously an appeal against the computer.

"It's their jobs," he said. "You can't get fired for doing what it says. You can get fired for using your own judgement. No one wants to take that risk."

He also helped me understand why Daniel Oliver could respond quickly but ElIJAH could not. I began to realize that the criminal justice system was like a live frog. If you pin down one piece of it, the rest becomes distorted. In the case of Greater London, they had pinned down parts of the frog by automating policing and the courts. The visible bits. The parts the public interacted with. The parts people complained about. The parts that would let politicians show they were cracking down on crime. Nothing had ever been done to improve the problems around the other parts—the prisons, or the systems for appeal and redress. Those only affected people society had already written off, and because they required human labour they were expensive and therefore under-resourced.

Surrey County had taken more than two years longer to investigate "my" crime. A lot of the data had been available to both investigations. ELIJAH certainly should—or could—have had the same post mortem data, the camera footage, all the physical samples. Yet somehow, that long-ago photograph of me with a friend who was now tarred with suspicion had been more important in its calculations than the actual crime. This is a bad person who is likely to commit crimes. How much does it matter if it wasn't this one?

I got word that a prison place was opening up. It may seem surprising, but that seemed like good news. I had been alone in my house for three years with barely any human contact. At least in prison there would be people. Maybe someone would help.

***

I was partly right. It had not been possible to fully automate prisons; prisoners proved too adept at figuring out how to hack and disable their robot guards. An advocate met me on arrival, my first in-person conversation in months. It was not uncommon, she said, for prisoners who, like me, had been imprisoned at home, to struggle to adjust to the lack of privacy. I was to call if I needed help.

The help I needed, I said, was legal aid—someone who could push my appeal. If I had that I could manage the rest—the noise, the constant presence of people, the lights...

Two weeks later, a solicitor came.

"I've looked up your case," he said. "That conviction is ridiculous. But you should have called a lawyer when the pod showed up."

"I didn't know if I could," I said.

"They count on that." He left in a whirl of optimism, leaving me daring to hope for the first time since that doorbell rang.

Then came his next visit. He had news. Amy Grant had used my case to get her own conviction quashed. She had successfully argued that she couldn't possibly be guilty if someone else had already been convicted of the crime.

"We will continue," he said. "We still have the physical evidence." But he sounded less confident than he had.

I come up for parole soon. The best I can hope is to be released back to my house with an electronic tag. It would be different from before. I would be allowed to go out, see people, find work, if I can.

My "hearing" will consist of answering questions on a computer screen. The solicitor has briefed me. It will ask if I accept my guilt. To move on, I must say yes. But that will reinforce the system's belief that its judgment of me was right all along, and will become a data point used to train it for the future.

I cannot ask ELIJAH what I should do. It has no social conscience.

Commentary

Trevor Burke KC

THE COINCIDENCE THAT in the forty-second year after my call to the bar I might have seen the first appearance there of Douglas Adams' Deep Thought does not escape me.

In September 2023, the Law Society Gazette reported that at a conference held by the Law Society, Lord Justice Birss described the year's breakthrough, generative AIs, as having, "real potential". "I think what is of most interest is that you can ask these large language models to summarise information. It is useful and it will be used and I can tell you, I have used it." According to the Guardian, it was the first known use of ChatGPT by a British judge to write part of a judgment.

Previously, the Guardian had reported that a Colombian judge had admitted to using ChatGPT in deciding whether an autistic child's insurance should cover all of the costs of his medical treatment. Judge Juan Manuel Pailla of Cartagena, is described as having asked the AI tool specific questions about the legal matter, such as: "Is an autistic minor exonerated from paying fees for their therapies?" ChatGPT's response was in agreement with the judge's final decision, concluding that the child's medical expenses and transport costs should be paid by his medical plan as his parents could not afford them.

In June, Legal Futures reported that two New York lawyers were fined after submitting fake citations generated by ChatGPT in a court filing, despite having asked the system to confirm their accuracy. Six of the cases cited were, in the words of the judge, "bogus decisions with bogus quotes and bogus citations."

How things have changed in 42 years.

Is Stephen Oram's "Ego Statistical" a glimpse of the future, perhaps?

A society policed by robots with access to private and personal information all available to detect, anticipate, and prosecute crime. Not just serious crime, but routine commonplace crime that our existing system simply cannot seem to detect and solve, let alone prosecute. Every day, month, or year countless street robberies, car thefts, burglaries, and other crimes are reported to the police. Most victims get at least a call from the police if not a visit to obtain a first-hand account of the crime. But thereafter, not much by way of resolution. Even if the police do manage to effect an arrest, trial dates post-covid can be delayed by as much as eighteen months, with only a fifty percent chance of conviction. Unimpressive statistics, some would say.

But the real question is, what price are we willing to pay to secure more arrests and more convictions? Do we sacrifice lawyers and judges and (human) juries to "get tough on crime"?

In Stephen's story, AI has advanced, and with the presumed consent of the general population a robotic police force is now deployed on our streets. Such is the technology, it would be safe to assume the clear-up rate for the crimes that so worry most citizens is much improved, and therefore the technology is popular. Bots with access to banking and lifestyle information, facial recognition, eavesdropping capabilities that monitor private conversations, all very *1984*. With little or no human intervention, the whole justice system has been delegated to a computer-run, cheaper and more efficient, model. A little bit of lip service to civil liberties restricting the use of evidence cleverly exposes how such principles can protect a criminal, as in this story.

The swift appeal and token compensation seek to mollify those concerned. This reflects a common thought, that civil liberties and the laws protecting such principles benefit the wrongdoer, as good, honest people who do nothing wrong do not need protecting from those who would abuse their powers. How wrong such views have proven to be over the years.

The real concern is, of course, that the general public will see it as progress. It is both cheap and effective and it works better than what it replaced. It will be sold, no doubt, on the basis that it reduces taxes and makes us all safer in our homes, which to many is an attractive argument.

So perhaps it really is a glimpse of a potential future.

An alternative title to Sophie Sparham's "All Born Machines" might be "Twelve Angry Jurors", reminiscent of the Henry Fonda film classic written by Reginald Rose, which I have long thought should be compulsory viewing for anyone called for jury service.

This story rewrites and revisits the tragic shooting of an innocent man, John Charles Menezes, on the tube just days after the 7 July 2005 terrorist attack, which killed fifty-two people. Eleven shots were fired, seven of them to the head, by undercover officers. No police officer was prosecuted but the Met Police were fined one hundred and seventy-five thousand pounds for health and safety breaches. The Crown Prosecution Service was of the view that there was no reasonable prospect of success in the proposed prosecution of armed officers confronting someone they believed was a terrorist likely to be wearing an explosive vest.

In Sophie's story, AI has developed to the stage where a robot chip can be placed in the body of a politician—or perhaps it is a human chip in a robot body, Whatever it is, it does not so dehumanise him that he cannot feel the effects of alcohol.

Otherwise, it is a conventional story of a juror's dilemma in retirement. A simple choice of guilty or not guilty is met with the comment "not enough options" reminding us of the old Scottish verdict "not proven", when a jury effectively sent the case back to the prosecution to come up with more evidence. The European Court of Human Rights opined that such a potential verdict, unique to Scotland, was inconsistent with Convention rights. "Not proven" verdicts have never been part of the English legal system and no one has ever suggested they should be, so the juror's lament cannot be resolved.

It becomes clear that the programming of the AI giving the fatal order was not adduced in evidence as part of the trial, depriving both defendants and jury from ever knowing how and why the AI made the mistake it did. No doubt the justification for such non-disclosure was public interest immunity. Disclosure can be denied in the public interest, a decision that ultimately falls to the trial judge, who has to balance the right of a defendant to a fair trial against the public good of not disclosing to the world at large how AI bots are actually programmed. If a judge orders disclosure the prosecution authorities face a dilemma: disclose and prosecute or decline to disclose and offer no evidence. There is no middle ground.

The Nuremberg trials swiftly disposed of a "following orders" defence. On the facts of Sophie's case, whilst evidentially significant, following orders ought not to provide a complete defence. The officers' defence must be founded on a principle—defence of themselves or others. Absent any "hostile" act by the victims, such as pulling a firearm, reaching for a firearm officers believed they possessed, or reaching for some form of trigger device for a concealed bomb, today's standards make it difficult to argue that the individual defendants raise self-defence.

So it becomes a question of trust. Were the officers entitled to trust the orders of the AI? Will the public ever trust a machine that makes a mistake, when the mistakes costs lives? Ultimately, what is the responsibility of the programmers?

At least we retain a jury system, a body of twelve armed with their collective "experience of the world", to decide criminal cases. Jury verdicts are widely accepted and always have been. Even horrendous miscarriages of justice rarely if ever call into question the jury system because it works on every level.

So whilst the development of AI seems inevitable, one hopes the fail-safe jury system will always keep it in check.

Ira Nayman's "The Programme Never Lies": identifying a suspect has long been a problem in criminal investigations. Well before the advent of CCTV, body-worn cameras, and doorbell cameras, we relied on eyewitness testimony and ID parades to prosecute people, often without any real corroborating evidence to support the correctness or otherwise of the identification. Numerous miscarriages of justice, especially in ID cases, led to judges giving every jury in an ID case a "Turnbull direction". This has been standard practice since 1977. It attempts to highlight human fallibility in attempts to identify strangers. The development of software that can take a known photo of a suspect and compare it with an image of a suspect committing a crime would obviously be welcome.

The moral of Ira's story is that whilst machines will have a place, good old-fashioned policing will need to supplement the process and find the often-absent corroboration.

Ira's protagonist's arrogance is apparent from the off—no investigation beyond taking a blurred photo to feed into the system. When the bots do not hand him the prosecution on a plate, he doubts the bot. This raises the issue of policing in the future. Will it replace age-old policing methods or supplement them?

Historically, the police have always welcomed and adopted advances in technology, as have the public. Fingerprint evidence was first accepted in a British court in 1901 and has been a mainstay of police work ever since. In the last thirty years, DNA evidence has proved equally effective in detecting and proving criminal cases. Of equal importance is the widespread public acceptance that such evidence proves what it is intended to prove. In court, no one can seriously dispute such scientific evidence. Whilst defence experts can and do sometimes question its relevance, the essential science is never questioned. But it takes time for such advances to be accepted; people are sceptical of science and often struggle to comprehend its significance.

In years to come AI will become an important tool for police, if it does not supplant them.

This story highlights the risk of inherent prejudice within the police and the hope that AI technology will remove inherent bias or prejudice. Ira's officer is fixated with K despite the obvious lack of solid evidence, his gut feeling born from simple prejudice and an element of jealousy. Even when evidence exonerates K, our officer uses this negative as yet more proof of guilt. His paranoid obsession does not go unnoticed. Lack of promotion and the fact that no one wants to partner with him suggest he is not highly regarded. Predictably, K is blamed for that as well. Our officer at times trusts the machines, but only when they confirm his prejudice and lend support to his obsessive beliefs. When the machines frustrate his efforts to arrest K, he rejects them.

Such is the nature of our policing that a rogue officer rarely makes a difference. Checks and balances ensure policing is never a one-man show, but individual prejudice can impact an individual suspect. John, Ira's officer, is but an extreme example.

In Wendy M Grossman's "ELIJAH", we see a fully automated criminal justice system for the whole of Greater London, which investigates and prosecutes a case within twenty-four hours. A system, cheaper, believed more reliable, and more efficient than what it replaced, is the basis of this story. It is built on the premise that the UK is now a federal-style democracy, not divided into states but counties, each with its own police force, its individual methods of policing, and its own completely independent court system. More American than British.

A murder, the corpse of which is found partly in Greater London and partly in Surrey, allows a contrast between older and newer, highlighting the pros and cons of both. The US-styled police bot appears ultra-efficient, and is incredibly fast at processing information and reaching a decision, but not necessarily the correct one.

Juries are directed not to convict unless "satisfied so as to be sure of guilt". We never attempt to put it in percentage terms, but in the future we discover eighty-three percent is more than sufficient to convict.

From its American caution and its inherent distrust of any suspect who is not living in a modern world of electronic gadgets that leave a footprint, the central character is lost in a system of algorithms that lack basic common sense and human intuition. Whilst it has the benefit of speedy injustice and appears to attract wide support, an innocent person is convicted in a system that does not begin to accommodate an appeals process worth its name. Even journalists, a traditional method of exposing miscarriages of justice, seem only interested in celebrity-type cases, and reject this one. No one seems interested in questioning the efficiency of ELIJAH.

Meanwhile Surrey received the same basic information, but investigated it in the traditional way, a real detective. However, a twenty-four-hour resolution in London becomes a two-year investigation, expensive and time-consuming, everything ELIJAH was designed to eliminate. But, based on the facts known to us, Surrey gets it right and the true culprit is eventually brought to justice.

Quashing the London conviction should be a straightforward process. Even in a federal system you cannot, or should not, have two people convicted of the same crime. But the problem is, quashing the London conviction exposes the faults and limitations of ELIJAH, and the appeals system within greater London. No court can question the commercially sensitive ELIJAH algorithm to correct it. A contract excludes this.

This attempts to interpret the doctrine ascribed in 1769 by William Blackstone that "The law holds that it is better that ten guilty persons escape, than that one innocent suffer (innocent person be convicted)." It is presupposed that any ratio presented should not be taken to indicate that it is worse to convict an innocent person than to acquit a guilty one. An interpretation presented as more adequate is one from an 1895 U.S. Supreme Court case which stated, "It is better to let the crime of a guilty person go unpunished than to condemn the innocent." This doctrine dates back to Roman law.

If nothing else, this at last answers the question what did the Romans ever do for us?

In Tehnuka's "Updated Intelligence", every police officer in the future will have a badge that can be updated daily and include updates to its code of conduct app. To avoid the need for a lawyer to advise a client once detained, AI is developed to allow the police to activate a remote lawyer who can advise the suspect directly. Lip service is paid to the principle of legal professional privilege, as the bot only dispenses advice when it is satisfied no human or machine can overhear the advice.

Policing by consent will always include the police playing an active part in any civil emergency. Looting has always been seen as a most serious crime attracting severe penalties.

When a refrigerator activates a warning on a mobile phone, the owner suspects a burglary and calls the police to investigate—of itself a perfectly reasonable request. The investigation skilfully blends future policing with all its technology with the good common sense of human beings who can read a situation far better than a robot. The good common sense of the police officers quickly determines this is a good-neighbour scenario, not burglary or theft. The automated enthusiasm of a machine kept in check by a human being is likely the way new developments ought to be treated and deployed.

But what of the coming decades?

AI is upon us and will not be stopped. Nor should it be and as long as it is properly monitored and regulated it can only improve the service judges and lawyers offer the public. Will such advances be of equal assistance to the police and security services? That is a far thornier problem.

AI has the potential to seriously impact our rights and undermine some of our most cherished beliefs and institutions. If the authorities can access all our smartphones, computers, and refrigerators, our bank accounts, credit cards, diaries, dating apps and Amazon orders, what sort of world will we be living in? The issue will eventually become how we control it and what use we permit to be made of it. A question for politicians, but a question we all need to ponder.

For my part it makes a barrister in a wig addressing a jury at the Old Bailey even more quaint.

Commentary

Jayen Parmar

WHEN SWITCHING OVER to catch the latest headlines, it's a common occurrence to discover policing events taking centre stage. Unfortunately, the spotlight often focuses on shortcomings, capturing public apprehension and eroding confidence. Regrettably, positive efforts in policing often take a backseat, overshadowed by a critical examination of actions and behaviours that reveal a lack of proficiency in achieving desired outcomes.

Undoubtably, when failures occur society expects transparency and accountability, prompting expanded media coverage to thoroughly examine the events and the corresponding responses.

This newsworthy pattern will never shift, especially when legal and social consequences influence public trust. This becomes even more pronounced when the narrative involves human elements such as children, families, communities, or marginalised groups, weaving a compelling dimension into the stories.

As you read further, it's imperative to bear in mind the scrutiny and challenges that will arise when implementing new technologies and AI to replace specific police functions. Policing draws attention and undergoes in-depth scrutiny at every level and is double-wrapped in layers of governance to meet regulation.

Confronted with challenges such as reduced year-on-year funding and the struggle to attract and retain officers, coupled with response incidents being documented for public scrutiny on social media, policing emerges as an exceedingly demanding profession. Despite these obstacles, officers derive pride from their work, finding fulfilment and satisfaction in safeguarding the public and resolving criminal cases.

Amidst these challenges, technology plays a crucial role in meeting demands and enhancing front-line services. Serving as a formidable ally, it aids officers in decision-making and expedites information gathering. The policing knowledge base is extensive, so much so that even the most seasoned officers cannot be expected to know everything.

New tech-savvy recruits are adept at navigating the digital landscape with their high-speed thumbs from an early age where the internet and devices have become indispensable aspects of their lives. Signalling a significant workplace generational shift, they now harbour expectations that technology will function more efficiently, placing high demands on its pivotal role to do most of the legwork and handle the majority of tasks.

The increasing utilisation of AI has the potential to reshape the operational landscape and cultivate a renewed interest in more intelligent policing. Could seamlessly integrating technology to manage routine police tasks in the background serve as a catalyst for enhancing both recruitment and retention?

AI prompts contemplation on the extent of an officer's involvement in a case—whether they might become excessively dependent on AI results, leading to attribution of blame on technology, rather than relying on their intuition and traditional police methods. Alternatively, there's the concern that officers might be discouraged from challenging AI decisions altogether.

The code of ethics in policing establishes and delineates the highest standards of conduct for all individuals within the field. The question arises: can we anticipate that artificial intelligence will demonstrate empathy and exercise judgment appropriately? Would we be confident enough in AI to reshape the profession's expectations, relying on decisions derived from predictive algorithms, extensive data analysis, and behavioural assessments?

Can AI develop a nuanced understanding when handling sophisticated and sensitive cases, adopting Hercule Poirot's discerning thinking style? I believe that this diversity of thought could significantly aid in solving cold cases, potentially expediting investigations and proactively preventing further crimes, with the added benefit of effectively halting the activities of serial offenders.

The landscape of UK policing grapples with persistent challenges in effectively engaging with under-represented and diverse communities, marked by the enduring presence of institutional racism. This long-standing issue reflects systemic disparities and biases that have, over time, eroded trust between law enforcement and regional communities.

AI holds the potential to both support and hinder efforts to address the challenges of race and diversity within UK policing. On the positive side, AI technologies can be leveraged to enhance objectivity and reduce biases in various aspects of law enforcement, such as recruitment processes, data analysis, and predictive policing. AI tools can be designed to minimise human biases and provide more equitable outcomes.

Yet, the danger lies in the potential for AI systems, if not meticulously crafted and overseen, to unwittingly sustain or worsen prevailing biases. Should the data employed to train AI models mirror historical biases within policing, these biases can endure in AI-powered decision-making procedures, resulting in the disproportionate targeting of communities.

As we take measures to prevent crime, its nature is bound to evolve, with criminals adapting and becoming more sophisticated in circumventing preventive measures. They are normally a few steps ahead and policing efforts are more reactive when cases spike, calling out a new trend. Considering this, what if criminals successfully infiltrate our AI network, causing widespread chaos and seizing control over our state, thereby manipulating the investigations? More disconcerting still is the prospect of innocent citizens facing irreversible decisions and wrongful convictions. Even worse if done without a trace and unnoticeable.

From the first Industrial Revolution to the current era of Industry 5.0, where we enter the age of AI and advanced technologies, whether now or decades into the future, considerations of the ethical imperative and regulation must be a priority. Letting this get out of control can have irreversible consequences, like opening Pandora's box of trust.

In Sophie Sparham's "All Born Machines", the story depicts the dilemma arising when officers cease independent thought and rely on AI for critical life-and-death decisions, shot dead on the spot as suspected terrorists. Algorithmic policing, designed to eradicate human error, cannot be solely relied upon. In U.K policing there is an established command structure for handling such incidents. The role of a Strategic Firearms Commander is to provide strategic leadership of operations which may require the deployment of firearms or less lethal weapons, ensuring the tactical plan can achieve the objectives of the operation before making the final decision, maintaining complete objectivity and separation.

On 22 July 2005 at Stockwell Tube station, Jean Charles de Menezes was fatally shot by officers who mistook him for a suicide bomber following the London bombings two weeks earlier. Mistakes in surveillance led to failing to identify Menezes. Based on suspicion, officers were authorised to prevent him from entering the Tube station.

This underscores the potential flaws in human decision-making. Solely depending on AI, particularly in matters of life and death, should be avoided at all costs. Leveraging it as a tool to aid decision-making and mitigate human error could prove to be a powerful secondary insight. Perhaps, under such circumstances, it might have played a role in saving Menezes' life.

In the realm of futuristic technology, where major corporations like the fictional STARK Industries in Marvel Comics provide our AI capabilities, it becomes imperative to address the legal challenges surrounding the responsibility for programming and designing AI. The boundaries of liability and trust must be carefully navigated, especially considering the AI's capacity to hold life-and-death consequences.

An important aspect to emphasise is that the defence put forth by the officers must be proven in the principle of self-defence, whether it be for the protection of themselves or others. That all-important human element must never deteriorate.

Wendy M Grossman's "ELIJAH" illustrates the supremacy of traditional policing over an automated AI solution designed for rapid decision-making. The AI calculates a probability score based on the available digital footprint of data. However, a digital native, deeply connected to technology, is unintentionally cataloguing information differently, offering a transparent audit trail for a readily explainable alibi. While automating services aims to reduce backlogs and shorten the timescales for convictions, it comes at a personal cost when errors occur. The repercussions are evident in the prolonged appeal process, which lacks automation and causes distress to innocent individuals struggling to navigate the system in their quest to clear their name.

The central message conveyed is that the outcomes hinge on the accessibility of precise and extensive data. As AI becomes increasingly prevalent, considering individuals who may not be complete digital adopters is crucial. In the face of resource constraints, the imperative is to use technology as an aid rather than a complete replacement.

Prioritising efficiency over accuracy, the debate between swift versus cautious, and the potential for rapid injustice versus prolonged justice arise. A conviction score of 83%, surpassing established thresholds, highlights the ease with which one can be deemed guilty when analytical scrutiny calculates a probability. The question emerges: will confidence in AI algorithms surpass our expectations to the extent that we unquestioningly trust their judgment, relying on probability scores to render verdicts with heightened success in evaluating the value of evidence?

Ira Nayman's story, "The Program Never Lies," serves as a chilling reminder of the enduring presence of institutional racism and racial hatred, which has seen minimal progress over time. This reality endures thirty years after the murder of Stephen Lawrence. The Macpherson report arising from that tragic event identified institutional racism and the disproportionate stop and search of black and other ethnic communities. Furthermore, it recommended a crucial shift toward police forces reflecting the diversity of the communities they serve, emphasising increased recruitment and promotion from these groups.

Seeking to improve diversity and inclusion via race action plans becomes challenging when AI models are trained on historically biased data or by individuals with racial prejudices. This complicates the task of changing perspectives, resulting in ongoing harassment and baseless accusations against affected groups. This erosion of trust is exacerbated when technology itself starts to fail them also.

The story highlights obsessive behaviour and stereotypical profiling, revealing that racial hatred and bias go beyond computer analysis. Essentially, Ira's character, K, becomes the victim of numerous biases, with little chance of being spared, particularly when those meant to protect us end up developing a passion to cause harm instead.

In this rare scenario, attention is drawn to the recent dark corner within the Metropolitan Police where Wayne Couzens and David Carrick operated in specialised units, through distinct events. Both individuals are now serving life sentences for their shocking crimes committed while serving as police officers.

While John, as depicted in Ira's story, clearly exhibits his paranoid obsession, his persistent pursuit and harassing behaviour go unreported. Distancing oneself from collaborating with a toxic colleague doesn't absolve one of the responsibility for safeguarding the public. At times, individuals with similar tendencies may eventually form alliances, giving rise to toxic cultures of bullying, racism, and misogyny within the boys' club, perpetuating a harmful cycle.

As our headlines continue to feature these narratives, a retrospective glance at the murder of George Floyd unveils a pattern where outrage and protests vividly illustrate the historical mistreatment of the black community by the police, a troubling reality that has been uncomfortably accepted, with justice often elusive.

"Updated Intelligence" by Tehnuka shows how the latest professional practice and legislation must be followed as part of the Police and Criminal Evidence Act. The lorebot in this story provides legal advice relying on an outdated database, promptly ending the investigation into a break-in and criminal damage.

Fascinating idea: a legal bot designed to interrogate suspects by assessing initial responses, conducting a preliminary analysis to reconstruct events, and prompting further questions. A generative score could gauge likelihood, supplemented by individual background information to provide guidance on subsequent actions.

Maybe this could be implemented through a mobile interface, streamlining the abstraction process for officers during initial interviews. The bot could then recap essential information to facilitate the conclusion of a report. This could help address resource constraints and function as a back-office task handled by non-police roles supporting investigations. By doing so, policing efforts can be focused precisely where they are most essential.

"Ego Statistical" by Stephen Oram, is a story that swirls the imagination into the future that defines a stark division in society, where the affluent, who can afford it, reside in a controlled environment governed by robots and an automated justice system.

The capability to swiftly identify, apprehend, and prosecute by accessing data on virtually everything instils confidence among residents. The presence of bots navigating the streets for cleaning and managing delivery orders exemplifies our readiness to incorporate them as active participants in our society.

In the societal desire for swift responses to police incidents, there is a call for the immediate arrest of suspects as soon as a crime is committed. Data centres churn at speed to analyse every transaction, identifying anomalies that trigger automated arrests through bots instead of human intervention. This integration aims to ensure a rapid response and increased convictions, envisioning a fully automated and robotic police force with no human involvement whatsoever.

The court proceedings unfold virtually, eliminating the need for any physical travel. Cross-examination is accelerated with the assistance of AI barristers representing both the prosecution and defence, expediting the process by focussing on the crucial and mutually accepted evidence, ultimately reducing the time and costs associated with drawn-out trials. Even the jury consists of AIs employing their models to reach a verdict with an 83.3% strong probability of guilt.

The result is a nullified conviction stemming from the historical scrutiny of data related to a drug-dealing operation. Joshua, who was present during the operation supplying the drug Stim, cannot be charged for the new offence. However, this development inevitably absolves him of the sentence he is currently serving.

The utilisation of data in AI demands a heightened level of consent, particularly when automating processes to such an extent that human interaction is eliminated, and decisions are driven solely by modelling. The question arises: can everything be analysed and accessed, or are there limits to what can be scrutinised?

This story also exemplifies those who seek the thrill of breaking the law and are always scheming their way to circumvent preventative measures to illicitly earn money, creatively finding loopholes and exploiting weaknesses.

A digital audit trail is deemed robust evidence, requiring every investigation to uncover this extensive footprint.

The utilisation of AI must broaden this dataset to extract numerous scenarios and possibilities, encompassing both historical and potentially unavailable data. Ensuring accurate decision-making hinges on this comprehensive approach.

As for a fully automated arrest, trial, and conviction, with no human contact, the jury is still out on that one.

In conclusion, AI is happening, irrespective of personal opinions, and it is crucial to thoroughly comprehend the concerns generated by this technology for its widespread adoption and use. These stories give you a glimpse into the future and the pitfalls that come with it.

My apprehension around AI revolves around the challenge of discerning what is real and what is the truth. As AI becomes more widely adopted, the ability to distinguish genuine information from artificial becomes a complex dilemma.

From falling victim to convincing deep fakes to placing trust in collectively curated evidence meant to bridge gaps in predictive analysis, there's a delicate balance with AI. It's imperative that AI doesn't spiral out of control to the extent that we begin questioning the authenticity of everything it generates. Moving to fallback positions will result in long turning points before trust and confidence returns.

In this context, having that human interaction is of paramount importance. As we stand at the crossing of advancing technology, the task of verifying the authenticity of information becomes progressively challenging, and reliance on human judgment becomes indispensable.

Delving into these stories offers a sneak peek into forthcoming AI integrations within policing. These dramatic transformations underscore how, regardless of the direction, full attainment of public confidence in outcomes remains unconvincing. Issues such as wrongful convictions, racial bias, and the efficacy of appeal mechanisms are all brought to the forefront, exposing the shortcomings of technology and AI and the regulation needed around it.

Harnessing AI in a positive light has the power to invigorate the cognitive imagination and freedom in our brains. By facilitating our concentration on intricate tasks, AI eliminates the drudgery of routine duties that often dampen our mental engagement. This boost in efficiency is especially pertinent in professions such as policing, where the use of AI holds the promise of significant gains in speeding up investigations and proceedings.

I am especially eager to witness how AI can enhance support for neurodivergent individuals and recognise inherent diversities in neurological functioning. Significant untapped power resides here, ready to be unleashed and enable the contribution of their unique perspectives to the world.

I wholeheartedly embrace AI, acknowledging its remarkable potential for positive transformation across diverse industries and in our personal lives. Simultaneously, I greatly advocate for prudent regulation and careful consideration of how data is shared in the realm of AI.

PART 2
Power and Energy

Milton Friedman's Heresy

DJ Cockburn

My old frenemy greeted me with "Hi, Simpers" when I opened the helicopter's door.

Don't shout at me in the comments, it was fuelled with green hydrogen.

I said, "Hi, Triz" and stepped onto the *Milton Friedman's* helideck.

She winced. Must have forgotten I wasn't the only one who had an excruciating nickname at university.

Then she said, "You're under arrest."

Which I wasn't expecting.

I pointed out that she wasn't in any police force and she said I was in a sovereign nation that had granted her the power of arrest and I said that turning a cruise ship into a tax haven doesn't make it a country if no government recognises—well, you get the gist. The half dozen men behind her were sweating in stab-proof vests and hip-holstered guns and I was alone and unarmed so it didn't matter what I said.

Which never stopped me from saying things.

"Does this mean you don't really want to discuss what the updated ecocide convention means to your passengers?" I asked as Triz and her goons marched me through the ship.

"Ecocide." She made the word sound like something she'd call a flunkey to clean up, which is how a finance bro with a penthouse on the *Milton Friedman* deals with anything from a stain on a jacket to a prosecution for high-level corruption to—if I was reading the situation correctly—me.

Which made Triz one of their flunkies and explained how she'd ended up aboard.

She's always had a gift for PR and she's been my number one sparring partner since we stopped meeting for coffee, but being a concierge to neoliberalism only makes you rich by normal standards. Not penthouse-on-the-*Milton-Friedman*-rich. Evidently, the penthouse-on-the-*Milton-Friedman*-rich know a good concierge when they see one.

They marched me to what looked like the ballroom but it wasn't laid out for dancing. The stage was dominated by a throne with two dozen chairs behind it. They sat me down on one of the two chairs seated below it and Triz took the other.

"Very theatrical. I take it we're being livestreamed," I said.

"You need to get your mouth under control, Simon," said Triz.

I wasn't Simpers anymore. We were getting serious.

And she hadn't finished. "We're not in the Students' Union now and I can't talk you out of an arse-kicking when you wind up the rugby team with your eco-warrior crap."

"That was *one time* and you'd wanted to get off with that neckless troglodyte for—"

"Shh!" She made a cutting motion with her hand.

A door opened and a liveried footman—I don't know how else to describe all that blue velvet and gold leaf—held it open and in trooped the doom brigade. A single file of figures hidden under hooded black gowns that would have looked ridiculous anywhere else. Trouble was, I wasn't anywhere else. I was in their fiefdom and nobody puts on a black gown to sing "For He's a Jolly Good Fellow".

The first man through the door sat on the throne and the rest took the seats behind it. They all threw back their hoods, revealing faces you'll be familiar with if you've been following me for a while: the two dozen billionaires who'd chosen to live on the *Milton Friedman*. The man on the throne was the man who'd turned a cruise liner into a country. He was peering down at me as if I was a fish he'd just landed. His trademark moustache drooped down to either side of his three chins, making him look even more ridiculous than when he'd hidden it under a hood.

If someone ever tries to intimidate you, 'ridiculous' is a word you'll want to keep repeating to yourself. Trust me, it helps.

I nodded to him. "Kasper Dick. It's a pleasure to meet you at last."

He pretended he hadn't heard me but gave himself away with a twitch of his moustache. It hadn't occurred to him that I might speak before I was told to. He was used to deference.

Triz stepped in. "A citizen of *Milton Friedman* is free to choose their own name. Our founder and first citizen is Hiro Protagonist."

"I'm sorry?" I asked.

"Hiro Protag... It's *not* funny."

"The prisoner will comport himself with the solemnity appropriate to the proceedings." Dick must have been miked up because his voice came from all around us, much louder than mine or Triz's. Whatever this was, theatrics were very much the point of it.

I looked at Triz. "Didn't you tell him about me?"

We all know about Dick's new name of course, but that didn't mean I had to play along. Not when I could learn something by making the room react to me. Triz's look of consternation told me I'd pulled them off-script, which would only matter if I was right about the livestream.

I learned even more from the liveried footman. He was biting his lip and struggling not to laugh.

Kasper Dick—I won't call him Hiro Protagonist—boomed again. "You, Simon Simpson, stand accused of economicide by the citizens of the sovereign nation *Milton Friedman*. All twenty-five of us will be both judge and jury. Theresa Luss will be your prosecutor. You may conduct your own defence. Do you understand?"

So Triz was not a citizen and she hadn't been allowed to give herself a silly name.

"You'll have to explain what economicide is," I said, "and how you have the authority to try me for it."

Dick nodded to Triz.

"Economicide is the programme you have ruthlessly championed over the last twenty-five years, both as a propagandist and a deep state conspirator."

"You mean as a journalist and a policy advisor?"

She ignored me. "You, your co-conspirators and the weak minds whom you have influenced have pursued a ruthless programme of authoritative legislation..."

I zoned out. I'd heard it all before and so had Dick and the permanent passengers who called themselves citizens. She wasn't speaking to them. She was speaking to the self-styled neoliberal partisans who'd appointed him their messiah and me their nemesis. It was a change from Dick's usual rants about genocidal taxation or the fascism of regulatory standards for drinking water but by the time Triz fell silent, I'll bet she'd bored half the livestream audience into googling funny cats.

"Forgive me, I think I dozed off there," I said.

Dick and Triz knew their audience. I was playing to the audience they'd overlooked.

"But I'd like to thank you. You're giving me full credit for governments around the world ditching the idea that economic growth is a cardinal virtue. You're also crediting me with making taxes, environmental lawsuits, and, now, prosecution for ecocide so difficult that you daren't leave international waters. You flatter me but I'll take it."

"I—" Triz had never been good at thinking on her feet.

"Your passengers—"

"Citizens."

I ignored Triz's correction. "—chose to live on this boat because it was getting so much harder to avoid responsibility for rising sea levels flooding Bangladesh, cyclones wrecking the Philippines, landslides loaded with mine-tailings—"

"That's beyond the remit of this court," boomed Dick. "The charge is the cost in freedom that your propaganda has ushered in. You have stripped the freedom from every citizen here with your trumped-up crime of ecocide. *That* is the case we're giving you the chance to address."

That's the trouble with being the face of a mass movement: you're the first target for reactionary punches.

"About that," I said. "The trial, I mean. What authority do you have? I'm on this boat by your invitation, to discuss how the updated ecocide convention—"

"Enough!" Dick's shout produced a squawk of feedback that made the passengers wince. "The *Milton Friedman* is not a *boat*. She is a sovereign state where citizens exercise jurisdiction and in this jurisdiction," he aimed his moustache at Triz, "the prosecution has questions for you."

"Yes. Right." Triz looked gratifyingly flustered. "First question. Why did you do it? Back at university, you were only an eco-warrior when you were drunk. Most of the time, you understood why regulation is the mortal enemy of economic growth."

That wasn't how I remembered my young self, but I let it slide.

"I grew up," I said. "You were there when it happened."

"I was?"

"It was a few years after uni. You were the public face of some asset management firm. I was in energy policy and we both ended up at one of those forums. There was one every week with its own forgettable acronyms and deadly dull subject. That day it was the future of UK energy."

"We both went to a lot of those."

"We went through all the usual. The gas guys wanted to extract hydrogen from methane and wanted the taxpayer to upgrade the mains so they could carry on with business as usual. The electric guys wanted to do more wind and solar and throw in a few heat pumps. You were nodding along and saying 'investment opportunities' and 'projected growth' at the right moments."

"This isn't about me." Triz's tone of voice begged me to leave her out of wherever I was going but Dick looked interested. Who doesn't want to know their arch-enemy's origin story?

"Then I said, how about we concentrate on insulation upgrades? Then we'd need less energy and we wouldn't need to fork out the billions you all wanted to spend. Remember that?"

"Vaguely."

"Everybody looked at me like I'd pissed in the punchbowl. You gave me your look that said you should have let your rugger boyfriend knock some sense into me a few years earlier—you'll never let me forget that, will you?—and repeated *less* like it was some sort of obscenity.

"Then I got it. You, them, everyone else, you actually *believed* in economic growth as the be-all-and-end-all. It was an article of faith for you. You couldn't have *explained* your creed that market freedom's the same as personal freedom. You'd carefully nurtured a blind spot around personal freedom being limited by how much money the markets leave the rest of us with after they've squirrelled the big bucks away in your hedge funds. When I talked about a world in which everybody could afford the energy they need without breaking the biosphere, all you heard was heresy.

"So if I've spent the twenty-five years between then and now preaching heresy, it's all your—"

"There has to be more to it." Triz learned how to shout down inconvenient truths from politicians who interrupted their way to their peerages. "You didn't commit economicide because I once said 'less' and you decided to hate freedom."

"Oh, I love freedom. So does everyone else who stopped voting for neoliberal parties when I showed them what they stand for. I didn't tell anyone what to do. I just showed up what you're doing and—who'd have thought it?—everyone who isn't a billionaire or one of their lackeys agrees with me."

"You might have fooled the masses," she said. "It doesn't make you right."

I really hoped this was being livestreamed.

"There's your problem. Right there. When the 'masses' you sneer at don't see you as the masters of the universe, you assume it's because somebody's better at fooling them than you. It doesn't occur to you that if you'd ever had to budget for your energy bill with a flood rolling down your street, you'd care more about the climate than some shareholder's dividends. You sit in front of your screens and trade things you theoretically own with no idea how they work or, more importantly, who makes them work for you. It doesn't occur—"

"This is beside the point," boomed Dick.

Behind the cloaked jury facing me, the sun slid along the windows and disappeared toward the stern. Someone else thought it was very much the point.

"Oh, I've barely started—"

"The time allocated for your defence has expired," said Triz, revealing Dick's low opinion of his audience's concentration span. "First Citizen Protagonist will now pass verdict."

"Let me guess," I said. "I'm guilty."

Dick looked around to receive a general nodding of heads and murmuring of assent. If you were watching, you saw two dozen men and women exercising their freedom to do what Dick wanted them to do.

Dick pulled up his hood. "The concept behind the *Milton Friedman* grew out of the world that you have helped to usher in. A haven for some of the most brilliant minds on earth whose brilliance is evidenced by the wealth they have accumulated, and was constrained by..."

And he was off. The same rant I'd watched him livestream a thousand times—to debunk a religion, you need to know its preachings—but then it had been my choice to give him my attention. Now I was his prisoner, he was trying to monopolise my attention and if there was one thing he should have known about me, it's that I don't respond well to monopolists.

His face was turning red, as it does when he delivers one of his angry monologues. I could see his colour changing under his cowl because the sun was now behind me instead of behind him. He showed no sign of noticing.

The sudden absence of Dick's voice drew my attention back to him. I backtracked for a moment to retrieve his last words: "...find you guilty."

What a surprise.

Then he said, "You were a sanitary engineer before you became a propagandist, correct?"

I have to admit, that surprised me.

"Yes, I worked in water treatment before I started challenging blind faith in the free market—"

"Give it a rest, will you?" Triz snapped at me.

"Your sentence will be served as the sanitary engineer on the *Milton Friedman*," said Dick, which was so unexpected that it almost shut me up.

"What? You're not going to chuck me over the side?" I did say 'almost'.

"We believe that every individual deserves the freedom to fulfil their potential," said Dick, "and we offer you the opportunity to fulfil yours."

"Ah. You mean that when you assembled the most brilliant minds on earth, you didn't think to include anyone who understands plumbing?"

Dick didn't answer. He stood and strode out followed by his citizens.

Triz waved two of the goons toward me. "Begum and Restrepo will show you where the sewers are."

"It's a boat, Triz," I said. "It doesn't have sewers."

She was already walking away.

"Would you like a cup of tea?" asked the goon called Begum.

That was when I knew I'd pulled it off.

Begum and I were on our second cup and well into our dissection of last year's Indian Premier League when the Brazilian Navy corvette hailed the *Milton Friedman*. If Dick had been listening when I asked him to consider the difference between owning things and understanding them, he'd have seen it coming. He'd have realised that his crew were men like Begum, who only worked for him because their homes were no longer liveable. The footman's struggle to keep a straight face had shown me the limits of their indulgence. Dick hadn't even realised he was testing the loyalty of the people whose misfortunes fed his fortune.

None of his brilliant citizens had noticed the ship turning toward Brazilian territorial waters the day after the São Paolo amendment made ecocide a crime against humanity. I felt safe enough to suggest that Begum and I go on deck.

Dick was still wearing his ridiculous black cloak and hammering on the door of the bridge. On the other side of the windows, the entire bridge crew stood with their backs to him. Triz was surrounded by half a dozen of the other black cloaks who were all yelling at once.

I wish the livestream had caught it. It was comedy gold.

Triz saw us and marched over. "Begum, get the security crew together. We're about to be boarded."

"Would you like us to fight the Brazilian Navy?" asked Begum in the tone in which he'd offered me a cup of tea.

"Yes, if necessary. That's what you're paid for."

"Would you like to fornicate with a goat?"

Triz gaped at him.

"Hi Triz," I said. "Looks like you're under arrest."

Legacy

Zed Badowska

CORNWALL, 2050

On the morning of Cornwall Spaceport's first commercial mining flight, Quentin Bancroft sat with his granddaughter in his late wife's garden studio, watching his house burn. From the top of the hill the explosion had been quite spectacular, and in the moments before he'd registered what was happening he had been struck by the beauty of it.

In the state of shock in which he now found himself, he couldn't decide whether he was more upset about the house or the vintage Bentleys in his subterranean garage that had been blown up to destroy it. He turned to Ada, saw tears creating rivers on her ash-smeared cheeks, and realised he didn't care a jot about the house or the cars as long as she was safe. He put his arm around her, holding her tightly as she sobbed into his cardigan.

***

Words spoken and written had changed things in the summer of 2035, when Ada, then six years old, came to stay with Quentin and Ruth while her parents attended an environmental summit in Glasgow. The first were uttered by Ada as she sat in the living room surrounded by books that had once belonged to her mother, Phoebe.

"What's a *po-lar* bear, Grandpa?" she said.

Quentin smiled affectionately and sat down next to her, lifting the cover of the hardback in her lap. *Animals of the Arctic* had been one of Phoebe's favourites. Ada had settled on a chapter called "Vanishing Habitats", her small finger hovering over a paragraph towards the bottom of the page. *Among the many animals that may one day lose their homes are polar bears and walruses.* Quentin remembered this sentence. When Phoebe was eight, she had given an impassioned speech about polar bears during her primary school's climate change assembly. Quentin had helped his daughter prepare the presentation, bought her the book so she could copy pictures and facts.

He felt the cold fingers of guilt in his stomach; Ada wasn't supposed to see this. Phoebe's generation had learnt from the mental health crises of the 2020s. They'd protected their children from the hate speech and misinformation of the internet, from the books and television programmes that told the truth about the world they'd inherited. Forest schools like Ada's were all the rage among those who could afford them, at which children were encouraged to be children, and web-based learning was eschewed until they were at least ten years old.

Quentin sighed and turned the page. "These are polar bears," he said.

"That's sad," Ada said earnestly, stroking the photo of a mother bear and her cubs. "I wish I could help them."

Quentin might have felt better if she'd asked more questions, to which he could have provided suitably sanitised answers. But she didn't. And with Ada's advanced aptitude for reading, he strongly suspected this was because she'd already understood everything else on the page.

The next words arrived a few days later, daubed across the house's white-rendered facade in what Quentin hoped was red paint: COMPLICIT IN GENOCIDE. Ada discovered them after waking up early and taking the dog outside to play.

Ruth deflected her granddaughter's questions about these words with exaggerated amusement at such a silly prank, while Quentin quietly called the police. Five other board members from the bank had been subjected to the same attack. They all knew the reason, of course. A disgruntled ex-employee had shared a list of the firm's historic investments on social media, a list that included multiple fossil fuel projects that had collectively released millions of tonnes of carbon dioxide into the atmosphere, at a time when the entire world was screaming for these ventures to stop.

Complicit in genocide. Quentin rolled the accusation around in his mind that evening, while he watched Ruth and Ada playing Hungry Hippos. Genocide was Adolf Hitler, Pol Pot, Idi Amin. It wasn't a semi-retired banker with a talent for making lucrative investments. In the few conversations he'd had with Phoebe about his work she'd never used the g-word. *You're assuming you need to have an overt intention to do wrong*, she'd once said. *You don't, Dad. Your choice to ignore the evidence makes you culpable. Your PR department can promote all the positive things the bank's doing as much as it wants, but they're meaningless if you keep doing the negative stuff too.* He'd buried these comments somewhere in his mind, convincing himself that his charity donations absolved him. Remembering his daughter's words now, spoken with love rather than anger, gave him pause.

Ada squealed with delight as her plastic hippo captured the last ball, and Quentin's thoughts drifted to his honeymoon. He and Ruth had safaried in Zambia, taken photos of hippos with cameras that weren't integrated into phones. He considered Ada's perception of the game she was playing, conscious that he wasn't certain which animals were left in Africa. Did she file hippos in the same mental box as dragons and unicorns? *Animals die out*, he told himself. *That's just what happens over time.* Today, however, his inner voice sounded unconvincing.

Phoebe and her husband, Matti, returned to collect Ada the following week. They were tired and subdued, and when Ruth asked how the summit had gone Phoebe didn't answer. Instead, she plastered on her biggest smile and asked her daughter what she'd been up to with Grandma and Grandpa.

"We read *Goodnight Moon* every night," Ada said after a short pause.

"I'm sure you did," said Phoebe, with a knowing look at her parents. Ada's favourite bedtime story hadn't changed in the past six months, and three or four readings were generally required before she'd consider going to sleep. "Anything else exciting?"

"Someone naughty painted the house," Ada announced, hands on her hips to indicate her disapproval.

Matti laughed and lifted her up. "We heard about that." He glanced at Quentin. "You and your mates made the news."

Quentin was aware of this. His face would have been plastered across video screens at the summit, and many of the people with whom Phoebe had been meeting would know she was related to him. He was also certain she and Matti would have agreed not to make a fuss about it, because they had never once directly criticised him for his work. *The way I see it*, Phoebe had said years earlier, *I can either spend my life being furious with you for the one part of your life I disapprove of, or I can accept that the money you made paid for my education, which has allowed me to do some good.*

Quentin smiled uneasily at Matti and shoved his hands in his pockets, and Ruth broke the silence by offering everyone tea.

Phoebe had met Matti in Australia during her PhD studentship. She'd been developing renewable energy projects for impoverished communities and he'd been working to mitigate the effects of climate change on Tuvalu, the Pacific archipelago on which he'd grown up. When she'd introduced him to Quentin and Ruth on a video call, she'd had to show them where Tuvalu was on a map. Ruth had remarked proudly that she knew about it from *Pointless*.

After finishing her PhD, Phoebe had joined New Dawn Fusion, an Anglo-Australian company exploring experimental techniques for clean energy production. Their technology could potentially provide abundant power fuelled by nothing but seawater, releasing helium as a harmless byproduct. The tech had been in development for years, a running joke in the scientific community being that it was always "nearly there". But they'd done it, in spite of false information disseminated by fossil fuel corporations, in spite of having to convince the public that nuclear power didn't always involve radioactivity. They'd done it, through global collaboration on an unprecedented scale. The first fusion power stations had been commissioned in several countries, and construction was already ahead of schedule.

Since then Phoebe had set herself a new challenge, leaving NDF to focus on downscaled reactors. In her view, powering entire countries was only the first step in the fusion revolution; the next was producing portable systems. The potential applications were numerous, from shipping to aviation to space flight, and her startup had received substantial cash injections from several private backers. But the initial funds had dried up quickly, and the lack of rapid progress had made investors nervous. Work had halted altogether at the beginning of the year, and the Glasgow summit had offered what might be the final opportunity for Phoebe to promote the company in person. No one had bitten. The tech was too speculative, too "out there", to make any money in the short-term, and there were hundreds of other green-tech startups promising more than Phoebe could.

As they sat in the lounge after Ada had gone to bed, Quentin dared to ask his daughter a question. "Was it because of me?"

Phoebe frowned. "Was what because of you?"

"You not getting any backers."

She smiled and squeezed his hand. "Your history doesn't define me, Dad. Most people with any sense really don't care that you're my father."

"Then will you let me do something for you?" he said. He scribbled a number on a piece of paper and handed it to her. "That's how much I can get for you in the next month, from pensions and some other investments. I'm certain you'd disapprove of most of them, but I want to help you build your generators."

There had been a time when forecasters were convinced there was no hope of carbon neutrality, let alone carbon negativity, without a period of extreme fuel austerity. They'd predicted the mass closure of airports, limitations in sea freight, mandatory dietary restrictions to reduce livestock emissions. None of this transpired. But other things, inevitably, did.

In the years following Quentin's donation, Phoebe was described by *Time* magazine as a visionary for her work in shipping and aviation. She was awarded a CBE. She accumulated millions of followers on the privacy-centric, not-for-profit, hate-free social media platform she and Matti had helped develop. And Ada—compassionate, intelligent Ada—began to contribute, incrementally, to her parents' tireless efforts to fix their broken planet by documenting everything they were doing.

She started by sharing video updates with Quentin through Phoebe's social media platform, determined to keep her beloved grandfather's ageing brain stimulated after the loss of his wife to Alzheimer's. Films of her parents and aunts and uncles building flood defences on Tuvalu while her cousins played in the sea. Her parents giving speeches at an environmental awards ceremony. Family "holidays" to help with land regeneration, wildlife conservation, retrofitting diesel fishing boats with solar panels.

Ada's videos became more polished once she started studying film-making in earnest, her documentation of the world's progress now shared with everyone rather than just Quentin. Events she'd once uploaded as separate videos were now combined in documentaries of increasing length, as she began to explore the links between them—wildfires, floods, marches against drilling for rare minerals, campaigns for a ban on disposable electronics and built-in obsolescence while thousands queued for the latest phones. The film she made at university won multiple awards.

It began with Ada's early footage of her parents' work, cutting to stills of news articles about the positive impact of this and countless other projects. Against a soundtrack of uplifting music she showed clips of the global celebrations when it was reported that these efforts were actually working, when renewables overtook fossil fuels, when energy prices began to fall. The music then changed to melancholy cellos and violins, the images replaced with stark white text on black: BUT HUMANS ALWAYS WANT MORE. A rapid succession of clips followed—happy couples with babies, models advertising clothes and cars and gadgets, production lines in factories churning out smoke, rivers polluted with factory runoff, forests destroyed and replaced with buildings and livestock, mineral mines at capacity, planes taking off and landing, workers making ever more products, faster and faster.

A voiceover accompanied the images: "Reductions in energy costs have led to increases in disposable income; that's the spare money you have after you've paid your bills. More people can afford luxury goods—phones and computers and cars with more efficient systems and batteries. Increased optimism and income mean people are having more children. There's greater demand for food and housing, for land on which to grow the food and build the housing, for building materials, for fuel to produce those materials, for minerals to make electronic goods, for energy to power and water to cool the servers storing our ever-increasing data. There's more digging for minerals, which damages the soil and releases more carbon. Trees—which sequester carbon—are felled, exacerbating the problem. Then there's more digging to make space for the carbon we need to capture from the factories producing all the shiny new tech. And because the cost of flights has plummeted, more planes are needed to satisfy increases in demand, new machines with better engines that use new fuel."

Silence, and a plasticine Moon appeared, happy face and heavy-lidded eyes.

"And then there's this," the voiceover continued, "the discovery by brand new spacecraft, which can fly further away more often, that the things we're running out of are actually within our reach." A rocket landed on top of the Moon and little figures in construction gear jumped out. "Even better than that, if we make holes on the Moon to dig up minerals, maybe we can fill those holes with the carbon we can't fit on Earth." The mini-figures drilled holes on every inch of the surface, filling them with black Lego bricks. The Moon cried a blue plasticine tear.

The final section of the film showed Ada in a boat with Matti and her Tuvaluan cousins. No speaking, no music. Just Ada's camera panning from one face to the next, and finally to small mounds of green in the distance. She cut to them wading onto an island, standing waist-deep in seawater on what was once a road. Shops and houses abandoned after the last storm destroyed any hope of gradual migration; a lone bird perched on the wheel of an overturned, floating car. Ada showed the boat's journey back to the Australian mainland. The Portakabins near the beach that the media had been told to refer to as "temporary accommodation" instead of "refugee camps". She focused on Matti: greying hair, jaw set, eyes red-rimmed. The screen went black, and words appeared one by one in red: We need to change our behaviour. Whenever you think, *I need this*, stop for a moment. Do you really, actually, *need* it?

***

The fire from Quentin's house had reduced to a smoulder, a few beams creaking and groaning before crashing to the ground. And that was it. A home gone, just like that. Not, however, the only one Quentin owned.

Ada wiped her eyes and looked at her grandfather. "I wanted you to know how it felt."

"I understand now, darling. I do." Quentin glanced with relief at the storage boxes behind him, filled with items Ada had been secretly hoarding since she arrived the previous week. Precious things. Memories she'd been kind enough to move to Ruth's studio before she blew up the house. Memories that a storm surge, a wildfire, a flood, would not have been concerned about saving.

Quentin had told himself that he'd built his carbon-neutral home to help the environment. He wondered now if that was ever true. He wouldn't have built it at all if the sea hadn't risen, eroding the coast on which his last holiday home had been situated. *We tell ourselves the stories we want to hear*, he thought. *Reframe things to make us feel better about them.*

One thing he knew to be true was his granddaughter's frustration. Her videos would never truly capture the emotion of the events contained within them. They were distant images of distant places and distant people who weren't real to those watching. To people like her grandfather, who had for decades buried similar images under more pressing local concerns.

In the distance they could hear a low rumbling, and Ada pointed towards the spaceport.

"The ship's taking off."

They watched it rise slowly, disappearing into the early-morning cloud.

Ada rested her head on Quentin's shoulder. "Goodnight Moon," she said softly.

The Bracelet and the Battery
Tim Kindberg

ONCE UPON A future time, in a land occupied not only by the people who were born there but by many others who have sought sanctuary in that land, there will be a parliament of proportional rule; and under that government there will live a young woman who calls herself Jacqui, although that is not the name her own people have given her.

It will be September, and very hot. And Jacqui will wear a bracelet around her ankle, for that is the decree brought down from the parliament: a constraint made in exchange for her presence in their land. She will wear it all day, every day, from when she sleeps (or tries to, in the muggy nights), to when she travels along the verdant streets, invisible to most but sometimes flitting a glance at a person who might also be a refugee, and who sometimes will reciprocate.

And everywhere that Jacqui will go, the bracelet will receive the transmissions of satellites to calculate and record her movements; and, near the cooling ice of the North Pole, a machine will check whether she has exceeded the geographic bounds deemed necessary for her usefulness. Violation will mean deportation, back to where the winds blow harder, the sun burns hotter, the sea and the floods rise even higher, the food is scarcer; and where there is no parliament of proportions.

One day in this future time, Jacqui will wake up hungry, like everyone without sufficient money beyond the Basic—whether or not they have bracelets on their ankles. This will be the third day of another food shortage. Despite the hard-won transformation to farming regeneratively and reducing livestock, crops have failed again, energy has failed too often lately, people are ill. The machines predict the shortages and the outages; many people like Jacqui, with bracelets, are reassigned to try to compensate. But there are limits to coping with combinations of exigencies: the weather will be cruel and mercurial; resources will stretch only so far; conflict will come and go in the lands beyond this land.

Let us fly into this future like a bird migrating in time, landing on a perch within a tree outside Jacqui's open window, peering through the shutters she left open overnight.

That morning, on waking, Jacqui turned back her sheet to touch the bracelet, which had been bothering her in the sweaty night; its low-profile plastic case was locked to her, heavier in how it pressed upon her soul than in its clasp around her left ankle. Her watch buzzed like a messenger she couldn't wholly ignore. Its screen flowered out with the weather, the energy, the food for the day. The heatwave that was making people so cross lately continued, with temperatures in the upper thirty degrees. An outage was likely at five p.m. for about an hour. Her rations would be available in the local food bank at seven p.m.

Her assignment was to spend another day caring for Sam, who lived alone and required care due to his learning disabilities and epilepsy. She was to report for her shift in the tower block where he lived, and this filled her with disappointment. She held misgivings about this man, with whom she was to spend the day alone. And while there was something to be said for an occasional change from her typical agricultural work, she missed the soft give of soil beneath her feet, the brush of leaves against her skin.

As one might check on a sleeping child, Jacqui looked across to where a bracelet battery was on charge, its amber light blinking. They had given her three: one inside the bracelet, a spare she had to bring with her everywhere in case that one gave out unexpectedly, and the one across the room. Given the outages and the variations in power that the algorithms assigned to every device, she sometimes had to leave them on charge for long periods.

Jacqui relied on her watch for maintaining her bracelet and keeping herself out of trouble. She meticulously followed its instructions to charge the spares, for the system demanded that it always knew where she was. She checked this morning's zone on her watch, which expanded and contracted according to her work routine, but always included the food bank and shops allotted to her. A few months ago, she had almost reached the point of friendship with someone who lived south of the river, and who would need to be registered in her zone so she could visit; but it came to nothing in the end, and their zones remained as they were.

To leave her zone, or to lose her bracelet's silent stream of location updates for more than a very short while, would be a serious breach of her conditions as a refugee. It wasn't so bad if that happened the first time; but it would be the second, in her case. Not that the previous occasion had been her fault; she wouldn't be so naïve as to fall for a battery scammer again.

She rose to shower in her tiny flat, thinking of that nerve-wracking time, and let the water wash her anxiety away. Mostly, the facilities in this land worked—if not immediately, then before long. She pictured her mother and father, working hard and queuing for meagre provisions. They had had to remain in her land, for here they accepted only the young and physically capable. People complained about the weather—too hot, too wet; but this climate was nothing compared to where she came from. She always tried to remember that most people here were not unkind in person, though their society looked inwards at this time of struggle against the raging Earth.

Jacqui mounted her bike and joined the multitude of pedestrians, cyclists, and riders of the electric three-wheelers they called shaws. She moved with them through the patches of shade beneath the trees and the bright sunlight between, amid the whirring motors, conversations, birdsong: sounds she loved about this land in whose ambivalence she worked.

As she rode her bike, she considered that Sam, whom she was to care for today, was maybe not one of the kind people in this land, although she allowed that he might simply be awkward in his loneliness, and stressed by the threat of seizure. Yesterday, his face had fallen when he opened the door to her for the first time. He needed company, but maybe she wasn't his cup of tea, as they said here.

Given the shortages, there was no point stopping for her usual snack on her way to work, so she headed straight to Sam's place and parked her bike, resigned to her empty stomach. Like yesterday, the lift refused to take her when she touched her watch to it, so she climbed seven floors of stairs. Sam didn't even say hello to her when she stood at his door, sweating and short of breath.

Perhaps he was just having a bad morning. She followed him as he shuffled to the kitchen. He took a single mug from the cupboard and filled the kettle minimally, one eye on the power display. Only when the water was almost boiling did he appear to think twice.

"Want one?"

"That would be nice, thank you. Where would you like to go today, Sam?" While he could exist in his flat by himself for periods, he could not stray far from it alone.

Every time she spoke to him there was a pause, or he wouldn't reply at all. It was difficult to know whether this was due to his learning disabilities.

"We could take the train somewhere nearby and walk into the fields—get some fresh air, see more butterflies, you know?" She felt excitement grow within her, and caution at the same time, lest it was dashed. Yesterday, he had broken a silence to exclaim at two butterflies on the lilac cones of a buddleia. With Sam, she could go somewhere new. There was a place which a fellow refugee had talked glowingly about recently—with marvellous cultivations by the river, she had said. They could take a train; in her case, for the first time after she arrived in this land.

He stirred and stirred the cup. "Alright then." He shrugged, handing her the tea.

The lift's doors opened when, after she prompted him, Sam touched his watch to it. It was hot and still when they emerged outside. They climbed into one of a straggling group of shaws nearby. Jacqui plied it expertly through the weaving electric traffic to the station, where they boarded a train.

"Sam, I need you to… you know." Awkwardly, he touched his watch to hers so that her trip would be sanctioned by his accompanying presence.

After Jacqui's attempts at small talk, they sat in silence, rocking gently in the carriage. As they gained the countryside, vibrant with food growing in the sunlight, she fell into thinking about the contrast with her desertified homeland. Her grandmother, a farmer, used to tell her about how much more fertile her land used to be. She sent money back to her family, but what could they buy when shelves were empty, and for much longer than here? The gnawing in her stomach was nothing compared to conditions at home.

Suddenly buzzing against her wrist, her watch stirred her from her reverie.

"That's strange," she said. "Got a bit of a battery problem." The bracelet had only two hours of charge remaining, when it should have been close to full. She was relieved to feel the heft of the spare battery in her bag. A green light came on when she pressed its button. She would find somewhere to swap the batteries when the chance arose, away from the stares.

They walked from the station through the crowds. Old, sandstone buildings caught her eye, but they proceeded on an unspoken route by the river that flowed out of the city towards the surrounding hills.

Sam said, "I want to see where the butterflies come from." She smiled, relieved that he hadn't wanted to remain amongst the crowds. He almost smiled back, but she could tell that he was thinking of the butterflies.

The houses soon merged into a patchwork of small plots lined with beans and green vegetables not yet ready for harvest, and wilder, wooded places amongst them. To Sam's delight, butterflies and bees crossed to and fro, settling on the flowering plants in the heat. Up in the hills, solar panels glinted, and two turbines rotated softly. She wondered whether the whole land looked as beautiful as this, trying to remember the videos she had watched before she came here.

They encountered fewer and fewer people as they made their way deeper into the countryside; eventually, they walked alone. But suddenly, with no one else around, three teenage boys appeared from a thicket and stood in their way. One, sneering and tough-built, stepped forward and removed a piece of grass from between his teeth.

"Look what we have here, lads. A refugee and her fancy man, I reckon. Only, he don't look too fancy to me!"

He indicated the cuffs of her baggy trousers. "Show us yer shackle, darling! We know yer've got one."

"You know nothing about me." She walked on but he blocked her path, his expression flipping into naked aggression. "I said show us yer shackle."

While he stood pinning her with his glare, he nodded to one of his friends, who moved over to Sam behind her. She heard Sam's muffled complaints and turned to see him cringing as the boy unstrapped his watch.

She kicked the ringleader hard in the shin. He spat in her face. "Run!" he called to his friends while grabbing her bag. She pursued them. But they skipped ahead over dips and fallen branches; they were faster than she was and knowledgeable about the terrain. She clambered through the thicket, heart thudding and branches scratching her. It was no use. Increasingly aware of Sam alone behind her, she gave up.

Sam was on the ground, unconscious in a seizure. His medicine was in her bag – gone, along with her battery. A fumbled search in his pockets yielded nothing. She had no spare clothing so she cradled his head in her hands as best she could despite his jolting movements, waiting to turn him over on his side when the seizure ended.

Meanwhile, her watch was vibrating with increasing frequency to notify her that her own bracelet's battery was finally dead.

When the seizure had still not ended after five minutes, she spoke into her watch to call an ambulance, thanking her god that the boys had not taken it. But Sam's seizure continued. She tried to calm herself and laid Sam's head back on the grass for a minute in order to hold up her watch. A dot was moving towards them, fifteen minutes away. No one knew the machines' threshold for letting a bracelet's silence go.

With relief she realised that Sam's jerking was slowing. After a while it stopped. She stroked his forehead and spoke to him – of whatever thoughts came to her about the vegetation around them, a red-flecked bird that stared at them from a nearby branch.

Sam had regained consciousness by the time the paramedics arrived. They wasted little time before taking him away.

"I need to come with him."

"Sorry, love. We'll take it from here. If you're a refugee, go for reassignment." How did they always know—think they knew? Did they have X-ray eyes?

"But I need to come back with Sam!"

"Not enough space in the wagon. Sorry." They lifted him on a stretcher.

She followed them to the ambulance by Sam's side, feeling guilty that he was to be separated from her. As they tilted the stretcher to take him on board, his eyes sought hers.

"Butterfly," he said. She moved closer, but the paramedic in the back pulled the door shut.

Jacqui rushed to the station, now thinking only of her dead bracelet. The passing bees and butterflies, the clean-flowing river which she soon rejoined hardly registered in her fraught consciousness. The instructions were to report her bracelet's failure in person within her zone. Sam, who presumably would recover soon, could confirm her story. But the algorithm didn't wait, and wouldn't necessarily take account of her circumstances. And people—flesh and blood who set the machines to watch her—were too busy, too hungry to listen for more than a minute.

On the train, a flood of homesickness overtook her; she desperately wanted to be back with her parents despite the strife at home, to exist on her own terms. The stares of the man in the facing seat only added to her feeling of oppression. She looked out through the window and fancied she saw that bird again, as if there were hope. Eventually she snapped.

"Look, I just want to be left alone, OK?"

"I see someone who is perhaps in trouble and I was wondering whether I could help."

"None of your business."

"We might be in some trouble together." His accent was strong, from another land. "If you tell me your worry, I will do my best."

"Got a charger—for a bracelet?" she scoffed, knowing he would not. Everything here was batteries, batteries. Charging happened in designated places, over time. And people guarded their batteries like gold.

"No, I don't," he said, raising a scuffed, khaki canvas bag from the seat beside him and placing it on the table.

"Got this, though." He took out a battery and pushed it towards her.

She opened her mouth to question him, but instead she grabbed the battery and made for the toilet. Seconds after she inserted it, her watch showed an image of a green band blinking around an ankle: "93%". She let out a long breath, imagining the radio pulses flying through the air towards the machines that watched her.

As she returned to her seat, the train was pulling into her home city. She closed her eyes and touched herself fleetingly in a prayer that the authorities would accept her tale.

"How can I repay you?"

She left him on the station concourse. The red-flecked bird flew off from a nearby awning, back to where it had come from, singing in a language.

Other Cheeses Are Available
Allen Ashley

JACK ARMSTRONG TOOK the bundle of wet washing—Hempocotton ™ smart garments—and carried them outside, where it was blustery but no hurricane. He carefully affixed the clothes to the communal washing line, making sure to give a few helpful tugs and pulls which would generate a small electric current for the extended household. "Every ripple helps," as the slogan went.

"You're up and about early, young feller."

It was his neighbour, Old Zander. By Crichton, did the guy never sleep? Oh, hang on, Zander had once mentioned lying awake worrying about the world that his generation had bequeathed. Jack suspected that if Zander had his tongue any further inside his cheek it would pop out like a worm after rain.

"Going to the game this afternoon?" the old guy continued. "Who are Arsenal playing?"

"Tottenham."

"Again? I can remember when they had games against the Manchester clubs and even Barcelona and Bayern Munich. Of course, that was before they put the clamps on air travel and the like."

"Sorry, Zander, can't hang around. Got *my* exercise to do."

Jack had his Pelly-Bike set up so that his pedalling would generate extra electricity for his Great Aunt Agatha in the Sunny Valley Care Home some five miles away. It was a civic duty that everyone of working age with a close or distant dependent relative undertook—keep yourself fit and create some charitable extra wattage via your efforts. He hadn't actually seen Aunt Agatha in a long time but she occasionally sent bland video messages to say she was eating well and, "Thanks to your efforts I can keep the table lamp on in the evening."

His home device pinged. An offer of a work assignment, one he could complete in under an hour. Cast your eyes over this report, check the algorithmic logic, and, crucially, give it a human endorsement. The AIs were infallible and everything always made perfect sense but people trusted—well, people. Jack skimmed through the text then deep-read before applying the yellow smiley face seal of approval. Zander had told him that the same logo had once been used on illicit drugs, and before that on badges protesting against nukes—"*Nein, danke*" had been the callout. Jack knew that the government still operated nuclear power stations and were coy about what percentage they contributed to the national grid and the insoluble pollution pile. But these power plants were far away and out of mind, whereas this task earned extra food credit that might buy him something fancy. Like cheese. Or pickle.

***

Zander wondered how best to occupy his time until offset hour, that enforced electricity-starved period of the evening when everyone sat at home in the encroaching dark and the increasing cold. A time when solo cubicle living revealed its true, isolating nature, even with neighbours all around. Doubtless, it suited the machines to keep human mental health unstable. Another job creation programme.

There was his growth station, out in the yard, bordering Jack's contraption. Zander's grandfather had boasted of growing enormous turnips and prize marrows back in the day; now, with the warmer climate, folks were encouraged to plant grapevines, orange trees, or genetically modified olives. Jack's crop seemed to be doing quite well this season. Across the allotted soil spaces, one could discern little splashes of bright colour punctuating the dull buildings with their greyish solar panels and tall white wind turbines. Like the first flickering of an Impressionist painting—before the pigments were banned as carcinogenic or net carbon contributors.

Zander had worked in the building trade, adapting to the changing requirements and acquiring a smattering of transferable skills. At heart, he was a carpenter.

"Noah," he muttered, "he must have been at the top of the trade. And old Joseph, Jesus's dad or stepdad or whatever you'd call him. Need to stay out of political trouble and find a woman for the list. Maybe Madame Guillotine—"

The capsule's intercom played a range of songs deemed suitable for his age range. It was the sort of sappy pop his late wife, Emma, would have vaguely liked. He punched the volume down as close as possible to zero, casually picked up his thermo-jacket from the back of the chair and looped it over the room sensor, which further deadened the irritating choruses. The system would soon start complaining in a soft, synthesised voice that did *not* remind him of Emma.

He found the tools he needed at the back of the cutlery drawer and prised open his handmade treasure box. A little favour here, some unaccounted credits there, a silent delivery by a dodgy geezer, and—he had some delicacies hidden away for quiet moments. He'd finished the Belgian chocolates yesterday. Today's treat to enliven the standard issue crispbread was an illegal, crumbly slab of Ecuadorean blue cheese.

You didn't need a knife, you could break it easily into mouth-size morsels. Savour one, Savour two. And—

The rough-throated roar of jet engines startled him. What on earth…? Oh, of course, it would be a military patrol passing over, perhaps accompanying the solitary VIP-plane allowed under offset rules. Shows of strength and defence remained necessary. The AI governments were still working on achieving world peace despite the great promise of equity that had swept them to power. Incurable national bias or something.

Salty. A slight moistness lingering on the lips. Worth all the effort and subterfuge.

He'd been wise and cynical and not voted for them. It hadn't made any difference.

***

Jack was momentarily startled by the rough-throated roar of jet engines. A military patrol escorting a VIP-plane. There was some seemingly good-natured fist-shaking and rough-throated catcalling from the crowd assembling for the match.

Daylight games had been the norm for several seasons now, but the rhythmic clapping, chanting, and stamping of the crowd booted the jumbo screens at each end of the ground into flickering and then pristine life so that team news and instant replays were available to the supporters. It was a bad-tempered, stop-start contest and, Jack reflected, maybe not simply due to deep-rooted local rivalry. Perhaps the over-familiarity of the teams in the London League had added an extra layer of contempt. Arsenal conceded early but won 2-1 in the end and their popular captain Chidoze McKennie won the "Sparky" award for most distance covered and, therefore, most watts generated.

On the way in, the robo police had hovered nonchalantly. The human officers were handling the sniffer dogs, mostly spaniels, stopping and searching any suspicious spectator. On the way out, the flesh and blood guys were in riot gear and the canines had become German Shepherds. Jack didn't hang around for any aggro, keen to walk home with the main crowd and arrive there well before offset hour.

He had ten minutes to check on his plants. The limes were still pretty small, and shouldn't there be six of them rather than five? He went back indoors, pressed the code for legitimate extra water rations, went back into his mini-garden with a half-full cup.

"You wanna get your washing in before our hour of darkness," said Zander.

By Crichton, the guy was a busybody. The sooner the Senior Re-Employment Bill became law, the better.

***

Zander woke to a message coming through on his device. He pressed "OK" to accept the minor energy surcharge for the call.

"Mr Proudfoot?"

One of those robotic voices synthesised from a couple of deceased actresses. At least there was a hint of Received Pronunciation in the tone.

"My friends call me Zander. Then again, you're probably not a friend."

"Mr Proudfoot? Pay attention, please. We need you to stop obscuring your home sensor. We are concerned about your welfare, Mr Proudfoot—"

He cut the connection. While he was spending energy credits, he decided to flick on the kettle for a cup of barley tea and check the news and ents on his device. Oh, here was "Judge Rudy"—an acronym, of course, "Rules Under Democratic Yielding"—the AI legislator with the Abraham Lincoln face projection. In the dock this morning were a few football hooligans involved in a dust-up at yesterday's game. Or maybe last month's. You had to give it to the machines: they were quicker at dispensing justice than the bewigged posh boys of the past. Slam the silly sods in The Cave for a spell without heat or light. Like offset hour but longer—and colder.

Zander eased open his cubicle door. The wind was stronger today—the usual hurricane remnants imported from the US and the Caribbean. He'd better go check on his fruit and vegetable mini-tower.

***

There was a "Message Alert" on Jack's device. He pressed "Accept". It was from Dear Aunt Agatha at the Sunny Valley Retirement Home.

"Thank you for caring for me. I am well and happy."

Her lips didn't move but her hand managed a few degrees. Probably a sync problem. What was it with old folks and new technology? Still, he should probably go and see her sometime.

As he pedalled out his energy contribution, Jack caught a few minutes of the latest "Judge Rudy" episode. A handful of football fans getting overly up close and personal and now being sentenced to a spell of solitary in The Cave. From yesterday or from some previous sporting encounter? Maybe it didn't matter.

The top news story concerned another airspace violation by a foreign power. The AI government immediately agreed an increased allocation from the fossil fuel reserve bank. They seemed to still hold quite a supply of the stuff.

Zander had once told him, "It's not fossil fuel, oil's actually a mineral. Coal is fossil fuel—like all that carbon in the Capture Bank at Ponders End."

Jack waited for some work to come in. Surely some AI protocol or machine learning conclusion somewhere needed that little yellow stamp of human approval?

***

By Crichton and the Park, that youngster next door could be really annoying. Wasn't he s'posed to be on his device earning a crust? But oh, no, he was out in the brazen wind and above normal temperatures fiddling with the fastenings on his grow station.

"I seem to be down a couple of items," Jack had stated. "What do you think the issue might be, Zander?"

"Squirrels. Blighters can get into anything."

"Squirrels? I didn't think they ate lemons. And I've never seen them or any other wild animals around here."

"That's the nature of wild animals, Jack. Sneaky, secretive. Ya don't often spot them."

But now the wind had dropped a little and the expensive automatic aircon inside Zander's cubicle was cooling him down a little. Another morsel of Ecuadorean Blue would help as well—

His door buzzed. He ignored it. Probably some drone delivery with a postcode mix-up. Couldn't tell their oh from their zero.

Another buzz. And another. Then the door sprung open.

A pair of robotic cops plus a human officer tightly gripping the leash on an energetic sniffer dog. What on earth?

"Mr Proudfoot, please accompany us to the processing room at the station."

"Why, you tinpot tin man? I ain't done nothing."

"We believe that you have been involved in the dealing of contraband goods."

"Dealing? I'm just like any other retiree, a mere consumer."

"Please come with us, Mr Proudfoot. It's not too far to walk. Officer Brettenback and Lassie will conduct a thorough search of your dwelling."

Lassie? Someone somewhere had a mean sense of humour. Zander swallowed a couple of times, surreptitiously (he hoped) wiped his mouth with the back of his hand, and followed the arresting officer out through the doorway.

At the threshold, he turned round and said, "And make sure you secure this place properly when you're finished. I don't want any of my neighbours coming in and nicking stuff."

**

For once, Jack was intrigued by his reading assignment. The concept had been fleshed out and elaborated upon by the usual AI collective but the original spark had been credited to a reward-worthy human, one Mr Richard Head. No, that had to be a wind-up, surely?

It was a brilliantly simple idea and one that Jack was surprised had not been mooted before. All those Bazalgette tunnels and the later improvements to the London sewers—prime potential for an untapped and permanent source of hydro-electric power. Genius. Jack thought through the typical puns he might add as a commentary—"No shit, Sherlock", "Sounds piss easy to me"—but in the end decided just to approve. We were being creative in this energy crisis, we really were. All hail the machines and the humans working so well together.

**

All the cameras in the courtroom operated on remote or automatic. Robotic cops guarded each corner. Two human police officers had upgraded their dogs from spaniel to German Shepherd. The canines were quieter than the drone recording apparatus. Unnervingly so. Judge Rudy projected its wise Abraham Lincoln countenance. Maybe it chose Biblical King Solomon on Sundays.

"Alexander Proudfoot, you are charged with a felony."

"With all the security you've deployed here, I thought I was being done for mass murder."

"Cease your flippancy. You have been caught in possession of an illegal consignment of Ecuadorean blue cheese."

"Consignment? I've only got a mouthful left."

A change of facial projection. Pretend kindness around the eyes. "Mr Proudfoot, why did you illicitly purchase this food item? Other cheeses are available."

"But they're all vegan and taste like shit. You can't get the real stuff in this country since the Methane Emissions Ban and the mass Cow Cull in 33."

"Mr Proudfoot, you have failed to consider the air miles and consequent environmental damage caused by your misdemeanour."

"It's not fair, Judge. The VIPs get limitless air miles."

"You are not a VIP, Alexander. You are classed today as a Nordic—Normal Dispensable Individual Criminal."

"But it's not a crime to eat proper food. And what happened to that notion of trade makes the world go round?"

"Mr Proudfoot, a combination of solar, gravitational, and astrophysical forces makes the world go round. We find you guilty as charged and sentence you to a period without heat and light in the construction you humans call The Cave. Court adjourned."

***

Jack saw Zander's trial on his device during his morning pedal-pounding. Before logging on for work, he went to check on his neighbour's place. Noticing that the door was unlocked, he had a little recce around the capsule. Without doing too much digging, he found a couple of items that had mysteriously gone missing lately. He retrieved them without fuss. Considerate to the end, he secured Zander's door from outside.

After yesterday's excitement, there were no new assignments today. The breeze was gentle and the heat was tolerable. This would be a good day to visit Great Aunt Agatha.

It was a longer walk than he remembered and he dipped further into his water ration than expected.

Jack felt that the robo-receptionist would have made a pretty human. She/it was probably based on someone long dead so maybe best not to go too far with that thought.

She whirred and buzzed almost subliminally then announced, "Mr Armstrong, I'm going to fetch our human counsellor."

The white-smocked individual who arrived bore a lanyard saying "Mrs Leggett". She looked at Jack and spoke with a voice as toneless as any mechanical's. "Mr Armstrong, I regret to inform you that your Aunt Agatha passed away six weeks ago."

"Six weeks? And you didn't inform me?"

"There were no bills outstanding and no personal effects of any value. But, yes, we rather messed up on the old-fashioned courtesy stakes there. System failure."

Jack gritted his teeth. "So, let me get this right. Every morning for the last six weeks I've sweated my butt off creating useable current for a patient who's died? And you've still continued to scoop up my energy?"

"See it as a charitable donation, Mr Armstrong. All for the greater good."

There were a few forms to sign "while you are here". And then he wasn't there anymore. Instead, he was at home starting to unplug all his controls and devices and looking for something with which to smash up the Pelly-Bike.

They'd arrest him, of course. Throw him in The Cave, that punishment that pushed you back into prehistory.

Maybe he and Zander would find a way of drawing on the walls and starting a fire.

Daylight Robbery

Prashant Vaze

LOWER MAGHREB, 2025

I'm at the bar keeping a glass with a blue fluid, an iceberg of fake cream, and a skewered cherry and cucumber company. The plan is to schmooze with the fellas from the conference banquet, including many of my biggest LinkedIn heroes. There's a small Arab dressed in a dress shirt, cufflinks, and chinos burrowed deep in a comfy chair. He's halo-ed by a poster of President Fayek standing outside his sand-coloured palace, the blue-blue sky reflected in his Aviators with the caption, 'Lower Maghreb welcomes delegates for the Africa Climate Week'. A couple of C-suites from multilateral development banks are locked in a tête-à-tête that I'm too sober to dare break into. I'm patient; I'll talk with them before my flight back to London tomorrow.

This morning, the conference organiser twisted my arm and got me to speak on a panel about the role private finance could play in Africa's decarbonisation. Not that I needed any persuading. I parroted my manager at Sahara Impact Fund's usual spiel. Plans to install solar panels across the desert, end poverty, and hit sustainable development goals. I guessed I must have been too convincing as renewable developers mobbed me straight after. To think, this time last year I was a newly minted lawyer wondering what I should do to pay off my student loans!

"Fortune favours the brave," says a British voice from the comfy chair. "Greetings. I'm Irfan Jouahri."

I smile noncommittally. I'd checked all the profiles of the noteworthy conference delegates and didn't recognise Mr Jouahri's name. He must have heard my talk this afternoon. "Don't get your hopes up. I don't sign the cheques at Sahara; I draft the contracts."

Jouahri gives me a 'poor lamb' look and glances at the two men deep in conversation. "Go and talk to them. You may never get the chance again."

I stiffen. "Do you have any idea how bad an idea that is? Pierre is the chief economist at the GCF, and Abbas is in charge of the MDB. I'm a rookie lawyer. I'm only here because my boss had to go to DC to meet investors."

"Your boss sent you because he believed in you." He shoves my stool, spilling me onto my feet. I'm in heels and almost topple over. I scuttle to catch him.

"Pierre, Abbas. It's so great to see you both." He clasps Abbas's hairy palms in his delicate hands. "It's been too long."

Abbas looks baffled but hugs Irfan.

To evade Irfan's grasp, Pierre stands and kisses me French style. "Well, if it isn't Ms 'green-the-Sahara', Dawn Lipsey."

"Sir, it's an honour."

Abbas knocks back his whisky and tips an imaginary hat. "I bid you goodnight. I have an early flight." Irfan takes Abbas's seat and closes his eyes.

I ask Pierre, "Wasn't President Fayek's speech inspiring?"

"I had to take an urgent call, so I missed it. Pray enlighten me."

"President Fayek said he'd transition Lower Maghreb from fossil fuels to solar power in ten years. Wow, amazing if he can pull that off! The Chinese are funding large solar farms to meet urban demand under Belt and Road, but he's desperate for funds for rural electrification for villages far from the grid. Villagers' power, such as it is, comes from diesel generators. I think Sahara Impact could help them…"

Pierre nods politely.

"But we don't have deep pockets; we'd need anchor investors to make it happen. We work overtime on due diligence and would take on the project risks. Around two million US? Can I perhaps schedule a meeting between your people and my boss to discuss this?"

Pierre shakes his head. "Don't be taken in by that crook Fayek. He grabbed the country in a coup five years ago and is operating a military junta."

"Yes, but he's much less corrupt than the last government and gets stuff done. Village girls attend primary schools; the anti-malaria eradication works; all one hundred social factions support him. He's doing all the things we like."

"Listen, Dawn. There's no point in me sugar-coating this. The Global Climate Fund can't fund you. There's no point in us getting out of bed for less than twenty million; it takes my people six months and ten internal committees to sign off on any deal. Plus, Moody's withdrew Lower Maghreb's credit rating after its default. It's not an investible country. And what will the villagers pay us back with? Goats? We want hard currency."

Surely, Pierre can't trot out all these excuses after his promises on stage. Hearing this powerful older man speak this way is soul-destroying.

Irfan says: "It's the original sin. Poor countries cannot repay loans in their national currency; they must repay in dollars."

"Sorry, which agency do you work for?"

"I'm just a guy staying at the hotel."

Pierre goes avuncular. "The issue isn't just about dollar repayments. It's because of the President's behaviour. The international community lent money to Lower Maghreb in good faith. He can't walk away from his country's obligations."

"And what about your countries' obligations? The rich countries signed the Copenhagen Accord in 2009. Fifteen years ago. Where is the hundred billion a year you promised the poor countries to help them stop climate change?" His voice is playful. "What about the aid money Western governments give you to disburse to Africa?"

"The aid money is earmarked."

"Yes, I know! For financing the closure of African coal-fired power stations. So, instead of using aid money to fund renewable electricity that helps Africa compete globally, you pay countries to close their coal power stations, which you lent them money to build. This reduces the amount of electricity they can generate. Then, lend them more money to build renewables. They get more indebted increasing their cost of borrowing. Genius! You get the green NGOs off your back, help Western exports and make lending to Africa more profitable for western banks."

I wait for Pierre's rebuttal of Irfan's hurtful accusations.

Instead, Pierre's voice hardens. "You are very well-informed for someone not working in the field."

"How much grant did you give Africa to close coal power stations? And how much to build new renewables?"

"I don't have those numbers at hand."

"One billion and zero!" says Irfan softly.

My mouth drops open.

"What exactly do you do? Are you a reporter?"

"I run a fund, SynTax Special Situations. We invest in European mortgage-backed securities."

"What's your assets under management?" asks Pierre, chuckling.

"Three billion."

Wow! His fund has more cash than the GCF and Sahara Impact combined.

A thin smile forms on Pierre's lips. "You're generous with other people's money. Why not spend the money you have a fiduciary duty to manage to save Africa?"

The waiters are whispering amongst themselves and pointing to Jouahri. One rushes over, his hands outstretched. "Mr Jouahri. It is an honour to meet you."

"You're mistaking me for someone else."

"No mistake." The waiter takes his phone from his jeans pocket. "This is a photograph of your brother who is my village's chief. You visited it and opened the solar power plant. Your generosity is transforming our village. Alhamdulillah. May I take a selfie with you?"

***

LONDON 2047

Even after all these years after leaving development finance, I get so mad watching the news these days. The Royal Navy contributed two frigates to the European Union's blockade of the North African coast. In a sickening escalation, an Italian frigate sunk a boat carrying 'fugees. Two hundred dead. The Italian Prime Minister declares. "Though we regret the loss of life, we will not launch an investigation into the incident. Africa's corrupt military dictators, not our brave officers, are responsible for Africa's poverty and overpopulation. I have one message for the illegal migrants. *Europe is full."* Several African governments threaten to leave the Commonwealth if the UK continues its support for the blockade. The King had reputedly scolded the prime minister in their weekly meetings.

My self-drive trike pulls up outside the Old Bailey. I instruct my DigiPal to pay the trike and inform me the moment my last witness gets in touch. I remove my VR and slow my breath to settle my mind. *Today is the big day, summing up, recess, and then the jury will decide.* There are a handful of supporters outside carrying placards in English and Arabic. One recognises me and embraces me.

My client, Irfan Jouahri, awaits me in the lobby, looking chipper. Glad one of us is feeling optimistic.

Eight months ago, he called and asked if I remembered him. *No* – I lied. I would be a comfortably off financial lawyer if it hadn't been for him. Instead, after our encounter, I researched his accusations and concluded that green finance, indeed my job, was just a green con for business as usual. Within two months, I resigned from Sahara Impact and joined a legal aid firm. Thanks, pal!

The financial regulator had closed his fund SynTax Special Situations and charged him with fraud. I told him my firm, Client Gaia, specialises in climate, not financial crime. He told me this was why he wanted us to represent him—his best line of defence was climate justice.

The case is cut and dried. For twenty-five years, the fund purported to invest in low-risk mortgage assets, providing a safe, albeit unremarkable return. Secretly, Irfan and his team had diverted an ever-increasing share of the fund to reforesting the Sahel and solarising the Sahara Desert in Lower Maghreb, the country of his birth. These investments provided dozens of remote villages with cheap electricity, animal fodder, and work. He got away with it all this time because the foreign exchange costs saved from avoided diesel imports provided the hard currency to compensate British investors.

He is a regular Mother Theresa. But instead of giving him the Nobel Peace Prize, Irfan is charged with fraud and faces bankruptcy and jail time.

I again check my mailbox for communication from my star witness. Bugger. In another couple of hours, it'll be too late.

The courtroom is packed with Irfan's supporters who cheer his entry; they wave flags depicting a green oasis in the desert. I also see Nigerian, Sierra Leonean, and Kenyan flags. The security staff stiffen when two or three suits representing the financial regulator enter to boos. The judge calls the court to order.

But the disturbance continues until Irfan raises his hands. "Please be still, brothers."

The prosecution and I each get half an hour to make our closing remarks; the judge will give the jury directions before they retire to decide. Irfan has already lost his livelihood, and worse awaits him. Instead of despair, he tells me, "But think of the millions of people whose lives I improved."

The prosecutor addresses the jury. "Jouahri told investors and the regulators he was investing in European mortgage securities. I asked how much he invested in mortgages. This is his response."

All of it, says a hologram of Irfan's cross-examination. *It was all indirectly invested in supporting the mortgage market.*

"I showed him the code numbers of the securities he pretended to have bought. All were fictitious."

The financial system is a complex, interconnected system. You don't have to buy mortgage securities to support the mortgage market.

"Instead of buying mortgages, Jouahri lent money to risky projects in sub-Saharan Africa and misappropriated profits. Listen to his tortured explanation."

I paid my investors for twenty-three years, outperforming my peers. My investments also removed 120 million tonnes of CO_2 from the atmosphere. This helps the mortgage market. Extreme weather has been the biggest reason for mortgage defaults, as it has caused insurers to withdraw coverage.

"This is a dog-ate-my-homework level of excuse. His criminal conspiracy was revealed when he failed to pay investors last year. Because Jouahri had spent earlier years' profits, there was nothing in the kitty to pay pensioners who rely on SynTax. Listen to his explanation."

I invested excess profits in planting trees, greening the Sahel, and providing the villagers with livelihoods.

"That's not an investment. That's misappropriation or *stealing* in plain English. Instead of reinvesting in safe European mortgages, Jouahri and his criminal company financed their pet projects. Hundreds of thousands of hectares of trees were planted, which provided the fund no financial return." He pauses and eyes the jury. "I asked him why he thought he was above the rules."

My only crime was not doing more. If other bankers had thought about their fiduciary duty as long and hard as I had, they'd have also realised helping people is cheaper than blockading them.

"That's a nice soundbite, but it's not a defence. Members of the jury, you heard the defendant admit falsifying reports to the regulators and misappropriating investor funds over a quarter of a century. The defence will argue that his motives were honourable. That he was doing 'good'." He spits the last word. "The rules are there for good reason. He took a gamble with other people's money and lost. Pensioners' money. You have no choice but to find the defendant guilty."

That was quick. I stand up and eye up each member of the jury.

"The facts in this case are not disputed. Instead, please ask yourself why the defendant did what he did and whether his actions were in the best interests of his investors. When the financial system is as fundamentally broken as it is, a fund manager has a duty to investors to use his judgement as Mr Jouahri did. Indeed, for twenty-three years, the fund has had stellar results, much better than its peers. I asked the defendant to explain his fund's marketing."

Financial regulations push pension company money into so-called safe mortgages and government debt. This pushes up house prices and allows rich countries' governments to overspend. If I told investors what I was doing, the vast majority would run a mile; those left would double the interest rate and make the project insure against currency devaluation.

"Members of the jury, you know the housing market isn't safe; it is collapsing. Thousands of British homeowners are in default as insurers withdraw from the market and their homes become worthless. Yet the regulations throw petrol onto the fire. I asked the defendant why SynTax collapsed two years ago."

Two words: climate change. Our tree planting protected Lower Maghreb from drought, but refugees started streaming from neighbouring countries. Two million live in the country's camps. The influx caused budget pressures; the currency collapsed, taking my projects with it."

The subject matter is dry, and some of the jury fidget. "For my last witness, I interviewed the celebrated economist Pierre de Couer, who helped shape the financial regulations. I asked if present rules stop pension funds from investing in poor countries despite opportunities to make acceptable returns."

A hologram of the silver-haired older man appears. "Mr Jouahri is correct that it is almost inconceivable for institutional investors to invest in projects in low-income countries, no matter how well the project is managed or its returns. The rules and conventions of finance do not allow it. Since retiring, I have worried that our institutions have focused on ensuring the pennies are safe while ignoring the risk of the system collapse. Jouahri has shown us that wise investments in poor countries can provide investors good returns. We should not persecute him for what he did but honour him."

The judge stops me. "Ms Lipsey, you have not offered any evidence refuting the charges. Your defence is essentially: *the rules are stupid.*

This is not a defence this court can accept, and I will direct the jury accordingly."

My DigiPal tingles me. I put on my VR glasses. Simultaneously, the prosecutor sits up and does the same.

"I know this is highly irregular; I have just received a document I have been awaiting." The judge splutters, but I press on. "President Fayek of Lower Maghreb, the current leader of the African Congress, has appointed my client the Africa Congress's Ambassador to the Court of St James. As you know, the King and his government are anxious to maintain unity within the Commonwealth and have accepted Mr Jouahri's credentials."

The prosecutor takes off his VR set and stands; an ambiguous smile descends on his face. He gathers his scattered papers into a unified pile. "The Crown withdraws its case."

Commentary

Richard Heap

ENERGY IS DEEPLY embedded in many aspects of our society and shapes how we live. How we use energy and where it comes from have undergone huge changes through time, enabling changes in national economies and standards of living. Dependence on energy is extensive, crossing economic sectors and policy areas, powering IT, communications, industry, health care, entertainment, and security. Ensuring an affordable, reliable, and secure supply is a primary objective for governments. Furthermore, natural energy resources provide wealth to the economy along with the industries and jobs that deliver them.

However, if we are to avoid widespread disruption to global society from the impacts of climate change and ocean acidification there will need to be fundamental changes to the energy system. As the environmental and societal impacts are hard to quantify, and are either out of scope of the markets, or have effects over very long timescales, the changes over the next few decades will have to be driven primarily by policy and political decisions. Short-term political timeframes add to the challenge of making these complex, long-term policy decisions.

While the need to decarbonise the energy system might be recognised and supported, the embedded nature of energy in society and the economy means that transition will expose tensions about what new technologies should be deployed, how they are funded, and how to manage the societal impacts. Multiple pathways have been proposed, but testing their underlying assumptions will reveal important aspects of the transition and tensions that will need addressing.

Insights into these aspects and tensions emerge in the stories, highlighting the need to think about the energy transition from viewpoints that go beyond just the technical and engineering challenges. While it is hard to predict how the future might develop, the stories explore how society might interact with energy and how attitudes towards it might change.

A couple of the stories pick up the role of innovation in electricity generation, which will be important in the transition. Allen Ashley's "Other Cheeses Are Available" explores micro-generation and how it could integrate into daily activity. This form of generation is already being tested in pavements and dance floors, and from vibrations in small portable equipment. While the amount of energy generated by each person from these energy-harvesting devices is small, as Allen describes it is enough to power electronic devices and charge batteries. In Allen's somewhat dystopian future, this small-scale energy generation could become a requirement to deliver services. Meanwhile, large-scale energy generation is being used by the state and controlling forces.

Micro-generation could have emerged in Tim Kindberg's story, "The Bracelet and the Battery", about a bracelet that harvests the energy from the person's movement rather than using batteries. While this may avoid the fear of the battery going flat, the darker side of the story is about the power of the state to control people's lives through access to energy. Limiting the bracelet to be dependent on recharging the batteries would add to the restrictions.

Zed Badowska's "Legacy" picks up on the potential of accelerating emerging technologies, in this case nuclear fusion. While questions hang over whether fusion could develop that quickly, the story highlights the challenge of gaining support for new technologies and where the large amounts of funding required will come from. Fusion is still under development, and while it offers the potential for producing large volumes of relatively clean electricity it may be many years before it can demonstrate sustained power output, after which further development will be needed to demonstrate its cost and economic viability. Even then it will take time to build these complex power stations at a scale that will have significant impact on the growing global electricity demand. It is also unclear if it could ever be used as a portable energy source.

In the meantime, existing technologies will need to be rapidly rolled out, supported by near-term innovation and development to bring down costs. Many of these will require specialist training. All this is feasible, but it will require concerted effort, with deep thought about how the transition will be funded and financed while also engaging with the wider context and potential implications that are highlighted in these stories.

That is not to ignore the potential for game-changing innovation that could alter the trajectory. If fully autonomous driverless cars become viable and acceptable, their adoption could transform the vehicle industry. It could transform car ownership, reducing the number of cars needed, with each one working full-time, rather than being parked for most of the day. It could have wide-ranging knock-on effects: changing the charging infrastructure, fewer cars parked on the streets, people working in the vehicles, changing how we travel across the country and go on holidays.

Zed's story also touches on the tension about where the funding for technologies comes from and the intent behind it. An example here is carbon capture and storage (CCS), which is supported predominantly by large emitters. Analysis suggests CCS may prove essential in the medium term to cut emissions from these economically important sectors as the alternatives are too expensive. Its development is also likely to prove essential for removing carbon dioxide directly from the atmosphere. However, there is resistance to the technology, as it is seen as a means for the fossil fuel industry to sustain its activities. Others argue that the scale of energy use is immense and not having CCS available as an option during the transition risks having to make deep and radical cuts in energy use if climate objectives are to be achieved.

Reducing the demand for energy can be an effective strategy. DJ Cockburn's story, "Milton Friedman's Heresy", highlights this as an important alternative pathway, and focuses on one of the challenges it presents. Insulating the existing building stock not only reduces the demand for electricity and its associated infrastructure, but also reduces the homeowner's energy bills. At a national level it improves energy security and reduces vulnerability to variations in the global energy markets. But, as DJ highlights, it will disrupt the commercial models of significant vested interests. Refurbishing the millions of homes in the UK will take many years, and the cost for each one will be much higher than a standard boiler replacement or upgrade to heat pumps. Delivering it will require political leadership to put in place long-term policies and address commercial interests. DJ presents the challenge that new financial structures and models will be needed to mobilise the transition. Attempts have been made to define the non-financial environmental and social benefits and impacts of the transition, but many are long-term and hard to value, and therefore are not captured by market analysis and decision making.

Transport faces similar challenges. Replacing the existing vehicle fleet with electric vehicles may be insufficient and does not address air pollution from tyre and brake dust. Measures may be needed to reduce car use. With individual mobility so embedded into the structure of our urban and rural landscape, and the favourable societal perception of car ownership, a mix of long-term measures will be required to promote the use of public transport and reshape town planning and access to services. Similarly, restrictions on the growth of aviation will require societal change. As Allen points out, the climate impact of importing exotic foods may restrict their availability.

We have already seen indications of the potential tensions with the opposition to the extension of London's Ultra-Low Emissions Zone (ULEZ), and to the deployment of Low-Traffic Neighbourhoods (LTNs). The political result has been to weaken policies to transform the vehicle industry and improve the efficiency of new-build housing. Houses that are being built today are fuelled by gas-based heating systems. These will need to be retrofitted within the next 30 years at a much higher cost to the homeowner than the build cost of a high-efficiency, low-energy new build.

Financing the transition is a huge challenge. Upgrading the nation's housing stock to low-carbon systems is likely to be expensive. Zero-percentage loans are being offered to provide financial assistance, but the overall scale of the funding needed is huge. As Prashant Vaze asks in his story, "Daylight Robbery", how might future risks from climate impacts affect the financial system? Will rising sea-levels undermine the values of property in floodplains, or even along the Thames? This raises further questions as to the cost and value of protecting assets and who should pay.

The core of Prashant's story is the link between national interests and development funding and the way risk and responsibility are framed and evaluated. The story questions the value of the funding commitments made by rich countries to support poor countries. The major funders are constrained by conventional thinking and attitudes to risk, so the funds are directed to cutting emission sources rather than being able to see the wider opportunity to support national development and build climate resilience. In Prashant's story, the lead character demonstrates the value of this thinking by diverting funds from his managed fund into tree planting and building solar farms. The effect of climate change on regional migration, which leads to the collapse of his investment scheme in the story, is already being seen today in the Sahel region. Changes in weather patterns have led to extended droughts bringing regional migration and conflict. In the longer term, as the impacts increase, these populations could migrate out of the region altogether, potentially into Europe. Finance is a key part of tackling climate change. Understanding how to mobilise it effectively and evaluate the risks will be vital.

Societal response to mass migration is alluded to in Tim's bracelet story. The consequences of failing to cut emissions fast enough, including from energy, could exacerbate existing societal concerns. Faced with growing migration, nations may still seek to benefit from the services migrants can offer but place harsh restrictions on their freedoms in order to manage their numbers.

Prashant's story also highlights the building of huge solar farms in sunny regions, particularly deserts. Projects such as these are already being developed, with plans to transfer the electricity into Europe via very high-voltage DC cables, which can transfer electricity over long distances with very low loss compared to conventional AC grids. In Saudi Arabia projects are exploring using electricity to produce hydrogen, which could be shipped globally or processed further to create synthetic fuels; the latter have similar properties to existing fossil fuels, enabling them to be "dropped" into existing infrastructures.

Many renewable energy sources have a much lower energy density than existing high-carbon fossil fuel generation. This may, in part, be offset by efficiency improvements in the system, but it will mean that equivalent generation will be more dispersed, with a greater land requirement. As a consequence, the infrastructure will be visible by more people and require more transmission pylons.

All of these stories emphasise that the impact of energy goes far beyond where it comes from and how it is generated. It has shaped our societies and interacts with many policy areas. Decarbonising the energy system will mean balancing a range of tensions between societal concerns, fairness, and technical and financial constraints. The long-term polices and interventions that will steer the transition will need to go beyond the technical and engineering challenges. Many of these issues can be subtle and hard to recognise and may not be regarded as being within the scope of decision makers. These stories bring valuable fresh perspectives to how we think about the future, and help expose the interactions and tensions.

Commentary

Dr Gabrielle Samuel

IT WAS AN absolute honour and privilege to be offered the opportunity to reflect on these five science fiction stories, which have done a brilliant job of illuminating a range of social, ethical, and legal issues associated with the future of energy, power, and technology. I thoroughly enjoyed delving into the stories, the futures they portrayed, and the different people, personalities, and relationships that inhabited them. At the same time, I was struck by the eerily similar thread running through each of the stories, with all of them, to some degree or another, acting as dystopian accounts of social, economic, and political hardships, with suffering and misery especially afflicting the poorest communities. As I read and re-read the accounts, these concerns were exposed by the writers in various ways—about the veil of green capitalism as a distraction from the march of economic growth and neoliberal agendas; in anxieties about the effect of these agendas on who wins and loses in our global economic climate; and in concerns about how these agendas contribute to climate harm, leading to an increasing number of people living as refugees. While each story is crafted through a particular lens, and with a particular meaning, in the below I give time to each story, one by one, to try to stitch together the commonalities between them, as well as between wider academic, social, and political discussions around these themes.

I begin with DJ Cockburn's "Milton Friedman's 'Heresy'"—a story of good 'economicide' (the destruction of economic growth agendas) versus bad 'ecocide' (environmental destruction). The story takes place on a cruise liner inhabited by a group of ultra-wealthy individuals who have shirked their responsibilities towards environmental harms by transforming their vessel into a tax haven—a self-declared country—on international waters, free from the purview of (inter)national environmental law. While on this ship, we learn about this future—one of extreme climate events ravaging homes, communities, and livelihoods, and underpinned by 'bad' tales of green capitalism, profit-making, and expendable environments. The ultra-rich care little for those affected by climate events, remaining wedded to the promise of neoliberalism to bring freedom to all. This fallacy of neoliberal storytelling ignores how freedom is more tied to socio-political structures into which one is born, than to individual choice. Propositions of freedom almost always privilege some, while institutionalising, and in some cases, imprisoning others. In this story though, 'good' wins out, with the workers revolting against their institutional structures, driving the cruise ship into national waters, for those on board to be arrested.

The economic/environment dichotomy was also borne out by Zed Badowska in "Legacy", though this time through a story of individual angst, with a guilt-ridden father/grandfather trying to self-justify his prior investments in fossil fuels in a world that has now been devastated by climate change: *"We tell ourselves the stories we want to hear,* he thought. *Reframe things to make us feel better about them."* In fact, this is perhaps something that we all do now—try to accommodate for our own eco-angst—whether through choosing to believe promises of sustainability that are more likely than not greenwashing, or carbon offsetting our actions even though we know it's just an excuse to maintain the status quo. There's even a growing academic literature beginning to explore what it ethically means to ignore that which we choose to not know. In this story, it takes the destruction of this father's own home for him to truly feel the pain of others—to bring the *global* to the *local*. As he watches his house burn, he reflects on his attempts to reconcile his wrongdoings through investments in climate action and activism.

Though this is more than a story of one man's struggles, through the unfolding of his angst wider ethical questions emerge: how should we balance investments that will help local economies versus their effect on the global? Is it wrong to ignore evidence if you know it is there but choose not to look? How much do we need to do to absolve ourselves from our own contributions to planetary harms? To answer these questions, it's nearly impossible to get away from questions of local versus global justice. Though I say, as someone who works in ethics, even with a wealth of ethical theories providing normative frameworks to guide us, decision-making remains riddled by questions of how to implement these in practice when resources are scarce and prioritisation is required. Whose voices are and should be heard? In "Legacy", and through the eyes of this man, Zed's story brings these questions to the fore.

Prashant Vaze's story, "Daylight Robbery", is another brilliant opportunity to explore the moral complexities at the intersection of climate change, power, and inequities, this time moving away from individual eco-angst to broader concerns about prevailing socio-regulatory structures that prioritise local economic benefit over global environmental and social good. In essence, this is a Robin Hood tale of a man, Jouahri, who for a quarter of a century has diverted low-risk pension funds that were supposed to be invested into mortgages, to high-risk renewable energy projects in Africa. Now on trial because he recently couldn't pay back investors, Jouahri is unremorseful about the communities he has helped and the carbon emissions he has mitigated. High-risk investments, he says, are unfairly determined by Western neo-colonial practices, and mortgage investments, anyway, are no longer 'low-risk' because of extreme weather events. Prashant asks us to consider this through his writing, and, in particular, who is right and who is wrong when regulatory systems provide perverse incentives that lead to more global harm than good.

However, it's the neo-colonial and geo-political undertones in Prashant's writing that I found most compelling, with descriptions of green aid requiring dependence on the West's approval of a country's political regime, and of capitalist economics, veneered as green aid, to benefit the rich rather than the poor. Such neo-colonial undertones were laid bare in Tim Kindberg's "The Bracelet and the Battery". This beautifully written story describes a girl, Jacqui, who has sought sanctuary from her climate-devastated land in a society which imprisons refugees to work. While Jacqui's life is affected by severe food and electricity shortages, at least the wealthy around her seem to have access to a functioning health and social care system (albeit based on refugee labour), homes fuelled by renewable energy, productive farming practices, a beautiful countryside, and an air of biodiversity. Similar to the other stories, the inequities between Jacqui's lived experiences and these future societies strongly remind us of how quickly human nations face inwards when resources are short, protecting themselves—the local—through nationalistic endeavours and neo-colonial practices that exploit the weaker. The future is different, yes, but the geo-politics and neo-colonial practices are the same. In scarcity, how will we balance environmental values without swinging too far towards nationalism and neo-coloniality?

In "Other Cheeses Are Available", Allen Ashley describes a future London, where AI (artificial intelligence) is governing, electricity and food are in short supply, and football matches are played locally because of air travel bans. Similar to some of the other stories, this future is one in which environmentally damaging behaviours are moralised (eating products that require air shipping is frowned upon), and sometimes criminalised (here we see imposed methane emission bans following a mass Cow Cull); and one in which inequities persist (the rich enjoy unlimited flying). What is it about Allen's future that is worrying? Is it the question of whether we will go too far in our moralising anti-environmental behaviours? Or how we can refrain from perpetuating existing inequities in times of scarcity? Or is it something else? Is it something around our relationship with electricity that emerges through his accounts of the future? In Allen's story, Jack, the main character, pedals on his exercise bike to generate electricity for his great aunt in her care home. What is happening here? How is our relationship with electricity changed and what does that mean in terms of our own responsibilities, our duties to those we love and broader society, to the social contract we have with society, and with human rights more broadly?

Before I finish, I wanted to briefly reflect on the way these stories, as a whole, portrayed the future of digital technologies (phones, AI, robots, surveillance systems). We often see utopian and dystopian media portrayals of AI and AI robots, and much of my own research explores the more sober realities behind such depictions. I was most struck by Allen's portrayal of AI in "Other Cheeses Are Available," which enacts these utopias/dystopias through descriptions of various AI/robot machines, all autonomous and capable, that are separate to humans but are able to work with them and even govern them. Allen's portrayals of these machines—which remind me of James Cameron's *Terminator 2: Judgment Day* (the one when Arnie was nice) and Edward Neumeier and Michael Miner's *Robocop*—raise perhaps fewer interesting questions to me than the questions of the here and now. I feel that when we jump too far ahead we forget where we are, and that we are already here, in a digitally-mediated society within which human-digital relationships define human meaning and understanding. Allen's portrayal of a 'robo-receptionist' exemplifies what I mean. This is a depiction of a science fiction future that hides the fact that we are already here: that we're already seamlessly (or unseamlessly!) interacting with 'robot reception-ists', as they become ever more integrated into our practices through software and apps at care homes and doctors' surgeries (and in broader society). To move our gaze to the future, then, hides important ethical and social work required to explore digital-human relationships in the present. Here, I was heartened by Tim's portrayal of AI in "The Bracelet and the Battery" as an algorithm being used to monitor Jacqui's where-abouts. When Jacqui is unable to report back to her permitted travel zone, this algorithm is unlikely to be able to account for her reasons, but also, those *who set the machines to watch her* are likely *too busy, too hungry to listen*. Socio-digital systems emerge through the everyday interaction of humans and 'the digital', and we can't separate one from the other; meanings of technology and the knowledge they produce cannot be separated from how that knowledge is used and how it is consumed. If we place too much or too little trust in technologies, or if we are just too busy to reflect, these are all aspects of our digitally-mediated society.

Lastly, I want to briefly circle back to a point made by Zed in "Legacy", a point I spend a lot of time reflecting on in my own work, and a point that brings much of what each of the stories has reflected on, at least to some degree: that *humans always want more*. As we move to make electricity and food sources more efficient, and as we reduce the resources we need to produce the same amount of products, without constraints, we alter our behaviour to use the 'extra' resources gener-ated from efficiency gains. As such, our energy/resource savings are less than expected, and in extreme cases 'backfire', leading to increased consumption. These are known as 'rebound' effects. Rebound effects are often viewed by policymakers as positive, because they drive economic growth, but their consequential environmental impacts are all around us, leaving questions about how to balance economic security alongside environmental protection. As Zed articulates in her story, efficiency gains in batteries led to reductions in energy costs that led to increases in disposable income, so that more people could afford to buy goods, leading to more environmental destruction. In the case of Zed's story, this was so much so that the moon needed to be colonised to gain more resources and dump old ones following the destruction of our own planet. How can we avoid such atrocities? A growing literature around ecological economics is beginning to offer alternatives, but we will have to wait and see whether such approaches can counteract our prevailing economic models over the coming decades.

Concluding, I thoroughly enjoyed reading these eclectic stories, each of which brought to the present the ethical, social, and regulatory issues we will likely need to reckon with in the coming years. The stories were ones of scarcity and inequity; a warning of what is to come without constraint of human behaviour, and without listening to those voices that often go unheard.

PART 3
Finance and
Digital Money

Don't Say That, You'll Make It Happen
Eddie Robson

LAURA IS IMPRESSED with the latest iteration of her desktop assistant. It could already scour media streams, identify what was relevant to her department, and deliver an edited highlights package. Now, after the update, it can also parse soundbites and interviews given by her department's ministers, correlate this with the online reaction, and let her know if they've had a total fucking car crash.

Jacob Faxton, Chief Secretary to the Treasury, was at a reception for business leaders earlier this evening. There wasn't supposed to be any media coverage, but a reporter from one of the late news shows was there and Jacob will talk to anyone who shows the slightest interest in listening to him.

"Look," says Jacob in the footage Laura is watching on her casting screen. Jacob is one of the younger Cabinet ministers, tall and rather doughy-faced, and he stands inside one of London's grander buildings, in front of an eighteenth-century painting. He's possibly had a drink. "What you have to understand is, this is all a different conversation in the age of the digital pound."

Everyone in the cabinet has been saying "the age of the digital pound" in every single interview for months, and even the advisers who told them to do this are sick of hearing it.

"The decisions we're now making are based on the best possible data," Jacob continues. "We no longer have to be led by forecasts made by economists based on, frankly, guesswork. We *know* where people are spending their money. We *know* where every pound is, compared where it was yesterday. So you can be sure we're making the right decisions for the country every single day."

Laura has warned Jacob statements like this are a double-edged sword. Because if you're making decisions based on the best possible data, and the economy is still in the toilet, that implies you're making shit decisions. The interviewer follows up with a question about a second quarter of negative growth and the economic effect of the ongoing transport crisis.

"Look," says Jacob again, putting on that fixed grin he does in response to aggressive questions; he thinks it makes him look unfazed, but in fact it makes him look flippant. "Good decisions can still be tough decisions. And it's a very complicated picture. You know, this isn't just about people. I mean, when you're talking about money, these days... there are systems at work, micro-adjustments being made by, er, algorithms..."

He has lost track of his own point. He should be asserting he's in control, but in going on the defensive he's straying close to stating it's beyond *anyone's* control, and so you can't exactly blame *him*.

"... and in the age of the digital pound... I mean, it's complex when so many systems run themselves, and now money can be put in and pulled out very fast, you have to make sure the system doesn't sort of run away with itself. But we have the best possible data and we're making the best possible decisions."

Laura closes the video and summons a car. She could just call Jacob, but when you need someone to know they've fucked up, nothing beats telling them in person.

"Can you please keep your voice down?" says Jacob. They are in his living room. Jacob wears his pyjamas and dressing gown.

"I'm not shouting," says Laura.

"I didn't say you were shouting. The kids have only just gone to sleep."

"Stop wasting time. Miles is going to be here in a minute."

Jacob winces. "Miles is coming?"

"Yes and you know how *he* feels about this project."

Miles is based at Number10 and handling implementation of the digital pound. He's an evangelist for it and whenever he's around, everyone else has to pretend to be one too. Laura doesn't believe big, showy political projects really work, especially not ones with this kind of technocratic bent. In her view the only thing that makes things better is boring sustained competence over time, and when someone comes in offering a magic wand she feels it will only make people less likely to seek effective, unsexy solutions.

"Look," Jacob says, "I know I was a bit unfocused in the interview, I'm sorry."

Laura hands him a transcript to show him just how unfocused he was. Jacob reads it while sipping some coffee which she is forcing him to drink so he can sober up. While he's reading, Miles arrives: a shortish, shaven-headed man whose easy-going manner belies his stubbornness.

"Well," Jacob says when he's finished reading. "These things always look bad if you leave in all the ums and ers and fragments and whatnots. What was I supposed to do, refuse to talk to him?"

"You weren't meant to go from saying we have more control over the economy than ever," says Miles, "to saying a minute later the economy runs itself and no-one really controls it."

"It's true what I said about micro-adjustments. All the financial services use them. They're all reacting to each other—"

"Based on parameters that have been set for them. They don't make their own decisions."

"I'm not convinced."

"Then you're fucking wrong," says Miles pleasantly.

"A lot of people," Laura tells Jacob, "have interpreted what you said as meaning that, between the digital pound and the financial algorithms, money now thinks for itself."

"That wasn't what I meant," says Jacob. 'Obviously."

"I know it wasn't what you meant but that's *literally* what people think."

"Um." Jacob screws up his tired eyes, then opens them. 'Sorry, do they mean money or the economy?"

"Both," says Laura.

"Most people don't distinguish between those two things," says Miles.

"But the money isn't... I mean it doesn't do anything," says Jacob. "It's just information, it just sits on a computer and people move it around. What do they think it wants?"

Miles shrugs. "To grow?"

Jacob raises his eyebrows wearily. "My job would be *much* easier if money *wanted* to grow."

"The point is," says Laura, "there are already enough people saying they don't trust the digital pound and won't use it. The banks still haven't given up campaigning against it." Before the digital pound was introduced, the banks suggested they'd have to charge for current accounts, because it would limit their ability to profit—but customers largely don't understand why, and don't care, and don't see why they need a current account that pays zero percent interest if they have a digital wallet. The messaging apps are stepping into the gap, offering to organise people's financial lives for them. "There's already enough misinformation coming from the banks without you adding to it," Laura finishes.

"You always get refuseniks with any new technology," says Jacob, "and on this there's always been a minority—"

"And we need to stop them becoming a majority," says Laura. "Which they will, if you keep on talking like that." This is Laura's area of expertise: she can read a crowd and tell what it's going to do. People trust her on it.

"So what, you want me to come out tomorrow with a statement that money *isn't* intelligent and doesn't have its own agenda?"

"No. That'll just make people think money is intelligent and has its own agenda," says Laura. "We need to reinforce the messaging and *you* need a solid line on this you can stick to, no matter how drunk you are."

It takes until four a.m. to hammer out the line and ensure Jacob is drilled in it, ready for any media appearances in the morning. And to his credit, he sticks to it well. The phrase 'We're on it' crops up a lot, as does the word 'dynamic' when talking about the data they're receiving and how they're responding to it. The question of why things still seem, economically speaking, rather shit, is deflected with three-point lists of what they're doing to turn it around.

Laura continues to gauge the mood and track the numbers. How many people don't trust the digital pound to work properly. How many don't think it's secure. How many have deep concerns about activity monitoring. How many are advising people to transfer their money into a new cybercurrency called Squirecoin which guarantees anonymity; the people recommending this are plainly on a commission for every customer they manage to send there. There are other, more elaborate reactions. A three-member art collective calling itself Eraza Pound keeps popping up in the media with stunts connected to the new technology: their latest is a real-time clock that uses the data to track wealth inequality, displayed in prominent locations around the country. An investigation into where they got the data from reveals they paid for it, so they appear to be well-funded.

But the mood and numbers are OK, and they get better. Apart from an obsessed minority, people get bored and move on. Laura is able to relax. Her job is to monitor public response and report on it, and the nature of that response isn't her fault—but in her world people have a habit of shooting messengers.

Then something complicated and not easy to summarise happens, something Laura hadn't anticipated:

The government's promises start to come true.

At first it shows up in economic data. This gives ministers some useful numbers to quote in interviews, but doesn't interest Laura: it means nothing if people can't feel it. In fact if they can't feel it, the numbers just annoy them.

Then, slowly, people *do* start to feel it. People can no longer see or hold their money, but they feel like it's going further. Confidence is higher than it's been in decades, even with automation causing frequent pockets of turmoil in the job market and climate change creating supply chain issues. Laura corrects for outliers and skewing factors, but there's no doubt: when she compares contemporary chatter with that from before the digital pound, the current mood is far more positive. And there's still almost a year to go before the next election.

Laura still maintains it's boringly competent decisions that make these things happen. But it turns out there *were* people making boringly competent decisions all along, and the new system has been making those decisions more effective.

Laura considers for argument's sake that she might be wrong, and looks back over the trend data her assistant fetched for her for any other things she may have previously dismissed. One thing in particular stands out, which she might not even have noticed were she not reassessing the period as a whole. There are always those in the political sphere and the commentariat who, during a crisis period, will trot out the line about not talking the economy down. It isn't something you tend to hear ordinary people say, because it's principally a way of shutting down criticism. This has changed. Laura sees it a lot as she looks through the data. People don't always phrase it quite like that, but the assistant is getting good at recognising the sentiment behind words and associating them with context, and it identifies an increasingly common response to any doubt or negativity around the economy is: Don't say that, you'll make it happen.

Laura raises this when she next speaks to Miles, and she brings examples of recent discourse with her to show him what she means.

"What are you talking about?' he says, not harshly: he genuinely doesn't know.

"Just look,' Laura says, pulling up the wordcloud she made last night. "You can see it in the verbs people use in connection with the economy. The language is more active than it used to be."

"People have always said the economy is *responding*, or *thriving*, or..."

"I know, I know – it feels nebulous, but I'm sure there's something there."

"Right," Miles says. "But so what?"

"It's like that thing we talked about, with the incident with Jacob." (Jacob is no longer in his post, having been promoted to Education Secretary and then made to carry the can when it emerged a number of schools had been granted academy status and government funding despite being entirely AI-generated.) "I think... people believe the UK economy thinks for itself now, to some extent. Like it's this big creature made of money which we all own a share in, but not enough for any of us to control it."

"Well it sort of is, in a way," says Miles, smiling.

"I *am* concerned about this, Miles. We agreed this was a problem before, if people think we're not in control."

"It was a problem *then*, because things weren't going well. But our numbers on the economy are good now, aren't they?"

"Very good, yes."

"I mean... I don't want to put out new messaging when people already have such a positive impression. Ultimately what you're telling me is people don't understand how the economy works—that's not new. It works to our advantage, sometimes. I say we leave it for now, Laura. We'll be on recess in a few days anyway. If it's still bothering you come conference time, we can pick it up then."

It's another hot summer, and London has felt half empty for weeks—anyone who can be out of the city already is. Laura is part of the substantial team summoned to a hotel on the Norfolk coast for a strategy conference ahead of the following year's election.

On the Friday morning of that week, during a coffee break, the attendees hear of Eraza Pound's latest conceptual wheeze, because the whole country is talking about it. They've posted footage of themselves transferring a million pounds into Squirecoin wallets—ten thousand in each wallet—and then writing the access keys on small blank pieces of card. They have proceeded to burn every card in a public display outside Canary Wharf tube station.

The chatter online is reflected in the room at the conference. The consensus in both arenas is it's obviously not real. There are many witnesses to the burning, but the footage of the money being transferred was surely staged or generated, and the cards surely didn't have real keys on them, just random strings of characters. Or maybe the money *was* transferred, but they still have another note of each key somewhere. It's an empty stunt.

Laura skips out on the next session and goes to her room to watch the unfolding reaction. The consensus is fractured as further information emerges. People have tried and failed to read the keys seen in the video, but they have gone onto the blockchain and found the money. A million pounds definitely went into a hundred real Squirecoin wallets, and Eraza Pound insist they do not have copies of the keys. They have effectively destroyed the money by making it impossible to reach. Those hundred wallets will remain on the blockchain as a statement on the value placed upon money.

Many people continue to believe it's fake and mock those taking it seriously. But others seize angrily on the notion the money has been destroyed. How *dare* they? Don't they realise what this could lead to? How *disrespectful* it is, after how well everything's been going? It takes little time for the death threats to begin and multiply. Some voices say no, if they still have the keys somewhere then killing them will mean they're lost forever. These voices are drowned out.

Laura rejoins the conference in time for lunch, where she sits with Miles. All the talk is still of the money-burning stunt: it is, after all, more interesting than the conference.

"I can't see anything else knocking it out of the news cycle," she tells Miles, "and public response is really heating up."

"It's not *actually* going to crash the economy, though. It's only a million pounds after all."

"Doesn't matter at this point. Someone is going to kill those artists for this."

Miles looks up from his plate with a half-smile and is about to make a witty reply when he sees her face and realises she's entirely serious. She reads crowds and knows what they will do.

"Oh," Miles says. "Right."

"I don't think it's an exaggeration to describe it as an act of atonement."

Miles looks back down at his plate and eats a few crisps. "How much of a problem is that? For us, I mean?"

Laura considers. "I see an upside and a downside."

Miles nods. "So do I."

A House of Cards

Kate Baucherel

THE CROWD PUSHED towards the imposing headquarters of the Ministry of Economic Futures. Cassie let her avatar be swept along, unresisting. She dared not shout but her headphones reverberated with the passionate cries of her fellow demonstrators. Tracking down the current virtual location of the Ministry had been no easy task, and the Resistance had moved fast to organise the demo before it shifted its location once again.

In front of her eyes, the building construct flickered. The cheers redoubled. The pressure on this virtual world's servers of thousands of demonstrating avatars, coupled with a determined Distributed Denial of Service attack on the Ministry itself from outside, was taking its toll. Ministry bots targeted avatars in the crowd, seeking real world linked identities that they could block and punish. Two avatars in front of her froze.

"Get out!" Will's voice cut through the noise of the crowd in her headphones.

Cassie didn't need telling twice. She warped away instantly, as they had planned. For a few slow, terrible seconds, she thought the access code hadn't worked. She held her breath, then exhaled with relief to find herself in an oasis of calm, surrounded by the avatars of her college class on their museum excursion.

The first painting she saw enveloped her, drawing her into its embrace. She stared unblinking at the canvas as the forms dissolved into brushstrokes, blocks of colour, and individual pixels. She was drowning in a sea of vivid blue, heart rate settling, calm at last.

"Cassie?"

The painting swirled back into focus. Cassie looked around into the far less interesting face of her avatar guide.

"It's time to log out," said the guide. "I hope you enjoyed the gallery tour. Please leave feedback on exit."

"I will, thank you," said Cassie.

The gallery faded, replaced by a wall of stars. Still lost in the stress of the demo and the memory of the painting, Cassie glanced at the five-star box and blinked. It registered instantly, transmitting evidence of her visit to the social feeds that recorded her life.

Hearing footsteps outside her door, she quickly pulled off the headset. The band that sat against her forehead was soaked with sweat. The mild disorientation of jumping out of virtual reality was lessened by the familiar surroundings of her childhood bedroom.

"How was the museum?" asked her mother, bright eyes darting around the room, always checking, always watching.

"It was good," said Cassie. "I liked the Klein."

Her mother made a note. "I'll add that to your feed," she said. "It will improve the Algorithm's score."

The Algorithm. Cassie's life was ruled by the Algorithm. Her every action and reaction, her passions and skills, were recorded and analysed by the Ministry's Algorithm. Exabytes of data compiled and optimised over a child's life enabled quantum processors to calculate all their possible futures. From the moment that they spoke their first word and held their first smartscreen, the Algorithm ran. While their predicted behaviour remained within the Ministry's norms, their careers, income, healthcare and state support were guaranteed and generous.

It worked for the majority, the happy, motivated, well-trained work-force who enjoyed the best quality of life in the hemisphere. A growing minority was not so lucky. Cassie vividly remembered the naughtiest child in her primary school classes, Harvey, who had been her best friend despite his occasional habit of sticking glue in her hair. The

Algorithm had *never* liked Harvey. He would regularly block the video receptors of the gentle little arts and crafts robot with play dough. Cassie had admired his streak of rebellion, and they had become inseparable even as his behaviour worsened. In fourth year, he kicked the substitute teacher on the shin. One day Harvey simply wasn't there anymore. Cassie cried for a week.

When she was older, she asked her mother what had happened to him. Her parents were furious that she even remembered him. The Algorithm was always listening, her mother explained later in a secluded corner of the garden. You didn't speak of those who had fallen. It might taint your record.

That was when Cassie started to question everything.

Her mother's voice cut through Cassie's contemplations.

"What are you doing now?" she asked.

"I'm meeting Will," replied Cassie. "We have an assignment to work on."

"I'll arrange your cab," said her mother. She was always in control.

Cassie waited under the grand portico of the house. The extensive front lawn and the sweeping driveway were slick with rain. Her family had done well out of the Algorithm. Three generations of talented politicians and policy makers had advanced the country's standing in the new world order and extracted life-changing wealth from the central bank through the Algorithm's beneficence. They were rewarded for being dependable, consistent, and successful. Cassie hated them all.

She was the wild card, the cluster of recessive genes that didn't want to play the family game. The first tentative results from the Algorithm when she was just a toddler had marked her out as different. Her parents had waived their right to a fourth child to avoid any risk of producing another mutation. Her mother immediately took control of every social feed on Cassie's behalf and supervised her closely, desperate to maintain the wealth and power of the family. If the Algorithm reacted badly to the mutation in their midst, Cassie could bring the whole house of cards crashing down.

Will's home was small and welcoming. His parents had only been funded for one child, as the Algorithm indicated they were unlikely to pass on the genes for significant economic contribution. They lived comfortably enough, unafraid of a system that they didn't really understand.

"He's in the den, love," said Will's mother with a beaming smile as Cassie bounded through the door. She handed her two bottles of soda. "Take these. I found your favourite flavour in the store."

Cassie curled up in her accustomed place in the big, comfortable chair by Will's desk. She gazed at the bank of screens on the wall and watched as his fingers flashed across the keyboard.

"Did you get to the museum tour before it ended?" he asked.

"Yes," said Cassie. "I caught the last room and left a rating. The class record shows I was there the whole time. Come on, fill me in on what happened after I left."

Will pulled a series of reports and film clips onto his screens. "Your tip-off about the server farm was crucial," he said. "The combination of the DDOS attack and the virtual demo disrupted some of the inbound data feeds. We've proved it can be done. And there's this, too." He tapped on another screen and pulled up a grainy video clip.

Cassie peered at the footage. Hunched figures plodded out of an anonymous building and away along damp pavements, ignoring the rain that soaked their hair and seeped through their thin clothes. A few looked up incuriously as a small group of people ran through the crowd towards the building, bent on disruption.

"Resistance activity at a real-world site," she breathed. "It must be one of the moderation factories. Where was this?"

"Not far away," said Will. "See the sign there? And the markings here on the road? I've matched the exact location from satellite feeds and CCTV. It's tagged as a research institute."

The footage glitched. A thin face wearing a manic grin filled the screen for a split second, then the video receptors blanked out.

Cassie gasped and jumped to her feet. "Will! Did you see that?"

Will nodded. "It was a good move, blocking the video to avoid the team being identified," he said. "Unlucky for him that he got caught on camera. The Ministry will be after him now."

"Oh, I hope he'll be okay," said Cassie, her heart beating wildly under a studied sober expression. She would have recognised that grin anywhere. It was Harvey.

***

Cassie's determination to help the Resistance redoubled. Although her mother followed her every move, checking her chip location and attendance records and posting Algorithm-boosting comments to Cassie's feeds, there were ways to escape the surveillance.

Her chip location was one thing, but Cassie's physical location quite another. A simple hack by Will sent dummy data to the network while Cassie explored the region. She worked fast to find the research institute and to help identify others, factories where rejects on the breadline spent their days plumbing the depraved depths of the social feeds, moderating what AI could not recognise.

At home, Cassie dug deep into the family records. She learned about her family's involvement in developing and honing the Algorithm, and her loathing for them and all they stood for grew.

"You're taking a lot of risks," said Will as they pored over the latest set of data she'd collected. "Are you sure it's worth it?"

"Yes," she said. "I've been lucky. My parents protected me. Other people don't have that chance." Like Harvey, she thought to herself. "The Algorithm decides they're worthless as soon as they can walk. I can make a difference with what I've learned growing up among those self-centred, pathetic..." She spluttered to a halt.

"They only protect you because it protects them," said Will. "What will you do when your luck runs out?"

"I'm ready," she said. "My coming-of-age grant is due on my birthday. It'll go straight into the family vault. They've made sure of that. Then

I'm no longer a dependent, just a burden. They won't want a mutation messing up their perfect scores."

"Most people celebrate when they turn eighteen," said Will sadly. "You'll be staring into a void."

"No, I won't," said Cassie. "I have plans…"

Will raised his eyebrows towards the door of the den. The walls in this house were paper thin.

Cassie took the hint and lowered her voice. "I'm ready to find my own way," she said. "What about you? You're taking the same risks, helping with the DDOS attack and passing on all the things I've found."

"The Ministry doesn't think people like me are a threat," said Will. "I'll be okay."

He turned back to his screens. Cassie curled deeper into the familiar chair, knowing that this may be the last time she would ever be in the place she wished she called home.

***

"Happy Birthday," chirped the entertainment hub in the corner of Cassie's bedroom, before playing a personalised message from her current favourite band. Cassie grinned. She knew it was AI-generated and she didn't care. Every year she woke to the same greeting, although the messages had changed over time in line with her listening habits. It was always the best moment of her birthday.

Cassie flipped open her smartscreen and navigated to the central bank's open ledger. A quick search on her ID number revealed that her coming-of-age grant had been transferred to the family vault overnight. It was time to go.

She took a long, luxurious shower, dressed as if ready for college classes, and made her way downstairs. She hid her bulging rucksack in a niche under the portico and went in search of breakfast. She was not planning to leave on an empty stomach.

Her mother was waiting for her. "Eighteen at last," she said, unsmiling. "You're on your own now."

"Thanks," said Cassie lightly. "No surprise party, then?"

Her mother pursed her lips and swept out of the room. Cassie laughed to herself. The morning was going exactly as she expected. Once she had eaten her fill, she retrieved her rucksack and walked off down the drive. She didn't give the house a backward glance. She was ready to embrace her new future.

Will's house was in darkness and the door was locked. Cassie frowned and tried the door again.

"Coming," called Will.

He opened the door and gave Cassie a strained smile. "Happy Birthday," he said quietly.

Two dark figures loomed up in the darkness behind Will. Cassie whirled around and ran straight into the arms of a third enforcement officer.

"Will?" she said helplessly.

There were tears in his eyes. "I'm sorry," he said. "This was the only way to protect my parents. They've done nothing wrong. I'm so, so sorry."

As the enforcement patrol led them away to separate cars, Cassie could hear Will's mother sobbing.

***

Days passed, stretching into weeks. Cassie was tired of repeated questions she couldn't answer about the Resistance. She learned in passing that her family had announced her untimely death and even staged a funeral. She asked about Will, but they told her nothing. She wondered about her eventual fate. Would she become one of those grey figures worn down by the awfulness of the online content they had to expunge? Would she simply rot in this prison, forgotten and fallen, a non-person?

Her dark thoughts were interrupted by distant shouting and the sound of running feet. Cassie pricked up her ears. There was a heavy pounding on the door. With an audible crack, it flew open. Smoke poured into the room.

"Cassie! Come with me."

Someone grabbed her hand. Blinded by the smoke, eyes streaming, Cassie stumbled out of the room and through the twists and turns of a maze of corridors. A welcome current of fresh air indicated they were nearing an exit. A shaft of sunlight penetrated Cassie's tears and she blinked hard, trying to clear her vision.

"Jump down," said her rescuer. "Two metres."

She could see enough now to judge her landing but stumbled all the same. The stranger's hand steadied her, and they ran together towards an anonymous cab that waited at the kerb. Behind them Cassie could hear shouting and sirens.

The noise cut out as the cab door closed and it moved smoothly out into the traffic. Cassie wiped her eyes and stared at her rescuer as he flipped a hidden panel open with practiced ease, tapped out a complex sequence, and sat back, satisfied.

"I've randomised the route and scrambled the cab's location," he said. "Hello, Cassie. It's been a while."

"Harvey?" said Cassie. "It's really you, isn't it?"

"In the flesh," said Harvey, flashing the old manic grin.

Cassie spun around in her seat, looking back at the smoke enveloping the Ministry building. "We have to go back," she said. "We need to find Will."

Harvey shook his head. "He's not there, Cassie," he said. "He's already with us. You'll see him soon. You're a bit of a hero, you know. The information you pulled together before you were both taken is dynamite. We weren't going to leave you to rot after that effort."

Cassie's head was spinning. She felt sick from the smoke. "I just did what anyone would have done," she stammered.

"But the difference is, you actually did it," said Harvey gently, handing her a drink of water. "Thanks to the work you and Will did, we know where and how to attack the Algorithm itself. We're fighting back, Cassie."

The city gave way to fields. Cassie closed her sore eyes. Eventually the movement of the cab rocked her into a deep sleep.

She woke to Harvey gently shaking her shoulder. "We're here," he said. "This is the headquarters of our Resistance cell."

They had pulled up in a small hamlet in the middle of rolling hills. The place was a hive of activity, carefully laid out to look like a normal farm to prying eyes. Sheep were bleating in the distance and a dog was barking.

"How far have we come?" she asked.

"About eighty clicks," said Harvey, "deep into the countryside."

Cassie stepped out of the cab and gazed around. She glimpsed silver antennas disguised by tall trees, providing independent connectivity from sympathetic satellite networks. Every roof was covered in solar panels, and high up on the hill wind turbines spun in the breeze. One of the barns was strung with lights and filled with comfortable chairs. She instantly felt at home.

"Like all the cells, we're self-sufficient for food and power and web access," said Harvey, leading her towards the large farmhouse, "and we have our own mining operation for Resistance privacy coins. No more Algorithm handouts. There's a whole new society being created across the country, right under the nose of the Ministry."

Cassie took a deep breath of the fresh country air. Her only possible future was laid out before her. She turned to Harvey.

"I'm ready," she said. "Let's take them down."

Update Needed

Alex Buxton

2035. NEW YORK, Friday evening. Trader Sammy Rain is about to tell Leigh he can get a reservation at Boulevard for them as his brother once had a thing with the maître d's avatar when their boss, Bellamy, sticks his head out of his office and sees them.

"Tu!" he calls, looking at Rain. "Step in here a minute, will you?"

Bellamy's mistaken Rain for Charles Tu, a trader who sits two floors down and is one 0x Protocol away from going postal. The mix-up's understandable, because Tu and Rain have almost identical digital foot-prints—they buy the same clothes from the same stores, live in the same area and hang out at the same bars. They even have similar-aged wives, and got married at around the same time, although Tu has a slightly more senior job and has a much better relationship with his father.

"Yes, sir," Rain calls back, rising to his feet.

"Jesus, Sammy," Leigh mutters as Rain makes his way across the room, "are you ever going to tell him your real name?"

Am I? Rain thinks, calling to mind *Telepar*, his favourite TV show. *Where's the drama in that? After that I've just jumped the shark.*

Rain smells a rat. He's only been in Bellamy's office a handful of times before. Something's wrong.

Bellamy's sitting behind his desk, looking like you could knock his socks off with a feather.

"Shut the door, have a seat."

Rain closes the door behind him but stays standing. *This is worse than season six episode three*, he thinks, still on *Telepar, when Toby didn't know about his son's leukaemia.* Bellamy takes off his glasses and rubs the bridge of his nose.

"Tu, I'm afraid your father's dead."

Rain stares blankly for a moment, thinking of his own father who he knows is in good health. He wonders if now's the occasion to tell his boss he's not Charles Tu.

"Oh," he says, playing for time.

"HR picked it up a minute ago," Bellamy goes on. "He hadn't been keeping up with the payments for software updates on his car, did you know that?" Rain shakes his head. Bellamy goes on. "They say that shouldn't affect safety, but then they would say that, given the number of crashes there have been recently. Oh—" he waves his hand at Rain, "—sorry. Anyway, the car had a bid accepted for emergency assistance not long ago, then they saw an automated payment to Bellevue, so, you know." Bellamy glances at the screen in front of him. "It looks like someone just applied for his life insurance."

Rain steps towards the desk. "Do you mind if I...?'

"Oh, no, of course not." Bellamy swings the screen around so Rain can see for himself. There it isn't, like the missing tooth in the face of the bum who sits on Thirty-fifth and Fifth and begs for spare tokens all day—the gap in the public blockchain where the missing payments should be. And there's the life insurance claim, the payment to Bellevue, everything. Rain can even see the subscription payment to keep this goddamn screen on. He zooms in. His eyes pass over the unfamiliar pseudonymous tags of thousands of payments. Rain's about to turn away when something else catches his eye, unconnected to Tu's father. It's a familiar tag—sip72z. It's the tag his wife uses that she thinks he doesn't know about from her private wallet. She'd made payments every Thursday evening to the Riverside Flower Hotel when as far as Rain's aware she has tennis lessons on Thursday evenings. What's more, she'd made the payments in digital dollars, not the hotel's tokens, which might be tacky, but would almost certainly offer better value. The only reason to pay in cash is to leave less of a trail.

"Have you ever heard of the Riverside Flower Hotel?" he asks Bellamy, swinging the screen back to him.

Bellamy shrugs. "It's a meta-hotel, decent token rate."

"Good to know."

"Listen, Tu," Bellamy says as Rain makes for the door. "I'm sorry for your loss, if there's anything we can do, if you need any time off..."

"Thanks," Rain tells him, "I'll let you know."

Fuck the blockchain, Rain thought, *I need to hear this from the horse's mouth*. Season two episode nine: Linda's affair comes out.

"Sammy!" Leigh greets him as he gets back to his desk. She's with Jackie, another coworker. They both have their jackets on. "We're going for sushi at Horse, but drinks first. Wild."

Rain grabs his own jacket. "I think I'll sit this one out. How will you get into Horse, anyway?"

"Piece of cake," Leigh tells him with a wink. "I know a guy. And yes, you are coming."

"Come on," Jackie whines. "I could eat a horse and chase the jockey."

The group bounces to the elevator. Leigh and Jackie are bickering about the merits of Dragon, a Pho place uptown.

"You're crazy," Jackie tells Leigh, "the food is out of this world."

"Who gives a shit? Hey, scoot over." Leigh shoves Jackie aside and punches the button for the lobby. "Name me anyone who's been there in the past six months who's been invited to one of Terry's parties."

"What did Bellamy want, anyway?" Jackie asks Rain as the doors open at the first floor.

"Oh, nothing," Rain says, waving at Tu who happens to be getting out of the elevator across the lobby. "Nothing important."

Wild has less class than a pig in lipstick and is twice as loud. They can barely hear each other speak, which is OK because they ignore each other anyway. The three of them sit at a booth and order negronis while looking about the bar and the dance floor for anyone they know. Rain has a headache. The thumping bass and the lasers dancing about the flailing limbs by the DJ booth are making him feel nauseous. Jackie has already made a scene by refusing to pay in Wild tokens at the bar. Leigh won't let it go.

"Why the hell wouldn't you?" Rain hears her shout over an extended mix of "Near Now" by The Cosmic Quasars. "It's like free money. If you pay in dollars you get *no* perks. You do realise cash is just for poor people and wars, don't you? You look like a janitor when you pay like that."

"I just don't want to pay the gas fees," Jackie blasts back. "That's all."

Leigh grimaces. "You're insane. You make it back with the discount. Listen—" she leans forward to be sure Jackie can hear, "—do you know who owns this bar? Sky Wing. I made twenty billion on their tokens today. You buy Wild tokens here, Sky Wing's go up."

"So I get to make you money?" Jackie snorts. "As if I needed more of a reason not to."

Leigh throws an ice cube at her and looks at Rain as the DJ turns the next track, something by Velvet Nebula, up several screaming decibels. "Hey, Sammy, what are you so quiet for?"

"What?" Rain cups his ear.

"I said," Leigh cries, "what are you so quiet for?"

"I think my wife's having an affair." Rain howls back.

"What?"

"I said, I think my wife's having an affair."

"Let's get some shots," says Jackie. "Cheer this bastard up."

"Good idea," Leigh roars, beckoning a waiter over. "I can't hear what he's saying anyway."

I can't believe she's having an affair, Rain thinks. It makes his piss boil.

Like everyone else, Rain lives in a small, grey two-room by two-room box on the outskirts of the city so it's close to the power banks for optimal rendering. He staggers home that night around nine, and goes straight to his headset without bothering to see where his wife is physically. He knows where he'll find her.

Their meta-home is spectacular, staggering. Rain had commissioned Anat Guadalupe at Reflex to build it from scratch. It has three floors, seven bedrooms, and multiple open plan living spaces that can change to suit the mood of the occupant with maximum ease. Everything is hand-crafted and bespoke, from the roof shingles to the doorbell chime. It had taken three months to build, and Samuel Rain considers it his finest achievement.

Once he's plugged in, Rain appears in the hall. He's standing on exquisite black and white floor tiles created with imported code from France, and looking at himself in the two wall-length antique mirrors in front of him and to his right. His avatar is immaculate, dressed today in a suit by Giorgio Armani with a casual, tieless shirt underneath by Burberry. Facially, it looks similar to Rain, with thick, chestnut hair and close cut, well-manicured stubble, but at one hundred and eighty-five centimetres is slightly taller, and more chiselled around the jaw and cheekbones. Rain takes the stairs to his left, still admiring the detail on the carpet tufts under his feet. The carpet alone had taken eight weeks to get right, and was made with code specially ordered from Puerto Rico.

Arden's on the third floor in one of the living spaces. She's nestled on a leather bean bag by Amara, perfect legs tucked under her and long, black hair falling over her face and hitting the light at an angle that had taken nearly two weeks to code just right. Everyone's avatar is beautiful, but Arden's, Rain thinks, not for the first time, has a face so hot it could boil potatoes.

She looks up from her book as Rain walks in.

"You're home late."

"Work ran on." Rain takes in the perfect room where perpetual golden hour light streams through two soaring arched windows and spills over his wife and the black marble table that today dominates the space. A chessboard made by Rechapados Ferrer in Spain sits midway through a game, with one of Rain's bishops dangerously exposed. He can't see anything out of place.

Arden's book disappears and she gets to her feet. "On a Friday?"

"Are you having an affair?"

She sighs. "Oh, Sammy, I was going to tell you. It's only a digi-affair, nothing serious."

The next morning they don't plug in. Instead, they sit in their physical bed and talk and cry until their eyes are as raw as bone. When he has nothing more to say Sammy gets up and packs a suitcase and an overnight bag while Arden tries to explain herself again.

"You're being ridiculous, Sammy, it was digital-only. It's not like we ever met in the real world. We've always said digi-affairs were fine. You think I don't know about the meta-bars you go to after work?"

Sammy zips up his Hermés overnight bag and snaps shut the clasps on his Carl Friedrik Carry-On Pro. "That's different. Looking at rendered tits isn't an affair."

Arden holds her hand out, but Sammy lets it hang. Her eyes fill with tears again. "Where are you going?"

Sammy hauls the bags off the bed. "I'm not sure yet." He looks at her. "It's the emotion. That's the difference. What does he have that I don't?"

Arden shrugs. "A lot more money. He's worth something, Sammy."

In his car, Sammy sets the auto drive to JFK and while driving, visits JFK's virtual ticketing desk. He scans the list of flights leaving in the next two hours and, for the first time in his life, chooses the cheapest. A chatbot with short blonde hair and pretty eyes smiles at him.

"Can I help you, sir?"

Sammy's avatar leers back at her. "I'd like a return flight to London, please. Make my return two weeks from now, but make the ticket transferable."

"And how would you like to pay?"

"United tokens are fine."

As soon as he's completed the transaction his phone trills.

"Sammy, Sammy Rain?"

"Who is this?"

"This is Chibuzo Miigwan from the Modern Maven human resources department. I see that you've just purchased a return flight to London. Is everything ok?"

What now? Sammy tries to make his voice reassuring. "Everything's fine, I'm just taking a little trip."

"Sir, I'm required to flag any signs of depressed behaviour I see in your records."

"I'm simply going on a short break."

"To London?"

Sammy's heart is racing. "I know it's not Costa Rica."

"Don't get on that flight." Chibuzo Miigwan from the Modern Maven human resources department tells him. "Going somewhere as dangerous as London is a flaggable activity."

"My uncle died," Sammy tells him. "I need to be with my family."

"Sure." For a moment Chibuzo sounds almost sympathetic. "You know, there are plenty more fish in the sea."

Sammy does have relatives in London, they're just all dead. He's never even been to England before. He stays in a cheap hotel in Covent Garden, working from his room in the day and cruising the bars that aren't boarded up at night. When he's been there for three days he starts a half-hearted affair with a young barmaid called Ashanti, but after three more days of crippling guilt he calls it off and sends a message to his wife confessing all. When he's been there a week, Chibuzo calls again.

"You're spending a lot of time in bars for someone dealing with a family bereavement."

"Grief affects people differently," Sammy tells him. "There aren't many bars left open."

"You should come back to work," Chibuzo says. "Whatever you're going through, we can't help unless we know."

"Don't worry," Sammy soothes Chibuzo Miigwan from human resources. "I'll be back in a week."

The next day he calls Leigh. She answers on the first ring. "Hey, where are you? People keep trying to take your chair."

"I'm in London."

"London? Isn't that in England? Didn't they go bankrupt?"

Sammy looks out of the window. From where he is he can count five people sleeping in doorways and two burnt-out cars. All the stores are boarded up.

"They did, Leigh, it's all up there on their chain."

"Do they have bums on the street, like New York?"

"Of course," says Sammy. "No one here has any money. They're just like the bums back home, but they talk in an English accent."

Leigh laughs. "The homeless people talk in an English accent? That's the most goddam pretentious thing I've ever heard."

"You haven't heard from Arden, have you?"

"No, why the hell would I?"

On the day of his flight back to JFK alerts of failed payments start pinging all over Sammy's phone like it's having a heart attack. He can't work it out—there's still money in all of his accounts. On the plane he puts his headset on for the first time in two weeks, but can't find home any more, just a blank space where his house has been. He reboots the system and tries again, but nothing. He sends a message to Arden. She informs him that her meta-lover has moved in and they've changed the locks. He's now homeless. He checks the failed payment notifications again.

Payment failed. Proof of address no longer recognized.

At the airport he grabs his Maybach S 1000 from long-term parking. He can't face going back to his physical house quite yet, so Sammy heads to the office instead. It isn't until he's pulled onto the freeway that he notices an alert on the dashboard.

Software update needed. Performance limited until payment received. Please send payment immediately.

His phone blares into life.

"Mr Rain, this is Chibuzo Miigwan. Did you know you've stopped paying updates for the software on your car?"

Sammy grimaces. "I haven't stopped, the last payment just didn't go through, that's all. Listen, I'm in the fast lane right now driving in manual." A truck in front of Sammy brakes hard. "I've got to go."

Sammy kills the call and pushes his foot down hard on the brake pedal. The truck's probably less than a hundred metres away and the car's braking too slowly. He's still doing seventy. It's not meant to do this, Sammy thinks, it's meant to just pull over and stop working or not start at all. He stamps on the brakes again. Too late.

The message blinks again on the dashboard:

Update needed.

Swipe Right

Eva Pascoe

As THE EARLY evening settled over Cnoxos City, casting long shadows across empty streets, Alix walked along in the rain on a dimly lit sidewalk. The soft glow of street neon gave her a sense of security as she made her way home from the East Town Hall office. Her skinny rescue mutt, Finely, followed her closely, sniffing and coughing, his wet nose irritated by the smoke coming off the nearby mountain fires. The muffled sounds of distant traffic and occasional footsteps echoed through the quiet city landscape.

Unbeknown to her, two menacing figures, concealed beneath dark helmets, on a powerful, black motorbike were moving up the street towards her. They had been casing her for several blocks, their faces hidden behind dark-tinted visors, and were closing in to strike. Before Alix could react, the pillion passenger reached out with a gloved hand, snatching her pink backpack with a violent jerk. The force was enough to nearly topple Alix off her feet. Her fingers helplessly grasped at the empty air where her bag had been just a millisecond before. Her heart pounded with fear as the two men sped away. Their motorcycle's engine roar fading fast into the distance.

Alix stood there for a while, stunned and shaken. Her breath slowly returned in panicked gasps after the suddenness and violence of the attack. She grabbed Finely up into her arms and cradled him, both trembling in the evening drizzle as the street fell into an uneasy silence.

For Alix, it was a stark reminder of how Cnoxos had felt before Mayor Klint had taken over. The old dangers lurked again in the shadows of the city's streets. The Cnoxos Crime Shield was a game-changer in this part of the city. A few years back, the town had suffered a wave of shocking, violent murders and was facing an exodus of all but the oldest citizens. Klint had campaigned on the promise of crime prevention with the introduction of the Crime Shield. It was a dense sensor network feeding data into an AI-based predictive crime engine that used a reactive force of drones and street closures when alerted by surveillance cameras. Danger signals interpreted by predictive crime algorithms would trigger drone responses in advance of any crime and the shield had radically reduced serious crime. Funded by the new, centrally-controlled digital currency, "Zilch", a special, smart-contracts fund for the city's services, Crime Shield paid for itself by saving hundreds of thousands in administrative costs alone. Afterwards, when the mayor also created Cnoxos' new City Bank, based on a private blockchain, Alix had landed her dream job setting up the Zilch team.

That was two years ago. Now, with the adrenaline from the attack still racing through her system, Alix's mind was filling with questions. Who were these guys, and why hadn't the Crime Shield pre-empted their attack? *Could it be down?* she wondered, searching her mind for answers. There was only one person she knew who might be able to provide them—Bob Steadman, a hacker and part-time anarchist who'd helped to set up Zilch and the shield back in the day. He was nearby. With Finley tucked under her arm Alix started running as fast as she could to reach him.

Bob lived in a cheap, lift-less building. It was not the first of his hide-outs where Alix had had to negotiate steep, narrow staircases. She rang the bell, pushing the button hard. "All right, all right, I am coming," Bob grunted as he appeared at the door with a half-empty glass of Johnnie Walker in his hand.

Alix's words spilled out as she described what had happened.

"Put your muddy dog down, I don't want its hair on my kit," Bob interrupted, pointing at a dense bank of workstations, screens flickering in the corner of what he called his 'artist's studio'. Alix ignored him and promptly borrowed one of them to log into Zilch's central money account, touching the authorisation pad on Bob's keyboard with her wrist to provide the required biometric Sweat ID verification.

"Have a look at this." Alix's shoulders tensed.

"Cnoxos central Zilch account is empty. Payments have been blocked since midnight. The Crime Shield sensors suppliers have disabled our network."

"What was in your bag?" asked Bob, taking over from Alix at his workstation. Using her log in, he set a swarm of audit crawlers to scanning Zilch's blockchain.

Bob Steadman was a man of few words but of eidetic memory.

"Didn't I see you in the Scramblers Bar with some guy a few days ago?"

Alix turned back, looking through the window at the rainy street five floors below them.

"I used Gambit, this new dating app, swiped right, and this guy's hologram came up on my card, so we ended up in a bar. He was from West Cnoxos, but we met only one time."

"What's your handle on Gambit? I think we should run some checks."

"Stop it, Bob. This is serious. While the payment system is blocked, the Crime Shield will stay down. And tomorrow the Central Air filters will stop too. That will be life-threatening for everyone in East Cnoxos with the heavy smoke coming off of Devil's Mountain. The summer drought has been longer than ever, the fires are so ferocious." Alix's voice trembled.

Bob turned to her and stared. "Your Gambit handle, please?"

"UptownRiches256," Alix replied reluctantly.

Bob turned back to his console and continued. "As I suspected. You were targeted. It was Zephyr, from The Thrashers. West Cnoxos mafia. He hangs out with my old ju-jitsu coach-turned-politician, Mr Alternator. Looks like Zephyr scrambled the algorithm and made his hologram pop up on top of your cards a few times, manipulating the AI recommender system. Easy to do, to be honest. He was stalking you on Gambit for a while. Did he end up at yours?" Bob asked without looking at her.

"We played chess in Scramblers. Then ended up walking to my place," Alix mumbled.

Bob continued, ignoring her response. "I know this guy. We were following him on a heist a couple of years ago. He discovered another hacking group's illicit entry to a bank vault. It was complex, but Zephyr diagnosed it and jumped in just before the original scammers. His timing was impeccable. The other guys got the blame, and Zephyr got the loot. Brilliant, really. And despite a huge bounty the money was never traced—ah, right, here we go!" Bob pushed himself back from his console, intertwining the fingers of his hands in a long, celebratory stretch.

"It looks like Zephyr dug into the central Zilch account with your credentials and sucked the payments out into one of the Thrashers accounts. That is why there was no Crime Shield. All payments to sensors' suppliers have stopped. And he's inserted some kind of feed to himself for any future payloads too, like a block for anyone trying to amend the fraudulent funds flow. I don't think I can undo it, Alix."

Alix cracked her knuckles. There were protocols in place for managing a breach like this, but ultimately responsibility for how to handle one was hers. She watched the wrinkles on Bob's forehead tightening. Blue lights from the flickering screens reflected on his face as he toggled screens.

"He swiped your sweat sample during that date. I can see he used your Sudological Bio Profile, Sweat ID, to break in. There must be a synthetic version of it now. Only a top lab can do that, so Zephyr's not working alone. His way into the system was with your credentials, then he emptied Zilch funds and re-directed all future payments to this designated account." He pointed at the screen.

"Dammit!" Alix exclaimed. "Is Zephyr's hack linked to my motorbike attack?"

"Not sure. But I can see from the Cnoxos camera ring that they were casing you for a while. Maybe some guys from the Credit Union sponsored this gang, hoping to get your sweat sample from your Gi and get into the system? Or a disgruntled cyber-security supplier trying to target the city's Queen of Payments?"

"Christ, you could be right—the Credit Unions lobbied hard against Zilch at the time. But they weren't the only ones!" Alix gathered her thoughts and turned back to look at Bob.

"First we must stop Zephyr from helping himself to the next chunk of the city's income. Can you identify his location?" Alix was calmer now. But she could see that Bob was unhappy with her request.

"Please?"

"This better be a paid gig. You know my fees." Bob mumbled, avoiding her eyes. "But if he works for The Threshers, for Mr Alternator, well, those guys are ruthless and not a match for me or you," he added with a sigh.

"Well, we know he's been trying to kill the Zilch payment system since it started!" shouted Alix, exasperated with his procrastination. She looked at Bob. "And it is not just the Crime Shield, it is also the Central Air Filters and our Mobile Clean Air units for emergencies in schools, everyone in Cnoxos East on a day pay schedule will suffer. The mayor worked so hard to get the police, firefighters, and bus drivers to trust Zilch. It will collapse tomorrow if Zephyr is not stopped." She spoke rapidly, gasping nervously for air.

She waited for his answer while Bob scanned through Zephyr's social media records.

"There is a photo of him streaming his Midnight Duel game. He dropped it on HealthyJunkiesGram a few hours ago." This was a closed, encrypted gaming platform, but not closed enough for Bob. "I can just see a neon light from the street shining onto his computer screen and reflecting in his glasses".

Bob ran the photo through the geodecoder.

"Now, if we enlarge it. Perfect! The neon is the logo of the SecuRex Corp in West Cnoxos. He is hiding in the small building opposite. It's Mr Alternator's business."

"Your old dojo buddy gone rogue?" Alix said.

"Yes, a few years ago." Bob replied, putting on his running shoes. "We will pay him a discreet visit. If we see The Thrashers, you will have to signal to Mayor Klint for more resources." Bob was already planning the route, remembering his old stomping ground.

As they crossed the bridge to West Cnoxos, Alix noted how smoky the city was on this side. The West had refused to join the mayor's schemes, as this section of town was further from Devil's Mountain and less exposed to smoke from the fires. They'd also accused the mayor of trying to sell data from citizens' payment behaviour to the advertising giants and decided not to adopt the Zilch payment system; no administrative savings meant no money for AirX filtration.

"Without the ventilation restarted, this smoke will be a nightmare," Alix explained as they reached Zephyr's building. "The central air filters, even the school's clean air shelters, there'll be no fresh air for any of them. They're just as dependent on real-time payment as the Crime Shield is."

Bob was running up the stairs faster than Alix. Zephyr's hideout was on the very top floor.

He forced his way through the door, finding Zephyr at the screens with his headphones on. His LED screens glowed ominously as lines of code streamed across at high speed. Bob pushed him off the chair, forcing Zephyr to the floor.

Zephyr's eyes widened in shock seeing Alix. "What are you doing here? And who is this?"

"I am the guy who is going to put an end to your little heist," Bob replied with a wry grin, trapping Zephyr in a vise-like headlock. "It's time to face the music."

Zephyr wriggled for a few moments. He was losing his breath, tapping loudly on the floor. Bob, never one for small talk, was making it clear that Zephyr's choices were limited at this point.

"Who are you working for?" Bob loosened his grip slightly to let him speak.

"For you. And for every citizen like you," Zephyr replied sarcastically. "Financial privacy for all!" Bob re-tightened his hold.

"Okay, okay. It's Mr Alternator. To stop your mayor. Bring down Zilch," he stuttered.

Bob spat back at him, "I hate to break it to you, but Mr Alternator is not a privacy fighter. Do you know where he makes his money? From your antiquated cash economy. Look at this neon outside. SecuRex is his company. SecuRex that supplies secure cash transport vans for all city zones. Thousands of bullion vans and bulletproof, reinforced lorries run in his fleet, a monopoly for West Cnoxos. You've been duped, bro."

Alix added, "SecuRex lost all of their East Cnoxos contracts when we moved to Zilch. That's why Mr Alternator started funding the Cash Freedom party, stirring impressionable dudes like you to fight his fights."

Zephyr looked at the reflection of the neon on his computer screen, processing what he had just heard. Alix could see him questioning himself. She pressed on.

"Time is running out, Zephyr. We know you are diverting funds, but some of them need to go to Crime Shield sensors. And to the air filters and smoke screen barriers. Right now!" She continued. "Look, your part of the city is ridden with crime and choking on smoke. Is this really what you wanted?"

Zephyr stirred uncomfortably. "Maybe. Mr Alternator has his own goals, and I have mine. They're not the same. But your centralised money and the mayor's control creep me out."

"Actually, I don't disagree with you on that," Bob said. "But the smoke is coming. Tomorrow, kids in schools will have no fresh air. Devil Mountain is burning and crime will return the moment the gangs hear that the Crime Shield is down. Do you think destroying Zilch and unleashing chaos on East Cnoxos is the way to argue for cash? For freedom? Is that what you signed up for?" Bob looked sternly into Zephyr's eyes.

Alix looked at Zephyr again. Surely once he realised Mr Alternator's true game, he would see his trust had been betrayed.

"OK, OK, let me go. I will help you."

Bob released Zephyr from his chokehold and sat him down in front of the computer screens.

"Time is running out, Zephyr. Get my funds back to paying for Crime Shield. And build back the city smoke protection. You know it's the right thing to do," Alix repeated, raising her voice a notch.

"Watch so you can learn something, old man," Zephyr said, turning to Bob, still furious with himself for getting duped so badly by Mr Alternator. Bob ignored the snark, but Alix knew him well enough to know he would get Zephyr for it later.

Zephyr flicked across his machine's interfaces and reversed the fraud he'd inserted into Zilch's transaction system. Alix watched as the Cnoxos central money gateway restarted, and could see the city's payments kicking in again when suddenly from outside of Zephyr's building came a roar of motorbikes pulling up. It was the Threshers coming after Zephyr to get their share of diverted funds.

"Crime Shield and Clean Air Barrier funds flow are back on. Done," Zephyr announced.

"Got to run now. Threshers are not a cuddly bunch!"

He pointed across the room to the fire escape stairs outside his window and stretched out his hand to Alix to help her jump outside. "You coming?"

She smiled, and a fresh storm of thoughts ran through her head as she climbed out of the window. *Maybe his Gambit app hack and my swiping right are going to work out after all,* she thought as all three of them ran down the rickety fire escape towards the hum of the city's Crime Shield drones, flying in the sky all around them once more.

Heritage

Wendy M Grossman

House of Commons Library
Research Briefing
Lessons from the Corinne McGrath Thompson Case
Standard Note: SN/HF/1326
DRAFT: 26 August 2047
Author: Nancine Tucker
Section: Health and Finance Section

The Kidnapping of Corinne McGrath Thompson

The 2038 kidnapping of Corinne McGrath Thompson is frequently referenced in Parliament. This briefing sets out the background of the case, which led to several changes in national law.

On 1 May 2038, the fourteen-month-old daughter of Paul Thompson and Olivia McGrath Thompson was abducted from her cot in a first-story bedroom in the family home in Hampstead. It was the first high-profile kidnapping case for some time, as 'ransomware' computer attacks afforded criminals a more lucrative and less risky option. However, by 2038 the collapse of non-state-backed digital currencies[1] and improvements in forensic tracing made ransomware attacks increasingly difficult to carry

---

1 It had proved impossible to eliminate fraud without government regulation, and none of the independent cryptocurrency businesses were able to meet the anti-fraud requirements. Efforts to create samzdat currencies found little traction because even criminals couldn't trust them.

out with any success. The Thompson kidnapping was the first sign of a revival of this type of crime.

For the next several months, all of Britain was gripped by the search for Corinne. Photographs were displayed in all public and private areas capable of receiving public service advertisements.[2] Cosmo![3] invoked the Police Visual Evidence Act (2027), which mandated device design to allow police to pull in images and video from Britain's hundreds of millions of cameras, including CCTV, personal devices, motor vehicles, and body-worn cameras, into its giant facial recognition network. Thousands of women were arrested who were spotted pushing strollers bearing babies of about the right age.

This case proved the first test of two relatively new laws. The first is the Biometric Inheritance Act 2030 (BIA), which came into force as at 1 January 2031. Second is the Child Ancestry Identification Rights Act 2033 (CAIRA), which came into force in 2034. The interplay of these two laws is poorly understood, not least because many believe incorrectly that CAIRA came first and inspired BIA. In fact, the two policies developed independently.

The rising number and cost of lengthy inheritance disputes and the development of DNA writing technology (formerly "gene editing") led to proposals to use DNA modification as a means of indelibly recording inheritance.[4] The proposal passed easily into law because it was thought harmless: adopting the technology was purely voluntary and its use affected only a small part of the population. As DNA writing was expected to become a standard medical tool, it was logical to accept

---

2 By 2038, this included all public and most private infrastructure, including most privately-owned vehicles.

3 Formerly the Metropolitan Police.

4 This technology could have been adopted much earlier. Even in 2023, it was possible to 3D-print a DNA sequence and insert it into a gene using CRISPR, although the procedure was slow and expensive, and required technical expertise. The advance that led to its adoption as national policy was the availability of portable, relatively inexpensive DNA writers that could be operated successfully with a modicum of training. By 2030, when BIA was passed, a number of these had already been purchased for hospitals for use in remediating genetic defects.

GPs' surgeries and hospitals as venues for making these modifications, as long as a financial fiduciary was present to witness and authenticate the transaction. It became common for banks and other financial service providers to form relationships with nearby medical establishments.

CAIRA, on the other hand, grew out of frustration with repeated rulings from the European Court of Human Rights, beginning in 2008, requiring the UK police to delete DNA samples taken from suspects who were later acquitted or not charged.[5] The courts ruled that selective sampling was discriminatory; the obvious solution was to sample the entire population and retain the database permanently to aid in criminal investigations. This proposal, first voiced in the 2010s, sparked public protests, led by vocal but misinformed 'digital rights' activists, and it wasn't until 2030, when the cost of supporting children abandoned in the continuing post-pandemic cost-of-living crisis[6] escalated to unacceptable levels, that the majority began to accept the necessity of sampling the entire population in order to establish with certainty the parentage of, and therefore fiscal responsibility for, all children in the UK, a proposal the press dubbed the "Boris Johnson law".

The new availability of DNA writing offered a solution to the long-standing objection that whole-population sampling would undermine the legal status of children in non-traditional families. This new technology, coupled with the passage of CAIRA and BIA, led to a Machinery of Government change creating the Department of Health and Finance, which merged parts of the Department of Work and Pensions with parts of the Department of Health.

To sum, both laws involve DNA sampling, but CAIRA is a read-only law, while BIA is a read-write law.

The interplay of these laws can be seen clearly in the Thompson case, At her birth on 22 February 2037, Corinne McGrath was DNA-sampled and her parentage verified (CAIRA). This formally verified the relationship between her and her parents in the eyes of the law. Subsequently

---

5 *S and Marper v United Kingdom.*

6 Brexit is often also cited as a factor.

and separately, she was also verified under BIA, and her status as the families' heir was recorded via a DNA update and stored in her body and in the central financial asset database.

At that moment Corinne became the repository of future wealth for both sides of her entire family, and her bloodprint was needed to unlock a variety of complex financial arrangements. Over time—for example, if her parents produced a sibling, or if the arrangements had to be changed for some other reason—those sections of her DNA might have been further changed under BIA. However, the sample collected at birth to establish her parentage under CAIRA would never be updated; those samples are part of the historical record, that is, her birth certificate.

After her BIA update, therefore, Corinne was, at least in the eyes of the state, a chimeric individual. There have been calls to update CAIRA to add samples taken later in life to the birth certificate, making it more of an accurate whole-life record. These have faded since BIA's repeal in 2041, which ended the use of DNA writing for financial purposes. However, because DNA writing is still in use for medical purposes, many experts remain of the view that the population should be resampled in adulthood, though they disagree about which ages would be most appropriate. There is public opposition to resampling from a small but vocal minority.

The McGrath Thompson family is one of the wealthiest in Europe. Paul Thompson's wealth derives originally from government contracts during the covid-19 pandemic; the family's holdings now include a significant portion of the world's personal protective equipment supply chain. Olivia Thompson, née McGrath, is the wealthier of the two; her family's fortune originated in pharmaceuticals but now sprawls across many industries. Both the McGraths and the Thompsons operate family offices to manage their wealth, and practice generation-skipping in handing on assets to minimize inheritance tax. As she was the only grandchild on both sides and the verified heir of both paternal and maternal grandparents, besides the personal aspects of the case there was great concern about her potential exploitation as a financial asset.

Unknown to the public at the time, and not widely known even now, there had been successful attempts to replicate the UK's financial

DNA-writing system and threats that the coders would publish their work as open source software. The police and security agencies considered it possible, therefore, that the kidnappers and technical attackers might work together to steal assets by altering Corinne's DNA in ways that might not be fully detectable or reversible. The details of these attacks remain highly classified and are held within the purview of GCHQ. They have never been published. However, the attacks, if not the same attackers, are believed to remain a threat to any similar system we might attempt today.

Expectations were that Corinne would quickly be found by the comprehensive police camera network and its state-of-the-art live facial recognition. It was also believed that any attempt to exploit Corinne's financial significance would be quickly exposed because her identity would be spotted at any authorised DNA writing location. The same would be true of visits for the purpose of medical care. The fact that she was not identified in any of these locations is one reason some believe the kidnapper was working with the hackers who had successfully devised the attack on DNA writing. Repeated audits commissioned by the McGrath and Thompson families have failed to identify any missing assets as of September 2040.

Instead, after two days a ransom email arrived at the Thompsons' home demanding three million pounds for Corinne's return and stating that payment instructions would follow. The email included a thirty-second video clip of Corinne playing in front of a TV showing the day's news. Attempts by digital forensics experts to identify the source of the email failed when the Sino-Russian service they used refused to provide account information.

Payment instructions came a further three days later. The kidnappers wanted the first twenty thousand pounds in thousand-pound Amazon Retail[7] custom cryptocurrency certificates, and the rest in two hundred and ninety-eight simultaneous bank transfers of ten thousand pounds

---

7 This was well after Amazon's breakup into Amazon Retail, Amazon Cloud, Amazon Advertising, and Amazon Bank. It is believed that the kidnappers avoided using Amazon Bank because its India-based headquarters made it subject to tougher transparency rules than applied to US-based Amazon Retail.

each to be sent in a mix of digital euros and digital US dollars from an account set up specifically for this purpose at Coutts private bank, where the Thompson and McGrath families were already known and had accounts.[8]

Further instructions arrived in due course in the form of a single-use smart contract chip card that could be plugged into the Coutts system and would execute the transactions. These single-use financial app chips had been spreading across dark markets for some years, based on technology US banks briefly used for authentication. The kidnapper warned that the chip would self-destruct if there was any attempt to read it before running the app it contained, and that attempts to log where it sent the money would also cause it to destroy itself, taking Coutts' accounts database with it. Technical experts argued that this wasn't actually technically feasible technology, but Coutts' insurers refused to sign off on making the attempt.

Police and security services agreed that in order to make at least part of the random traceable a portion should be paid in digital pounds, which were due to be withdrawn in 2039 after a pilot of eight years. The digital pounds' cryptographic design had proved to be insufficiently future-proofed against the development of quantum computing. In addition, all encryption in the use in the UK is subject to clauses in the Online Safety Act (2023) requiring assured government access. The combination of the technical flaw and government policy made a central bank digital currency system fundamentally unsecurable in the UK.[9] Police hoped that using this time-limited form of payment would force the kidnapper into the open. The family was persuaded to agree.

Corinne was not returned after these payments were made. Police hoped that the modes of payment afforded two possibilities for tracing the kidnappers. These were the Amazon Retail certificates and the

---

8 The question of whether Coutts or its other clients had a connection to the kidnappers was never investigated.

9 There is currently no plan to revise and reissue the digital pound on the basis that it is not commercially viable. The reasons for the countervailing success of digital euros and digital US dollars are unclear.

tranche of digital pounds. Both would trigger alerts when spent. The certificates proved to be a dead end; they were resold via various legitimate and illegitimate services and tracing their use led only to innocent bystanders who purchased them at a discount and knew nothing of their original owners.

Following the trail of the digital pounds proved more fruitful, and they were quickly traced to Dev Patel, the owner of a small independent grocery store in Twickenham. Patel claimed to have found the money in a wallet stored on a USB stick he found on the floor of his shop, but based on his access to the ransom money, Patel was arrested, tried, and convicted in 2042, and imprisoned for life. Many remain unconvinced that he was in fact the kidnapper, and even after his suicide in prison in 2044 members of the public continued to campaign for his exoneration.

The Corinne McGrath Thompson case led to the abandonment of the nascent system of DNA asset verification and the repeal of BIA, for a number of reasons. First, it appears that the attacks on financial DNA writing can't be remediated; at least, GCHQ has given no indication if so. Second, Corinne's use as "wet ransomware" was tortuous for her parents, and the fact that she has never been found has left them in a permanent state of uncertainty with limited financial resources.[10] The case led the public to believe that the policy placed their children at extreme and unnecessary risk. Both CAIRA and BIA were introduced as measures to protect children's rights; the irony that they created harm for at least one child has been widely noted.

The case also ended the debate about police access to all cameras in the UK. While turning on the network did not help find Corinne, the police successfully argued that had the network been operational on that fateful night, her abductors would have been identified immediately, and the abduction could have been stopped in progress. This argument was given further weight when the police revealed the number of infractions AI analysis of the collected video footage was able to identify that

---

10 For example, the Thompsons have said publicly that their financial uncertainty has left them unable to bring their Hampstead house fully up to net-zero codes.

would otherwise have gone unpunished.[11] As a direct result of this case, the decision was taken to turn it on permanently. An amendment to the Police Visual Evidence Act ensures that all cameras sold in the UK today are automatically joined to the national network whenever they are active by installing the app at the time of sale.

One reason the case has remained alive in the public mind is the fact that Corinne was never found, giving the press and the entertainment industry the opportunity to frequently revive the case as an enduring mystery. It is also regularly cited in debates about the revival of the use of DNA for recording financial assets and the prevention of inheritance fraud.

---

11 For example, over the months of searching for Corinne the national camera network enabled the prosecution and conviction of more than 100 cases of incorrect recycling.

Commentary

Martin C W Walker and Izabella Kaminska

SOME OF THE greatest works of speculative fiction are not based on extrapolation of current trends or anxieties about the present but upon ancient history. The *Foundation* series by Issac Asimov and the *Dune* books by Frank Herbert were both based on the period between the collapse of the Roman Empire and the rise of new empires and belief systems including Christianity and Islam. Looking back can be a very effective way of looking forward because so much of human history seems cyclical. Nations, empires, and religions rise and fall, but humanity as a whole never seems to fall all the way back into a simple hunter-gatherer existence except for some isolated tribes. If we look hard enough amongst the fragmentary evidence of those collapsed civilisations, we can learn a great deal about many aspects of human nature including about our love of and belief in money.

In 410 AD Alaric led a Gothic army that captured and sacked Rome. The Goths did not attack Rome out of a desire to destroy the Empire but in order to be part of it. After all, where else were the Goths going to spend the hundreds of thousands of gold solidi they had previously extorted from Rome? Whether money exists as records in an electronic ledger, pieces of paper, or bits of metal, some or all of its value comes from being able to spend it somewhere. Even the intrinsic prettiness value of gold and silver is boosted by nations minting them into coins or hoarding them as reserves in vaults. It's only when things get really bad that human beings, if largely cut off from the rest of humanity, revert to using genuine commodities as medium of exchange.

There is a very real question regarding what form money would take after a collapse of our global civilisation. Would bitcoin become the currency of the dystopian future? A genuine Doomcoin. (Assuming sufficient power remains, alongside Starlink satellites for crypto mining and the operation of minimal communications.) Even then the question remains, "Why accept it?". Maybe the survivors would immediately resort to commodity money, but which commodity? Rice, AAA batteries, paperback novels (life will be pretty dull with no Internet or TV)? History also tells us people can cling to old mediums of exchange long after they have no real meaning. Somalia's shillings continued in use long after Somalia collapsed as a functioning nation, steadily declining in value until their market value eventually equalised with their value as scrap paper.

What does this mean, though, as we reflect on the themes in the stories about digital money? In Eva Pascoe's somewhat dystopian "Swipe Right" the state is so bankrupt the only way it can find to fund clean air and safe streets is by squeezing out the credit card companies from processing payments. The fightback against the state comes from a rapacious private security firm, supporting those who fight back against the CBDC in the name of privacy so they can keep collecting and delivering physical cash. Perhaps, though, the real theme in "Swipe Right" is the limits of financialization.

Maybe in the city of Cnoxos, that's the only economy left over other than the ruins of a financial centre. Literally the only economic activity is moving money around, whether in digital or physical form, with a few scattered gyms. Did you ever notice the large gym in Lombard Street? Someone, presumably China, keeps supplying the inhabitants out of habit with food, energy, hot pants, and so on in return for bonds they know can never be redeemed. Like a baker in some part of ancient Britain still selling bread in exchange for coins minted by Romans that had left hundreds of years previously.

The theme of financialization and the ultimate "tokenised" economy also runs through Alex Buxton's "Update Needed". Should the little people, including us, really be allowed to own anything? A tokenised world means the little guy (well, almost all of us) has to keep spending their income on feeding tokens into all their "possessions", none of which they really own. This is the world many poor people still live in. Home is rented, furniture purchased on hire purchase, car is leased, and energy provided by feeding a meter. Historically, extractive economics made it very hard for poor people to advance in life. In "Update Needed" even the superficially prosperous really own nothing. The twist of this ultimate in financialised futures is that the proliferation of different tokens for different purposes means fungibility of money has collapsed. Surely this means the "democratisation" of finance? The end of the monopoly of the "Fiat money state". Well, let's look back to look forward.

The real story of Jesus driving the money changers from the Temple is as much based on monetary economics as religion. Even in the first century there was a large Jewish diaspora. Jews travelled from across the diaspora including regions outside the Roman empire to pray at the great temple. One of the great misunderstandings of the ancient world was that coinage solely derived its value from the commodity value of the precious metal in coins. This was not entirely true; a portion of the value came from the power of the nation minting the coins, just like the dollar today. As people travelled further away from their home nation, the value of their coins dropped in value, eventually to just the value of the metal contained in them. Jews reaching Jerusalem from say, the Persian empire thus needed to change their coins for local money.

A world of many tokens for many purposes creates a huge market for financial intermediaries, trading against the changing relative value of coins and extracting more commissions and spreads. The financialised, "own nothing" world screws the little guy of their last few pennies paying money to yet more middlemen to convert from one token to another.

Kate Baucherel's "A House of Cards" is a crypto fundamentalist's dream of dystopia. The all powerful "Algorithm" determines whether each individual has earned their place within society. Though the society seems superficially capitalist, the desire of the state to accumulate every possible scrap of information about every individual (no matter how trivial or worthless), the fact that all wealth flows out of the central bank to the chosen few, and the belief you can predict the future contribution of everyone is basically the Soviet Union recreated by Big Tech. Naturally there is a resistance. The resistance are self-sufficient in food, carbon neutral, and big on "privacy coins".

It's quite understandable why the Resistance cut themselves off from the presumably atrociously executed central planning of the "Algorithm", but who are they economically connected to? Who are these subsistence farmers buying their solar panels from? Maybe they have an army of "influencers" convincing the rest of the world their coins have value. Perhaps they are more like the remnants of other fallen civilisations that, instead of trying to rebuild with the ruins, retreated into the jungle, growing ever more like a lost hunter-gatherer tribe in the rainforest, ignorant of the existence of the rest of humanity and moving towards a future where burnt-out GPUs will eventually be worn as talismans around the necks of shamans. Their purpose forgotten but their magical qualities amplified.

Wendy M Grossman's "Heritage", in spite of being written in the form of a Civil Service memo, is a wild tale of kidnap, DNA hacking, and money laundering. The story is perhaps the most unbelievable of the tales of digital money with quotes like the following, "Further instructions arrived in due course in the form of a single-use smart contract chip card that could be plugged into the Coutts system and would execute the transactions. These single-use financial app chips had been spreading across dark markets for some years, based on technology US banks briefly used for authentication. The kidnapper warned that the chip would self-destruct if there was any attempt to read it before running the app it contained, and that attempts to log where it sent the money would also cause it to destroy itself, taking Coutts' accounts database with it."

Or at least, it would have been until a few years ago when ransomware attacks became a routine experience for everyone from unlucky individuals to major corporations and governments. The ideas of Decentralised

Finance ("DeFi", smart contracts, and "programmable money") where no one has ultimate control of money are captivating to many in the conventional financial sector. The wild journey by which many banks search for innovation, any innovation, while neglecting to upgrade their legacy infrastructure could lay the foundation for a future like that laid out in the story. Perhaps the mundane path of having records of ownership stored in conventional databases that are properly backed up and have every possible security precaution built around them is not exciting enough for today's Fintech evangelists?

"You can't argue with progress" is the likely response of the evangelists. People preoccupied with solving today's real problems as opposed to problems as yet unknown that could arise the future (an argument actually made for CBDCs) are already likely to be described as "Boomers", a term being used synonymously with "Luddite". Turning back once more to the ancient world, we have to remind ourselves that the forward march of an idea is not the same as "the march of progress". Bad ideas can gather supporters for decades, if not millennia. Thales made many believe everything was made of water. Aristotle placed the earth at the centre of the universe and it stayed there in many people's minds until the Renaissance. And let's not dwell too much on the wasted efforts of the alchemists, lest someone launches an initial coin offering to fund renewed research on the topic.

Which takes us to Eddie Robson's "Don't Say That, You'll Make It Happen" which describes an eerily familiar point of view.

"In her view the only thing that makes things better is boring sustained competence over time, and when someone comes in offering a magic wand she feels it will only make people less likely to seek effective, unsexy solutions." Somewhat reminiscent of what we wrote to the House of Commons Treasury committee back in 2018 about the over-enthusiasm for blockchain: "The Danger of Magical Thinking – Ultimately Blockchain 'Magical Thinking' may be a long-term threat to the UK finance and technology sector because it distracts from solving real problems."

The themes running through the story are very reflective of present-day preoccupations: a government obsessed with creating a digital pound but not entirely sure why; the idea that financial system is some kind of "creature" that is making all the decisions about the economy, where people are passive onlookers; and performance art as a particularly lame and annoying substitute for social activism. Though reflecting on much of the recent "progress" around digital currencies, it might be more warranted to worry about central banking as a form of performance art with its endless CBDC experiments, governments as passive on-lookers to inflation and stagnating growth, and the "creature" as a manifestation of ChatGPT's reliance on poor-quality data.

But what do all these stories say about money? Perhaps it simply shows a failure to learn from history. The Roman Empire showed a preoccupation with money over hundreds of years. It went through multiple cycles of hyperinflation and attempts to restore sound money but in the end it was fundamentals that destroyed the western empire rather than monetary policy. An empire built on growth and extraction of wealth from conquered territories reached the limits of growth. With undeveloped lands to the North and South and an assertive Persian empire to the east, it could no longer fund itself by exploitative expansion. Technological progress and productivity crawled to a halt. Cutting off the economic hinterland of eastern empire from the west left little real economy to support the military-bureaucratic complex of the western money.

Money is important, as anyone with a mortgage, credit card bills, or car lease payments can testify. Tinkering with it is not necessarily the solution to our problems, but just in case all else fails, there is still work to be done on designing a proper "Doomcoin" to help us recover after the collapse.

Commentary
David G W Birch

I OFTEN TELL the same story to people who are thinking of writing about the future of money. It is the story of Edward Bellamy's classic *Looking Backward 2000-1887,* a best-selling Victorian slice of time-travel future fiction. The book has a special place in my canon because the time-travelling protagonist is told by his host that there is no such thing as cash in the year 2000. Instead, he says, the populace use "credit cards".

The author then goes on to describe what are in fact offline pre-authorised debit cards, but no matter, it is an imaginative prediction a generation before the Western Union charge card. In fact, given that the book fails to predict television, computers, airplanes, or the knowledge economy, that prediction about the future of money is quite impressive. The author has the character reflect on the nature of the currency itself (anticipating the end of the gold standard a generation later and the post-Bretton Woods world to come) by saying that:

"This card is issued for a certain number of dollars. We have kept the old word, but not the substance. The term, as we use it, answers to no real thing, but merely serves as an algebraical symbol for comparing the values of products with one another."

Writing at the time of the gold standard and globalisation, money as an "algebraical symbol for comparing the values of products" is an impressive leap and it must have seemed unsettling to the readers. A more unsettling question appears later in the book though, when the time traveller asks his twenty-first century host a key question:

"Are credit cards issued to the women just as to the men?"

and is told

"Certainly."

This is a wonderful illustration of the general principle that science fiction is not really about the future at all, but about the present: the retort "certainly" is clearly intended to surprise (perhaps even shock) the Victorian reader. The fact that women have them is a much more interesting and much more important prediction than the existence of the cards themselves.

Why do I bring up this particular prediction? Well, it is because the important point is that technology of the future money is not as important as its social context and its unspoken commentary on its use. What does our future money tell us about the future us?

(This is why, as a rule, social anthropologists are the most interesting people to talk to about the future of money, rather than, well, me.)

Writing about the future of money is difficult, which is why I admire all of these authors for trying to find the equivalent of that shocking question, to tune into the voice of future money. If you start from the position that the way that money works now, which we can lazily label "Bretton Wood II Money", is a set of temporary institutional arrangements that will soon be forcibly reorganised by a combination of regulatory, demographic, technological, and business changes then this artistic endeavour is actually rather important.

What those arrangements will be reorganised into, of course, is the 64,000 Bitcoin question.

There is a future with no money, therefore no institutions. Remember when, in *Star Trek IV, The Voyage Home*, Captain Kirk and his crew try to get on a bus in 1980s San Francisco:

Spock: What does it mean, "exact change"?

Kirk: They're still using money. We need to find some.

While it's tempting to imagine a post-scarcity future where money (as a system for allocating scarce resources) has vanished and the vast communist galactic super-state takes care of everyone's needs, I don't buy it. Some things will always remain scarce and desirable, like your attention span, and money will remain necessary. But what kind of money and what kind of institutional arrangements will be needed to support it?

In "Don't Say That, You'll Make It Happen", Eddie Robson made me think about those institutional arrangements right away by making the point that commercial banks are against central bank digital currency, not only conspiracy theorists, although I did raise an eyebrow at the use of cards in a mimetic echo of Bellamy. But the story did fuel my imagination to the point where I thought about creating a bitcoin wallet, writing the secret keys down on a piece of paper, and then burning it so that anyone could go to the blockchain and see that the value is there but completely unusable. I think this might be even more of a political statement than the pile of ashes created by KLF a couple of decades back.

Given that I am sure biometrics will have a role to play in any future of trade, exchange, and finance I thought that Eva Pascoe's clever use of sweat in "Swipe Right" as an identification mechanism was rather fun, but her idea for front-running bank robberies was even more fun. She is definitely on to something by making us think about how stopping payments stops everything else. I wonder how long it will be before her Cash Freedom Party replaces the Monster Raving Looney Party as Britain's effective opposition party.

(By the way, when the Monster Raving Looney Party first stood for Parliament in 1964 two of their main policies were votes for eighteen-year-olds and all-day opening of pubs, both of which are now law.)

Kate Baucherel's sophisticated take in "A House of Cards" on "the Algorithm" and the relationship between human behaviour and the algorithm made me reflect again on the choices we will soon have to make around AI.

Ethereum founder Vitalik Buterin's musing in a blog posting on techno-optimism on the paths open to us caused me to read the story again and re-enjoy the plot shift in the middle. On the one hand, this was a salutary tale about the Global East Germany that we seem to have opted for (how Erich Honecker would have loved TikTok) but on the other hand it was a great story about people.

The use of location data, or more specifically bogus location data, is already part of the daily cyberwar going on around us all the time—indeed I recently wrote a piece about how ships (for example, tankers carrying sanctioned, Russian oil) do this all the time.

(Incidentally, one of the reasons why I love the movie *Aliens* so much is that it seems a very realistic version of the future, so I wonder whether there will be a single state algorithm in charge of things or multiple warring algorithms of corporations competing for resources that include Unobtanium and human attention.)

Biometrics are an inevitable part of the future and so is biotechnology. Gene editing is the next 3D printing, so Wendy M Grossman's tale, "Heritage", has already got me fantasising about a Netflix sensation. The idea of individuals having more than one lot of DNA in their bodies (my son, who has a degree in genetics, assures me it is true) brought me up short and I don't understand why it's not already part of a James Bond film.

Anyway, it's a thought-provoking narrative that takes us from Amazon gift certificates to quantum computing, from people with multiple DNA profiles to real smart money in chips.

(Wendy left me thinking that making all cameras have an app on board, just as all drones have to have certain characteristics, was interesting, and I can imagine it being extended to include appending unforgeable digital signatures to every image, something that is desperately needed right now!)

As a crude measure of impact, I thought about Wendy's story half a dozen times while reading the MIT Digital Currency Initiative's recently published *Framework for Programmability in Digital Currency*.

In "Update Needed" Alex Buxton's central conceit is that there will be different kinds of money, money for the rich and for the poor. But the story isn't really about that, and its emotional depth (I really did want to know what happened to the characters) actually left me reflecting more on future relationships and the nature of physical and virtual intimacy. I am sure that you will find yourself as conflicted as I did in trying to shoehorn the burgeoning virtual into the mores of the physical.

Alex got me thinking that in a messy and unpredictable but realistic future (when it will be bots taking care of most transactions, not people) there will indeed be many different kinds of money. Most of us will neither know nor care which currencies, which baskets of digital assets, or which "stable coins" are being exchanged in a transaction.

The noted Fintech investor Matt Harris, a partner at Bain Capital Ventures, wrote in Forbes that fintech would mean the end of money as we know it. He wrote that rather than money as we know it, in the future "our assets will be one hundred percent invested at all times". In this vision of the future of money, transactions will be settled through the transfer of baskets of assets between counterparties without the intermediary of money. That world, in which assets are constantly on the move, may sound crazy but I'm sure that Matt is right. This view of the future of transactions, that money is an intermediary that disappears because assets can be traded as money-like instruments, is what got me interested in the future of money in the first place, many years ago.

Way back in 1994, I picked up a report from the Centre for the Study of Financial Innovation written by the late Dr. Edward de Bono, remembered by many as the inventor of "lateral thinking". It was called "The IBM Dollar" and it was based on de Bono's vision that IBM might issue IBM Dollars that would be redeemable for IBM products and services, but are also tradable for other companies' monies or for other assets in a liquid market. The difference between IBM stock and IBM money, to continue this example, is that IBM stock is a claim on something that is exchanged through intermediaries. But IBM money is, well—what we now think of as a digital asset, a token. A bearer instrument, not a claim on something else.

When first I read de Bono's ideas of tens of millions of tokens in circulation, constantly being traded on futures, options, and foreign exchange markets, I was shocked: shocked because I immediately realised that he was right. Remember, he was imagining this before the internet, but thinking deeply about what the future of high-speed electronic networking and high-powered cryptography would mean for financial services. He had come to the conclusion that if you could exchange baskets of these liquid assets directly between counterparties *then you would not need to exchange them into money first.*

Now this apparently strange world of money-like assets in continual motion might at first seem unbearably complex for people to deal with. But that's not the world that we will be living in. This is not a world of transactions between people. It is a world of transactions between my machine-learning AI supercomputer robo-advisor (or more likely my mobile phone front end to such a cybergenius) dealing with your machine-learning AI supercomputer robo-advisor to work out what basket of tokens it wants from you in return for one of my books, or a day of my time at a workshop or a speech to your conference.

These robo-advisors will be entirely capable of negotiating between themselves to work out the deal. Dr. de Bono foresaw this in his pamphlet, writing that "pre-agreed algorithms would determine which financial assets were sold by the purchaser of the good or service depending on the value of the transaction... the same system could match demands and supplies of financial assets, determine prices and make settlements". He also wrote that the key to any such system would be "the ability of computers to communicate in real time to permit instantaneous verification of the creditworthiness of counterparties".

This last point is rather important, and Alex's story reminded me of Matt's bold prediction. Matt said that "once identity is solved, credit risk becomes easier". This is because of the nature of reputation in an online world. Reputation, such as credit history, that is immutable and available to any counterparty, becomes the fundamental transaction enabler with the potential to displace the incentive functions of commercial banking.

All of these stories did succeed in making me reflect on the impact of the transition to virtual worlds and digital identities and I therefore very much enjoyed reading them. I'm not sure if I am any closer to understanding what finance will look like in a world of digital identities, digital assets, and reputation markets, but I will certainly take some of the questions raised here back into my own thinking on the future of digital financial services.

Rereading all of these stories and going back to my introduction, then, maybe the shocking question for the readers of today is not what the new money will be, or whether women will be allowed to use that new money in the metaverse, but whether any of us will know the answers. Transactions exchanging digital assets between bots may have nothing to do with us at all. We may never learn what it is that the robots value, what they are using for their medium of exchange, and why they have chosen any particular store of value any more than my cats understand what I exchange at the supermarket to get their tuna treats.

PART 4
Health and Longevity

Signpost to Normal

Rosie Oliver

"The Atlantic Ocean?" Dylan asks. "Wow! All that detail." He stares down beyond the safety rail onto the six-metre diameter model of blue going through to red translucent three-dimensional streams, swirls, and vortices flowing in a contoured shallow basin. His normally cool green eyes are afire like emeralds in bright sunlight.

This seal of approval from an ocean expert at the Meteorological Office is what Kendra had been hoping for. Yet her happiness is dulled by a cocktail of painkillers, life-extending telomerase, and chemo-targeting drugs. Contentment is all she feels. Her consultant had warned this would happen if she chose the 'second-best treatment' for her aging. The 'best' has an unacceptable side effect for her.

"Yes, it is." Her forced grin covers for her stifled enthusiasm. "It's not complete if you'd like to think of it that way."

"Oh?" He keeps staring through the glass at the airtight solid and fluid sculpture. His head turns this way and that, his eyes seemingly tracking strange paths of thoughts and the sculpture's details. "That's incredible. You're so close to modelling the Atlantic Meridional Overturning Circulation as it was before—"

"You can say it. The ice melt bursts we've been experiencing." The latest had been another deluge from Greenland's Helheim glacier that further stymied the AMOC. The only thing that keeps northern Europe warm enough now is global warming.

A quiet grunt escapes her throat. Her emotions are now so blunted she can accept such realities. Yet they are still strong enough to channel into this artwork, her last masterwork, before her treatment stops being effective and she is forced to 'upgrade' to the proper anti-aging regime. She shivers at the thought. It was, and still is, hard to believe. Yet, the other creatives who have had the same treatment confirmed it. She believes it is really a psychological effect of living longer. Or is this her way of hiding from the truth?

"Which year are you modelling?" Dylan interrupts her thoughts.

"2004."

He nods, tossing his brow's curls. "Makes sense."

She would have preferred the mid-twentieth century to get a better sense of history, but this was the AMOC's earliest reliable data set. No use on dwelling on what might have been.

"Still got that mess to sort out in the northeast." She points to her sculpture's warm North Atlantic Drift splitting into the Norway and Imminger Currents. "No matter how I change the sculpture's air patterns and river flows, I can't get a strong enough warm current going up over the mid-Atlantic ridge and around Iceland's west and north coasts. Ends up pulling the Iceland Sea's gyre too far southwest, making the flows up Norway's north coast all wrong."

"I noticed, but you are fighting the physics of flow miniaturisation."

She knows that only too well; the details had given her enough sleepless nights.

"You should be proud of what you've got right," he continues. "It's an incredible achievement."

"It's not good enough." She thumps her fist against the rail. It triggers a spasming fit down her right arm. Not now! She grabs the safety rail to calm it down. "Can you suggest a solution to that mess?" She points to the Norwegian Sea with her other hand. "Anything, except placing a swirling rotor where the Iceland Sea gyre should be."

"Why not? It solves your problem."

"It's cheating."

He whistles appreciatively, sweeps his brown curls back and stares at the troublesome area. "I'd have to do some serious computer modelling to understand this. Still..."

She waits for him to say more.

"Have you tried to model today's Atlantic currents on here?" he finally asks.

The question surprises her. "No. I wanted to show how much better the past was, not imitate your work. What would be the point?"

He turns to lock eyes with her. "To be frank, we're desperate for new ideas on how to get the ocean currents out of their self-reinforcing configuration back to the old AMOC's zigzag. Using this might just signpost us in the right direction."

"How? This sculpture is just a representation, and a rather sketchy one at that. You could end up wasting your time pursuing a useless line of investigation."

"We've got nothing else. I mean it."

"But—"

"Look, this has already shown you where the source of your problem is. Maybe, just maybe, a sculpture of today's currents can do the same for us."

Perhaps he has a point, but could she really help? And does she have enough time left to do so?

"If you did turn your talents to our current problem," Dylan continues, "we'll use our computer models on your historic one in return. No guarantee of an answer for you, or for us for that matter, but it's a quid pro quo of time and effort. Are you interested?"

She stares at the mesmerising blue and red flows churning around Iceland. It has been four frustrating years of focusing her artistry to get this close to the 2004 currents. True, knowledge gained from constructing this sculpture will help develop the 2050 flows far more quickly. Yet he was offering her time in his own way. Would it be enough?

Her right arm flinches again, not as bad as before. This will happen more often, damn it. She needs to get off the chemo-therapies that are causing these spasms, and would if it were not for the consequences. Time is definitely running out for her to complete this artwork. She gulps.

"I want this sculpture for my work. You'll have to build your own. Obviously I'll share construction details with you."

"We can certainly do that. So, you're in?"

"As you say, a quid pro quo."

***

The waiting room's music soothes Kendra's nerves, but not her headache. It has been there seemingly forever and is getting worse. She wants rid of it, its induced blurring from constantly incipient tears and its tightening of her neck muscles. Her painkillers, like all previous types, have become useless. A new, stronger prescription is needed to keep her on task: finishing her sculpture and helping Dylan improve his, especially as his model was proving particularly difficult to alter. His latest focus is trying to force the warm Florida Current eastward to rejoin the Gulf Stream. Maybe he is right about the higher sea levels causing the 2050 configuration of currents to be annoyingly persistent. Yet he has to break it to get the AMOC back to normal to cool the world. Her hindering headache must go.

The music's beat quickens slightly. The wall-screen's turquoise slow-moving wave-lines move a touch faster against a background of fuzzy stars. Auto-psycho-prepping her for imminently seeing her consultant, not that the tempo-upping enlivens her. The dampening effect of her drugs successfully counters it.

A petite dark-haired woman opens the door and spots Kendra on the corner sofa. "So sorry to have kept you waiting," she smiles. "I'm Doctor Swainswick. Unfortunately, Doctor Effingham was urgently called away and asked me to take his place."

"Oh." Kendra quickly stands. "I can come back later."

"That won't be necessary. I'm up to speed on your case and concerns. If you'd like to come through." She stands back holding the door open.

She steps towards the doctor. Her ankle is so stiff she crashes her foot onto the floor. It takes a moment to gain full balance. The slightly raised eyebrow on Swainswick's face means her clumsiness has been noticed. She smiles at the too-clinical-looking expert and hobbles into the consulting room.

"What brought you here?" the doctor asks once both have settled into comfortable chairs either side of a veneered desk.

"My headache. It's getting worse. I was wondering if you could up my painkillers."

The doctor glances through the notes on the desk's raised hologram screen. Her eyes and fingers work in counter-tempo. She finally sits back, chin on fingertips. "I've just double-checked your latest blood tests and scans."

She sits up straight. Words like that are never good news. "What's wrong?"

The doctor takes a moment. "I'll get straight to the point. Due to the cocktail of chemicals we're currently putting into your body, your AI-driven nanites are no longer able to keep your blood pressure from rising. That's the immediate cause of your headaches."

There is hope. "You can deal with that, right?"

She slowly shakes her head. "Not this time. We've tried all the possible treatments."

The finality of the statement slams into her, utterly destroying what few dreams she has left. A scream of frustration is stillborn in her throat. A choice has to be made; one she has avoided facing.

"Your body can no longer tolerate both the telomerase and the chemo drugs simultaneously. It was always a balancing act that would reach the end of its viability at some point. And, well, this is now that point."

She nods numbly. This is it.

"I wouldn't say this unless you needed to hear it. You've gone beyond it. You've got liver cancer. The type that comes from clearing the body's extra gunk out. We can cure that, but only if you come off the telomerase."

A sob escapes Kendra.

"I think you know what this means." The doctor pauses. "The anti-aging works by replacing all your body cells beyond a certain level of aging or deterioration. All of the cells you were born with will be cleared out and—"

Like those that make me creative. A yelp escapes her. She bites it back from turning into a full-blown scream of "No." She does not want to hear the words from the doctor, not now. "Doctor Effingham has already explained the consequences to me."

"So I gathered and believe me, I understand your reluctance."

"Do you?" Taking the treatment would make her more normal, submerging her life into the crowd. But it would take away what defines her; being a fluid sculptress. And now, she had Dylan's needs to factor into her decision.

A weak smile crosses the doctor's face. "I suppose not deep down. But whichever way you look at it, you must come off the telomerase to reduce the aggressiveness of your cancer. Even if you don't opt for anti-aging treatment, it'll buy some time, not a lot, but some."

"How much longer?"

"A few days, maybe even a fortnight."

She needs more time than this to solve her sculpture's problem. So does Dylan. And so does Earth.

"Of course, if you take full treatment," the doctor continues, "it'll allow us to cure your cancer as well."

This really is it. "Bottom line is I either lose my life or my soul."

Swainswick opens her mouth to say something, but immediately closes it.

There might be one last hope. "How long have I got to decide?"

"The sooner you opt for anti-aging treatment, the easier it'll be for you."

"Obviously, but that doesn't answer my question."

"To be on the safe side, two days, certainly not more than three."

Kendra sits still, stunned. Time and the world go by. Die to have a chance of saving the world or live for however long waiting to die from global warming effects. What a choice.

***

Kendra's sore eyes are the price she is paying for being awake over twenty hours. Dylan's assistants had gone home hours ago. Moonlight tinged with the amber glow of essential streetlighting streams through the windows to merge with the low glow of the eco-strip lighting. It is enough to see his sculpture by, its modelled currents stubbornly fixed in its globally warmed loops. He has not been able shift that U-turn of the warm current to above the latitudes of the British Isles.

She rubs her temples to ease her headache, not that it helps much. His is definitely the more impossible problem to fix. Best to stick to solving her own sculpture's mess around Iceland. She turns and step by slow step makes her way from the safety rail of Dylan's sculpture to her own. The strip lighting adjusts, darkening his fluid sculpture and brightening hers.

Her eyesight blurs, making her stop halfway across the floor to close her eyes. She hears the distant night traffic and the quiet whirring of the sculptures' pumps, smells the hints of floor polish and stewed coffee, and feels her body has become stiffer and more clogged. The last has gone from being a nuisance to a serious impediment. Her meds will not hack it. She has to struggle on. Damn it, time for self-pity can come later.

She slowly opens her eyes and gives them time to focus on currents around Iceland in her sculpture. The orange current approaching from the southeast is turning bluer, colder as it travels through volcanic islands and up past the west coast into a sharp increase in darkness. That is the trouble with AI-controlled strip lighting; sometimes it mismanages a patch.

Her eyes are drawn back to those volcanic islands forming the Vestmannaeyjar archipelago. They are outcrops of the North Atlantic Ridge. The current must flow faster over it, which makes it lose more heat through extra evaporation, albeit a very small amount. It would make hardly any difference to the mess northeast of Iceland. But what might affect it could be the large amount of extra heat from strong volcanic activity over a long period of time, like when the most southerly island, Surtsey, was formed. Those volcanic rocks have been cooling for over twenty years now, passing less and less heat into the seawater. If only—

Her mind flips. A turning point. This is the key. For her creativity this is a typical moment of sudden realisation. For the currents, it is that little extra push to make the warmth go much further along the current. Placing a heater along that part of her ridge will sort her sculpture out. She is sure of it.

Her eyes widen. She turns to stare back at Dylan's sculpture. What if that same heat source is inserted into his? It would send the nearby cold currents deeper that would create a domino effect of changing the direction and extent of the shallower warmer currents.

Would it really work?

Her heart pounds with excitement. She checks her reasoning. It is the answer. The only thing to work out is how much heat is needed. That can be done by trial and error.

Her head hurts more. She pulls out her smartphone and rings Dylan. No answer. Of course. Not at this time of night. It goes to voicemail. "Know what's wrong with my sculpture. Lack of heat from volcanic activity along Atlantic Ridge southwest of Iceland. Pretty sure if you inserted same into your sculpture and computer modelling, it would tip your currents to get the Gulf Stream back to its old course. In reality, all it would take is to bring up some lava from under the Earth's crust."

There, she has done it. Her breathing becomes more rapid. An ache feeling like a tight band develops in her chest. She staggers towards a safety rail for support.

Her head pounds. Phone still in hand, she duplicates the message to send to his staff.

She feels faint, and her legs become too weak for her to stand. She slides down against the safety rail's balustrade and ends up sitting, leaning her back against it.

Dylan will know how to find the right place for drilling for lava. Then the AMOC will revert to what it was, even with the high sea levels. It will take a couple of years, but he and the others will get there. She will not live to see it.

The pain in her chest explodes, and her left arm straightens out. She had made the right choice, keeping her creativity to save Earth from the worst of the greenhouse effect.

Despite all the pain, Kendra smiles.

I Am Not, Until I Am

Jesse Rowell

ASH VARLEY COMPOSED herself before activating the Live Again's immersion. She felt like she hadn't slept in days working on this code release. *You can do this*, she thought as she gestured toward the constant cameras hiding in the recesses of her office.

"Third January 2040, 9:14 AM," she instructed.

Images flickered to life, and the fans that cooled the holographic units stirred up dust. *That's all my dead skin cells*, she thought in dismay. *My body is sloughing toward infinity with each passing year, and soon enough there will be nothing left. Except the memories. Memories never turn to dust in the silver-trance.*

The projected silver light gathered around her, a beta recording from fifteen years earlier. Her four-year-old son sat on the floor playing with plastic figures. *This is what consumers had wanted*, she thought. *To coax ghosts from Live Again's servers and watch their past-persons play out their lives.*

"Strawberry Shortcake is dead," he said, his small, assertive voice coming from speakers. He set the doll's body on a miniature tea cart.

"How?" she watched herself ask in the holographic reconstruction of the event. The images of her son and her own body stitched into objects of light as the shimmering surfaces of inanimate objects, life's clutter, hovered in midair.

"She was shot, and now she is dead." Her son gathered two other Shortcake characters around the tea cart.

"Who shot her?" she asked in unison with her recording. She watched her past self smiling, a visage of love reflected in quicksilver.

"The aliens." He pointed at a football, pretending it was a spacecraft. "I will shoot them." He picked up his slide whistle and held it like a gun. "P-kow. Now they're dead."

Ash winced. Her son's face had collapsed inward forming a gray, concave surface, streaks of light sinking into the absence of data. Beta had been buggy in playbacks, consumer data corrupted by the anonymization of health data. She looked at the faceless figure for a moment before flicking her wrist to return Live Again to passive mode.

Like cloud photo services from a quarter century earlier that harvested their customers' BMI and weight, Live Again's cameras captured personal health data and used machine learning to predict future pathologies. Disease detection through the air, the liquid atmosphere that flowed around people, had been turned into a virtual ultrasound that packaged clinical data and anonymized it for data brokers and health insurers. She had transformed people into the wearables they once wore.

The room felt empty without the memories of her son playing around her. They called it the silver-trance, the mind dipping into pools of mercury as recorded events repeated, holographic forms of family long gone, their bodies of silver light dancing around furniture as they lived out the same moment forever. Forever capturing consumers' health data, real-time haptic and therapeutic feedback for users who had upgraded for the feature.

It had saved lives. AI-driven interpretation of clinical images made for faster depression diagnoses before suicidal ideation could occur. She remembered the shock of getting an alert that her son, aged fourteen and no longer pretending slide whistles were guns, had been flagged for risk. She hesitated to call up the memory and enter the silver-trance again. You can do this, she thought, and gestured at the wall to activate the immersion.

"Twenty-fifth August 2051, 6:33 PM."

She watched her son's facial expressions twist, his shoulders sink. A silent agony playing out in light. He held tight his long locks of hair, which he had refused to let her cut. That was the moment she understood. Her ex-husband, Chip Bragg, had been less than understanding, spitting invective and blame over losing his son.

Ash had modified Live Again's admin controls to erase her ex-husband from playback. *Erasure is necessary*, she had explained to the Chief Technology Officer. *Live Again should not force users to relive trauma.* Chip, after inflicting a lifetime of hurt on her and their son, had slunk off to join Guiding Light and their crusade against Live Again. She held up her hand to pause playback and looked at her son.

"Sweetie." She tried to control the tremble in her voice. *I helped create this goddamn machine*, she thought. *I shouldn't be getting this emotional.* "I'm sorry..." she trailed off. Talking to ghosts was supposed to be therapeutic. She reached into the light and grasped empty air.

"Hey!" Her Scrum Master banged at her office door. "I've been pinging you for the last twenty minutes. Didn't you hear me?"

"No," Ash answered. "I was busy."

"Well, another defect came up in test environment. It's misdiagnosing appendicitis again. We need to recalibrate data interpretation."

And by we, she thought, *he means me.* She felt like she hadn't slept in days.

***

The rain smelled good against the concrete steps as Katie Bragg stepped out of Guiding Light. *A perfectly timed baptism*, she thought, her prayers answered for an end to the California drought. The spritz ended when she reached her car parked on the baking black pavement, and a stifling heat settled back over her like a blanket.

"Oh, well," she laughed, smiling at Alma Stirling, who walked briskly past her. "Guess we'll just have to pray harder."

"God is good," Alma said without looking back, her heels crunching against pavement gravel as she raced to get out of the heat.

"Yes." Katie slid into the air-conditioned interior, sweat sticking to white leather. "He certainly is. He—" She paused as she thought of Chip, her poor, sweet husband. "Carmelo. Please drive home."

"Confirmed," her car said. "Home on Highland Drive. Estimated time of arrival, 2:38 PM."

She kicked off her heels and felt the cool air against her feet. Carmelo purred as it exited the parking lot, charting a route away from the high-rises towering over the Castro District. Most of them belonged to the Live Again campus or complex, or whatever they called it these days, the sprawling research and development center for health sciences and wearable technologies.

A ping alerted Katie to an incoming video call from Alma, or Miss Stirling, as she insisted people call her. Alma had been assigned to mentor her as a new congregant of Guiding Light, help guide her away from the temptation of wayward paths. Katie liked having a life coach help her make decisions. It reduced the complexity of life, even if some of her advice seemed old-fashioned.

"Hi, Miss Stirling. Long time no see."

Alma didn't laugh. All business, as usual. "Why wasn't your husband in attendance today? Chip is supposed to be helping with PAC donations." Her head filled the video frame on the windshield, streaks of cloud behind her face. The map below showed her location traveling in the opposite direction. Alma was undoubtedly monitoring her location in real-time, which made her laugh. *Does she think I'm going to go party with all the Live Again techs down in Castro?*

"He's still under the weather. Bed rest, for now."

Alma frowned and peered closer into the video frame. *If her face gets any closer*, Katie thought, *she'll pop through my windshield and press her nose against my chest, her chin on my lap. The job of a mentor, I guess.*

"He has not accompanied you to church for the last three months. A married woman, an attractive woman at that, attending church without her husband is not a good look. You're still giving him the medicine I gave you, right? Colloidal silver and ivermectin?"

"Aw, ya think I'm pretty?" Katie teased. "You're so sweet."

"This is important, Mrs. Bragg. Are you giving him the medicine?"

"Yes," she lied. Something had started to turn his skin blue-gray. It made him look like one of those Live Again recordings come to life. The silver-trance, her husband called it, grumbling about how his ex-wife had helped develop the technology. People mesmerized by the past as it collected their health data. It made her shudder. The recording of a wife sitting next to her dying husband. She didn't want to end up like that, a soulless reproduction of her authentic self.

"Good." The frown lines slackened around Alma's pinched face. "Try giving him oil of oregano, too. A tablespoon when you get home, and another before bedtime. I will call for more prayer warriors."

Katie nodded. Alma's support, though abrasive, gave her hope. It made her happy to be embraced by the church community. Their centuries of wisdom. Guiding Light felt like wearing custom-fit clothing that she never needed to take off. *Why Live Again when you can be born again?* Alma often quipped.

"Carmelo," she said. "Please increase the temperature by three degrees."

"Confirmed," Carmelo replied. "I am raising the temperature to 68 degrees Fahrenheit."

"You're so polite to your car," Alma finally laughed. "Katie and Carmelo. Anyways. When are you planning on having babies? A quiverfull is a blessing, and your husband is still nearly twice your age, isn't he?"

Intrusive questions, but Katie had prepared herself for this. "Oh, my dear. We are guided by our Lord and Savior. He will decide when the time is right for us."

Frown lines returned to Alma's face as she thought over her mentee's retort. As she opened her mouth to lay out admonishments, arrange them like curios on a coffee table for Katie to consider, an alert from Carmelo broke the tension.

"An accident has been reported ahead. You are still on the fastest route."

"Sorry, Miss Stirling. I have to take Carmelo off self-drive. We'll chat later, okay?" She ended the call before she could reply.

Alma's face dissolved to reveal the Dwight D. Eisenhower Highway, off-ramps choked with traffic. There was no escape. She heard plastic and glass crunch under tires as Carmelo approached the accident, somebody's car crumpled against a guardrail. Foamy effluent leaked out of its rear where firemen had extinguished a fire.

"Your heart rate has risen, but you need not worry," Carmelo soothed. "Vehicular accidents are rare. Please sit back and enjoy a selection from your playlist." Light guitar strumming came from the speakers, a country song about prison life.

The crash was by God's design, of course, but she didn't like how it reminded her of the inevitability of His design. A broken man waited for her at home, a man crippled by the design of his own body. She had pretended not to see the blood in the toilet, around the same time he had asked for a Live Again unit. With Alma's coaching, Katie had convinced Chip not to trust the science. 9G radiation, government control, luciferin in the silver-trance, and whatever else those perverts did with the technology. No technology should stand between God and your soul.

Chip had trouble getting out of bed now, and he wore the same clothes for days on end, his favorite sweatpants and country band T-shirt. He groaned when she tried to motivate him to move, and he said things that scared her. She prayed as she had been taught to do, and he remained in the dark of their bedroom, waiting for grace.

***

Every year it felt better. Her dead name anonymized along with all its old health data scraped out of her life. Deep learning models sluiced her past for patterns and pathologies because what are we humans if not test subjects for machines to analyze? *They can have my past,* she thought. *I am not, until I am.*

Rachel Varley stood in the Castro District. Her home. Childhood memories of rainbow streets, open-air bookstores, and sidewalks stained with beer. All driftwood bones now, pushed up against Live Again's corporate campus. Guiding Light watched from the hills above, waves of humanity crashing on the streets below.

She remembered the terror of thinking she had to choose between the two. The siren song of churches offering erasure, or medical sciences that offered the opposite. Puberty blockers had helped calm the waters. Helped slow down time.

"Young lady." A security guard held up his hand as if the power of his palm could stop people from streaming into Live Again's corporate campus. A dreamland where techies shuffled along basement corridors with bloodshot eyes as their holographic ghosts played hide and seek. "You can't enter here without a badge."

Strangers gendered her correctly now, which was a relief, something others perhaps considered incidental. She remembered the joy of hearing her mother's voice say her new name, her real name, much to her father's disdain. Fuck him. Chip had left them to marry some sexpot model who had turned born-again not long after consummation. He deserved all the regret in the world.

"I'm rescuing my mom," Rachel told the guard. "She's been trapped in there for the last three weeks." Live Again's scrums blurred people and process. Each passing year had reduced her mother to a shadow of her former self. *There's just never enough time*, Ash had told her. *I work for machines that steal away my future.*

"Yeah, they're preparing for the next big release. You're not getting inside. No visitors during crunch."

Another guard approached her, this one restraining a German Shepherd as it pulled against its leash. The dog sniffed at the hem of her dress. Bomb threats against Live Again had increased, the anti-science crowd inflamed with fresh panic and violence.

"I'm not a visitor." Rachel pointed at the web of skin between her thumb and index finger. "I've been chipped."

A handheld scanner acknowledged her clearance with a trademarked melody, and the guards fell away to monitor the river of techs returning from lunch. She joined them, swept into the bustle of half-heard conversations, alerts pinging for attention, and the clomps of Vans against stairs. Noises ebbed as she walked deeper into Live Again's research facilities, its dimly lit hallways, cool air whispering through ceiling vents.

Twenty years ago, wearables had tracked patterns of movement, extractive technology that harvested consumer data. She remembered that funny chatbot clinging to her mom's wrist, warning her about uneven gaits and lactic acid. Anonymized data, patterns and pathologies, silver bullets in the silver-trance. Live Again had promised it all.

This is the part they hide from the public, she thought. Recordings of the terminally-ill hobbling up and down passages, in and out of cavernous offices, shimmering datasets that had trained Live Again's deep learning models. Their faces had been fragmented for data anonymization, broken reflections on broken mirrors. Rachel walked through their silver light, the sound of their breathing washing over her.

She opened the door. Her mother didn't look up, immersed in an old recording. Rachel watched her doomscroll, light moving across her face as shapes shifted. One of the shapes, a younger version of herself, stood in front of a medicine cabinet mirror. Forever looking into that mirror, and trying not to look into that mirror, and trying to pass through it to find herself.

Her identity had been about presentation back then. The shirts she wore. The music she listened to. The beliefs she believed. Until it was not, and she had realized in a terrifying moment of blankness that she was trapped in something that was not herself. Her face, her hair, her genitals, but they were not her own.

Her mother touched the face of the immersion, its silver light illuminating her fingers. Rachel stepped through the doorway and into the form. She stood still for a moment, remembering the past, and she smiled as her mother's fingers brushed against her cheek.

"It's me, Mom" she said, and reached up to hold her mom's hand to her face.

Startled, Ash fell to the floor, the silver-trance broken. Rachel knelt down to help her up.

"It's okay, Mom. You rescued me once. Now it's my turn to rescue you. Let's get the hell outta here."

Ash and Rachel skirted the silver reproductions of themselves, cameras and scanners turning to follow them out. Ash flicked her wrist to put Live Again into passive mode, and the immersion ended, their ghosts returning to their servers.

Journey to Brindisfarne Abbey

Eva Pascoe

BRIDGET'S MONTHLY PILGRIMAGE to the Chapel was her only time away from Brindisfarne Abbey in the nine months she had spent there. As she pulled her shawl over her greying, windswept hair, her thoughts turned again to Ella—she would have been thirty years old today. A large wave broke against the gabions, releasing a high spray of cold water that woke her from her daydream. It wouldn't be long before the rising tide cut off the misty island and its crumbling gothic building from the mainland. She hurried her pace. It wouldn't be good to be late today.

As she stepped onto the beach, the dense seafoam behind her engulfed what was left of the path to the Chapel. Though she had made the trip several times, the sense of relief from the safer ground beneath her feet on this visit was far greater than before. As she looked back at the waters for the last time, she hoped her prayers would soon be answered.

The haptic belt secured to her slim tummy had felt more active as the months rolled by. She felt a simulated kick. In the near distance, she heard the ringing of the bell, its deep, rhythmic sound spelling urgency. The familiar voice of Seamus, the Abbey's caretaker, followed, his grisly baritone bellowing, "Huxley Hall! Six o'clock."

Walking purposefully through the cloisters, Bridget could see the Great Hall's entrance ahead of her. Inside, gently illuminating the intricately decorated mediaeval walls with a warm, green light were eight evenly spaced glowing pods.

"Aidan," Bridget said softly, greeting the dark-haired, hunched figure sitting by the first pod. She placed a soft hand on his shoulder, "I am sure she will be a great windsurfer, just like her Dad."

Aidan gave her a tentative smile before taking a long swig from the bottle of Brindisfarne Mead clutched in his hand. Made by the Abbess in her leisure time and prescribed to remedy "neurosis" or, as in Aidan's case, give a light boost of courage.

Bridget and Aiden had bonded over their shared struggle during their time at the Abbey. His husband had passed away before they could have their second child. It had always been their dream to raise two children together—one biologically his, the other biologically his partner's. Aiden had spent much of the last nine months on the island volunteering at the terrarium at the back of the Abbey. Unlike Bridget, he had the knack for turtle care and seemed at his most peaceful while tending to the bale. He had a gentle manner and was a doting parent to his daughter, sharing his curiosities with her. Together they aided the production of the turtle waste extract—a key biomimicry compound for Brindisfarne's Ovarian Reanimation research.

For Bridget and many others like her, the ORA project was the only remaining hope for having a child, for a family. The epilepsy medication that prevented her seizures and allowed her to live a mostly normal life was lethal to a foetus yet she had dreamed of raising children ever since she was a young girl. But the trauma and heartbreak after losing little Ella, the breakdown of her first marriage shortly thereafter, and the depression and struggle forming new relationships that followed had left her feeling cursed. It had taken years to open herself up to someone new. And although the Brindisfarne trial meant risking that the curse would strike her again, it was also a chance to heal her deep wound and to start a family with her new partner. She knew she had to at least try.

In Bridget's pod, little Eleanor was floating cosily in her synthetic womb. Ten tiny pink toes were wriggling, and a wrinkled face was discovering new expressions for the first time. Watching her grow from a sack of cells to this mature form had been the most unexpected experience of Bridget's life. Nothing compared to the love she already felt for her child. They had created quite a bond, thanks to the haptic belt. Whenever Eleanor's small legs kicked out at the womb, leaving a trail of bubbles in the amniotic fluid, the haptic belt would shudder against Bridget's abdomen in a simulated touch, and the rush of endorphins made her feel a growing closeness to her daughter. She couldn't wait until the moment when at long last she would be able to hold the baby against her skin for real.

The pod's display showed 'Status: Complete'. The children were finally ready to enter life outside the pods. The air felt tense as the nuns busied themselves with preparations at their stations. The Abbess took one last look at the array of instruments and over at the glowing pods. Each nun held their jet beads and gently murmured a prayer to their respective pod. Though science was at the foundation of the project, spirit and belief held just as much power to the nuns as the empirical evidence. Even Bridget, who was not religious, whispered a short prayer. At this moment, there was no such thing as enough luck.

The delicate walls of the synthetic wombs began visibly contracting— the pods emulating the movements of the female reproductive system. At the core of the programme was artificial intelligence software that had been trained with data from healthy live births. ORA had been pioneered by the Abbess herself, a woman of deep faith but also of deep scientific rigour. The technology combined innovative biomimicry with artificial intelligence to reanimate egg production for older women and create an external birthing chamber. If this trial succeeded, countless people like Bridget and Aidan would be able to have their own children. Everything was riding on a good outcome today.

"T minus twenty minutes," declared the Abbess from the bridge overlooking the pods. Bridget felt her haptic belt activate, sensing her child's increasing movement in the final, pre-birth stages. But as she reached down to touch it, the surge in activity abruptly stopped. The background splashing noise heard throughout the hall reduced, then halted. Bridget looked to the Abbess for her calming reassurance and was instead met with unfamiliarly anxious eyes. She had never seen the Abbess unnerved like this. Frozen with dread, Bridget's vision began to blur. She needed to stay present and began focusing on the sound of Aidan's voice. He was shouting.

"What's going on?" he exclaimed. "What's happening?"

Seamus had told Bridget that, months before, in one of the early trials, a radical protest group had hijacked control over two of the pods and caused them to lose their babies. The thought that it might be happening again was enough to make Bridget's greying hair turn even whiter.

The Abbess turned to the nuns: "Keep these babies stable while we activate the backup generator." Bridget didn't know much about the science of external wombs, but she did realise it was a delicate practice that balanced on a knife's edge. A power disruption would surely affect little Eleanor who was still voyaging through the artificial birth canal. She was sick with fear and grabbed onto Aidan's arm. He grabbed hers back. They were in this together, whatever the outcome.

She held tightly on to her breath as the array of indicator lights began to calm and the tiniest glimmer of relief crept across the face of the Abbess.

"The second generator is up and running. That should buy us time we need, but we have to focus. This doesn't go backwards, Sisters. As well you know!"

The specially engineered amniotic fluid that mimicked the nurturing environment of a mother's womb splashed around inside the transparent casing of the pods. As the walls of their synthetic wombs began contracting and started to push their babies out, Bridget's anxiety grew again. If she couldn't focus on the birth, she feared her mounting stress could trigger a seizure.

Aidan pulled her aside. "It will be fine, just stay with the pod," he ordered her calmly, and gently wiped the sweat from her forehead. She looked back towards Aiden's pod and the gathering crowd of nuns around it.

"She is having a little trouble," the head nun called to Aiden, as suddenly a high-pitched call through the Hall's narrow windows shattered the tension between them both.

"Longboats, approaching the shore!"

Beyond the protective walls of the Abbey, protesters brandishing painted signs with words of condemnation gathered outside and demanded a halt to the programme. "No to ORA! Close the Abbey! Close the Abbey!" Their chants were growing louder and made their intentions clear—to disrupt the miracle of these births, to spread fear of the ORA, and tarnish the Abbey's name.

Seamus, who had rung the alarm, was now preparing the defences. His squad of defence drones kicked into gear. The hum of the motors rose quickly from the roof. Within moments their nimble, spirited engines had catapulted them right into the danger zone. The protesters barely noticed as the black nets fell, seemingly from nowhere, only becoming aware of them as their limbs became entangled and the fibrous netting released its calming vapours. Giggling like teenagers zoning out from their first joint, they slowed and stopped their climb, sliding to the ground beside the wall like intoxicated beetles.

As the last protester succumbed, Bridget could hear Aidan's baby crying from inside the Hall. Finally! She swung herself around to see him receive his child, grinning from ear to ear.

Looking back out of the narrow stained-glass window and scanning the coastline below, Bridget could see the Police marine units arriving on the shore in their black rafts. The chief officer of the Coastguard was a traditionalist, having previously warned the Abbess that hosting the programme would endanger the village. He was also, however, quite dutiful, and mandated to pick up the protestors.

"Leave their boats for now. They can be used for accessing the Chapel at high tide," he commanded. Bridget thought she saw a crack in his steely façade. He had some respect for the work being done by the nuns, she was sure of it. She thought back to her last prayer at the Chapel earlier in the day and thanked herself for making all those pilgrimages through the fog and the rain.

Back inside the Abbey, her birthing team's focus had stayed locked to their task, despite the swell and subsequent ebb of wailing sirens and the failing electrical systems. Bridget turned her attention towards her pod. She could see Eleanor's tiny head passing through the birth canal simulator and wondered if her adrenaline had started to spike yet. This step was crucial in the birthing process as adrenaline would jump start her initial moments outside of the womb, allowing her to clear her lungs of amniotic fluids and take her first breath of air. It hadn't. The pod's balance of hormones and biomechanical controls were failing. A lump of terror rose again in Bridget's throat.

Eleanor's forward progress had stalled. After a few long minutes of struggle, the attending nuns placed the birthing bot on standby and prepared for a caesarean section—a sub-optimal final step, but the correct solution to save a baby stuck in the birth canal. Yet just as the team was about to proceed, baby Eleanor emerged from her cosy cocoon and lay crying in the hands of her attending nun. The team cheered loudly. Bridget felt faint. Hearing a sudden rushing in her ears, she fell to her knees, her body utterly overcome with emotions, and all her prayers answered. With trembling hands, Bridget touched the fresco on the wall and thanked whatever was out there that was looking over her.

"Eight pounds on the dot!" announced the Abbess, looking proud as she lifted the baby from the scales. "Just as we predicted!" The Abbess made cooing noises at the little form and turned, smiling softly as she carefully passed daughter to mother. Skin to skin. The tiny body in Bridget's arms wriggled beautifully with life. As their skin touched, Bridget took what felt like the deepest breath for as long as she could remember. With her daughter's limbs folded in tight, almost as they had in the pod, she settled hungrily onto Bridget's breast, a small line of dribble connecting her tiny lips to her mother's body.

This was the moment she had been waiting for and warm tears escaped Bridget's eyes. She stroked the small tuft of reddish hair that covered her daughter's head. It was like silk. Her husband was a redhead. She held their newborn close to her body and pictured him. This was their baby, born from love and a tiny sprinkle of scientific magic. She was perfect.

The Abbess quietly removed Bridget's haptic belt. "You will get it back afterwards as a keepsake. We just need to complete tests and take all the data out."

She packed it into a special pouch and set it to one side, gazing first at Eleanor, then around the hall and back to Bridget. "Look at them, these tiny visitors from the future. If only they could tell us what is to come."

After she had finished feeding, the Abbess gently lifted baby Eleanor from her mother's chest, wrapping her in a delicately crocheted swaddle blanket and placing her in her new cot. Some things were best done in the old way, thought Bridget, reaching out and gently touching her mother's handiwork. The stitches spanned three generations, rising and falling now with Eleanor's tiny breaths.

The Abbess put a hand on Bridget's shoulder as they stood together, admiring their creation. "You have a strong soul, Bridget. This special child was meant for you. May you both have long and prosperous lives."

The ocean wind raised goosebumps on Bridget's pale skin and she hitched the blanket up to cover as much of the baby in her arms as possible, rocking Eleanor gently, protectively. As the deep, victorious sound of the bells rang out from the Chapel in the distance, Aiden joined them, cradling his new daughter in his arms.

The Abbess was looking out at the water now, and sighed a small, bittersweet-sounding sigh. "The success of this trial, of our dream, it is real now. Our work, our labour, of so many years, completed." She turned back to Aiden and Bridget. "If I asked you to take on our invention and offer it to others, would you do so?"

Bridget stared at her in disbelief. Aidan did the same. The Abbess continued, "Now that ORA helped to deliver healthy babies, we can patent our technology. And I would like to gift you and your children, and all the future lives of the extraordinary children it would potentially bring to life, the rights to our ORA. Would you accept?"

The value of that proposition was more than Bridget could fully comprehend. She had finally become a mother, she had thought, to one beautiful, baby girl. But now potentially to so much more. She looked at the Abbess and then back at Aiden, waiting for his answer.

He pulled the swaddling protectively around the baby girl in his arms.

"So, Bridget. I guess I will have to teach you how to look after those pesky turtles after all."

The Theseus Stone

Jendia Gammon

A SHAFT OF early morning sunlight cast dappled shadows on the toes of Galena Lane where she sat holding a now-cold cup of tea. She was tired. Night sweats had kept her kicking off her sheets, then dragging them back over her body as she cooled down. Even more challenging: the dreams. Dreams of her mother and father, younger, still alive, in the garden of the rural home of Galena's youth.

She tried writing the memory-dream down while the tea still bore some warmth, but it faded quickly. Like so many of her memories of late, they fragmented in broken shards, some sharper than others, cutting her. And yet so hard to recall when she *was* ready, when she *wanted* to see her parents in her mind clearly. Ultimately, she abandoned the dream journal, returning to her manuscript. She refused the help of the AI assistant, which she'd left only as an emergency feature. At one point, it prodded her for a break, intoned that her thoughts were degrading. Sickened by the intrusion of that statement, she unplugged everything in her home in disgust. That prompted an alert to Auratanno. Its tentacular product awareness detection systems sounded a shrill warning throughout her home and echoed outside. So she reconnected everything and stared at her manuscript, eyes stinging. She took her tea outside.

All I want is to feel whole again. I want them NOT to fade. Why can't I see them anywhere except in my dreams? That fade so fast—

She knew why: menopause. The hot flashes, memory distortions, and broken recalls formed a warped debris ball in her tornado of hormonal fluctuation.

It's not like there weren't solutions. This was the 2050s. Every imaginable hormonal manipulation existed. Nanoviruses altered protein production, yielding elaborate cocktails of hormones, new and artificial, tailored for every individual who wanted them. But a few individuals rejected that interference in favor of natural aging. Galena wasn't quite sure what she wanted to do.

Still, she suffered. Her closest friends now questioned her judgment for refusing to act.

She stared at her mug. It was embedded with clouded amethysts, clouded like her own memories. She had always adored crystals. They reminded her of her father, who would bring her back special stones he'd found on his world travels. She had an entire shelf dedicated to them, enclosed in glass. Occasionally, she would open the case and admire them, turn them over in her palm, observing striations, occlusions, and pits. One was a little iron meteorite.

She considered.

There was a Remaker implant, nicknamed the Theseus Stone by ardent skeptics. It controlled longevity and aging, converting and rejuvenating the body and mind repeatedly, arguably remaking the person in the process. *But does it remake their soul?* Galena wondered.

I don't know if I want to be altered. I don't know if I want hormones or augmentation. But I do want THEM. I want to see my parents clearly again in my mind.

The world outside was harsh, too hot to linger during the day. Morning offered her one chance for normality. All her plants were bought with resilience in mind. Local trees were chimeras, amalgams of heat-resistant plants with original trees, planted years prior in some places by forward-thinking urban planners. She was fortunate to have any, she knew—and it was *because* of her parents that she did. They had loved gardening but witnessed the harsher climate unfolding. They chose sustainability. For that and many other things, she was grateful.

The Theseus Stone. Or the Remaker, as its manufacturer, Juventason, billed it. She ruminated. If she could piece together the best memories of her parents, would she finally feel at peace?

The sun's strength told her it was time to go inside. She set the half-empty, cooled tea on her small kitchen counter and gazed around at her apartment. It shimmered here and there with its Aurotanno devices, ever recording her, ever "protecting" her. It adjusted the windowpanes to repel daylight, while shifting the spectrum of interior light to mimic daylight as she'd once known it from childhood. Warm, but not sizzling. Creamy-gold.

But it was a sham. Her whole apartment represented a facsimile of comfort. She knew partly this was due to her own grief. All the apps and devices in the world attempted to remove that from her, but she resisted.

And yet—

She picked up a small hexagonal block from her kitchen bar. Iridescent letters winked back at her: *"Remake yourself today! Get your very own Remaker. Open now!"*

Her fingers slipped, so that she touched one of the facets of the hexagon. It opened. She dropped it as if stung. A little holographic version of it hovered and rotated above her sink.

"Welcome! We're so pleased you've chosen a Remaker of your very own. One of our representatives will be with you shortly to guide you to your readjustment appointment. Hold on to your precious memories. Remake yourself today!"

She felt sick.

Readjustment appointment.

She didn't like the sound of that.

Then her door chimed.

An image appeared on it, displaying what was outside: a hovering bot, with bulbous, "caring" eyes, humming in what its makers considered a charming voice.

Galena quailed. "Here already."

She considered not answering. But if she did not, and the bot persisted, Auratanno would enact unpleasant scenarios: alarms, feedback to Juventason, etc. She felt trapped in her own home. She covered her eyes and fought back a sob. Then she shook off a couple of tears and said to the door, "Enter."

With a singsong little voice, the little drone chirped, "Thank you for opening your mind to us! We at Juventason welcome you to your new, better future, remaking what you once lost."

It turned appealing shades of soft violet and emanated gentle tones. She stared into its gleaming, vacuous eyes as it hummed.

"So...what do I do?"

The bot turned an ethereal shade of periwinkle blue. "Please follow me. You'll be escorted to the lab."

A tremor coursed its way through her at the word "lab".

That all sounds experimental.

Shouldering a crossbody purse, she said nervously, "Well, I hope you've got all the kinks worked out of this process."

The drone-bot then turned vivid pink, and for a wild second, Galena wondered if it were—embarrassed?

"We call it a 'lab' to honor its creators and their research legacy. But the Juventason facilities present as a spa or salon."

Galena rolled her eyes. "How glamorous."

An ovaloid, hovering car pulled up outside, its door opening like a beetle wing. Inside, a gleaming white seat beckoned, surrounded by fine bottled water, snacks, and fruit, and enhanced by soothing music. It bore no driver, being a drone like many transports these days. Yet the little bot assistant entered the craft to dock into a small port in the front. A step unfolded for Galena. She nervously stepped aboard; it bobbed more gently than a boat on calm water.

The seat extended a strap across. She sat motionless, palms sweating. The beetle-wing door closed. Her home fell below her as the drone car rose to join the appropriate sky-course. Then the interior changed, so she could not see where she was going. She tensed.

"Why can't I see where I'm at?"

The bot hummed.

"We want to ensure our valued clients arrive relaxed and refreshed," it replied.

Galena smelled something floral in the air.

Honeysuckle.

Fragments of her childhood flooded back. The bot watched, its bulbous eyes dimming. Another fragment of music echoed forth, triggering more memories for Galena.

"Ah." She sensed the craft's descent without seeing its destination. "You're already assessing me, from all this."

"This is part of the process of readiness for implantation," concurred the bot. Galena shivered, clutching her purse to her chest. "We will dock soon, and an assistant will guide you to the salon."

The car opened, a stair extended down, and Galena met a glossy-faced young woman in a white suit, with golden fingernails and dark violet, towering hair. From her earlobes, tiny hexagons swayed gently in the hot breeze. Galena gazed all around her, finding the facility bright and manicured. Faux, large gemstones of various colors erupted from iridescent white, amorphous architecture. Succulents and thick-leaved trees dotted the corporate landscape. The iconic Remaker gem symbol stood out above the glass doorways, with "JUVENTASON" shimmering on one of its facets. It presented sleek yet somehow sinister to Galena.

"Welcome to Juventason, Galena Lane." The young woman smiled with overly white teeth and wore a plastic, stiff expression. She stared unflinchingly into Galena's eyes.

Galena felt shabby and outdated before this young woman.

"I'm Violet Chance. I'm delighted you've joined us today at Juventason. Let me guide you to the salon."

"The lab, you mean." Galena chanced a grin, masking her anxiety.

The smile Violet returned was so superficial that, in another circumstance, Galena might have laughed. But here, she felt unmoored.

Violet walked ahead of her. Looking back, Galena discovered the car and the bot had disappeared, presumably docked elsewhere. The glass doors opened, and Violet turned to give another perfunctory smile.

Galena walked in, clutching her purse, feeling even more underdressed. Music in the form of electronic piano, harps, and other instruments wafted throughout. The interior of the building shone as smoothly as the exterior, with water features tucked in corners. People dressed in white intermingled with hovering bots. Some guided what Galena assumed were patients. Everyone—literally every person there—smiled.

That can't be too *bad, right?* She pondered this as she followed Violet. Everyone greeted Galena warmly. It didn't have a medical feel, much less a laboratory feel. It did seem like a high-end spa.

Violet led her to a podlike extension with vines draping over it outside. Inside, divans, all white, were lit by soft, warm, shifting hues. Two people stood waiting for her: Galena sensed authority in one, an older woman, but with a smooth, unwrinkled face, white and blue-striped hair, and sharp, dark grey eyes. Her younger assistant bore short, magenta hair and bright, violet eyes, and held a small, clear plastic slate.

Violet nodded, turned, and left. Galena stared at the two individuals.

"Greetings, Galena Lane," said the authoritative one. "I'm Doctor Marden. This is my nurse, Shev Ranger."

"Hello." Galena creased her brow.

"We understand you're ready for the Remaker implant," Dr. Marden continued. "We're so pleased that you've opened yourself up to *reclaiming* those precious memories we know you've missed so much. We will help your system readjust and enter a much more comfortable state."

"My *system*?" She disliked this. She wasn't a system. She was a person.

"Come this way, please," offered Nurse Ranger.

Galena followed the nurse into a softly lit alcove with a reclining chair. The nurse gestured for her to sit. She did so...still holding her purse.

"You can set that on this table," suggested the nurse.

"Do I have to?"

"You won't be needing it," Dr. Marden said. "We'll need for you to sit very still. Don't worry, the *Emanation Cocktail* will relax you. No need to hold on to anything."

A spike of anger shot through Galena.

"Isn't that the point, though? I'm here so that I *can* hold onto my memories. So that I can hold on to Mom and Dad even though I'm aging."

Her palms sweated more. A surge of heat followed, creeping up the back of her neck, then across her chest. The bends in her knees sweated. She realized her armpits likely visibly soaked her shirt.

Hot flash.

"Is everything all right?" asked Dr. Marden. "I'm getting an alert that you're having fluctuations."

Galena then went cold.

"Wait, you're…you're tracking my hot flashes?"

Dr. Marden sat beside her and clasped her hands under her chin, resembling a librarian, studious and calm, ready to give information. Yet the effect chilled Galena.

"Wouldn't it be better to do without this…antiquated suffering? We're so glad you've chosen the Remaker implant. This has been my life's work. Here at Juventason, we're changing lives for the *better*. I'm so pleased we'll help you regain what you've lost. Piece your precious memories of your parents back together. Release you of the awful symptoms of menopause."

Galena's ears rang. She could hear her own pulse.

"If you'll just offer a scan consent," Dr. Marden glanced up at Nurse Ranger, who brought forth a small device for Galena to place her eye against.

She recoiled.

Dr. Marden leaned back, mouth in a thin grin with no teeth exposed.

"Shev," she said, "let's let Ms. Lane relax. Bring in some water, won't you? Ms. Lane, Shev can take your purse. You won't want to have it with you during the procedure."

Galena squeezed the purse against her and blazed again with another hot flash.

"I want to keep it." Her mouth went dry as sawdust. Shev returned with water, and Galena gazed with longing, but resisted taking it. She clung onto her purse like a shield.

"May I ask why?" Dr. Marden, glancing down at the worn bag.

Galena reflexively squeezed it, and out fell a small object. It tumbled down under the chair she sat in. Shev quickly retrieved it and held it up toward her.

It was a little acrylic picture. On it two faces smiled: her parents, Seb and Jess, holding a baby between them. Galena as an infant.

She seized the picture, stood, and shook her head. Her eyes then fell on a little dish on a side table. There, a tiny little crystal in a gelatinous medium writhed back and forth, as if alive.

"That's it, then." Her voice grew in strength and timbre. "The Theseus Stone."

Dr. Marden dipped her head. "The Remaker, you mean."

"No." Galena surprised herself with her emphatic tone. "It really *is* a Theseus Stone. It could restore me, maybe. It might even bring back my memories."

"It will, I assure—"

"But maybe not all the good ones."

"We can tailor—"

"Some memories were meant to fade." Galena slid the little acrylic picture of her parents back into her purse. She stood with her chin high and threw her shoulders back. "We were meant to fade also. I wouldn't be me anymore. I'd be 'remade'. I don't think I need to be."

Dr. Marden shook her head, laughing softly. "We have the power to make our lives longer, with less suffering. Wouldn't you want that? Don't you think *they'd* want that?"

Realizing the hairs around her forehead were now soaked from the sweats, Galena stared into the doctor's face. Maybe she could stitch back together the moments in her life in which she had been with her parents as a whole family. *My parents raised me to be independent, and only wanted what was best for me. I get to decide what that is. Not some company.*

"I can't answer what they'd want, other than for me to choose what makes *me* happy."

She patted the shoulder bag.

"And I have them here with me, always. I don't need to recreate that. I'm their daughter. They live on through me. And I'll live on as *I* choose."

She turned away from Dr. Marden and Nurse Ranger then, discreetly using her watch to hail an actual cab. Rare as they were now, they did still exist. She walked quickly yet confidently out of the Juventason building, ignoring the confused and surprised stares from too-perfect people. People who she assumed had been "remade".

She met the cab at the curb and turned to look back at the cold face of Violet Chance staring at her from the door, her arms crossed in front of her abdomen, and finally with a flicker of some emotion on her forehead that Galena could not quite discern. She entered the cab, with its tired-looking human driver bearing a five o'clock shadow and no patience. The vehicle smelled like illegal oil. She grinned.

"Nice place," he said gruffly. "You work there?"

"No. Do you need my address again?" she looked uncertainly at the dashboard's old tech.

"I've got it," he answered. "What brings you over to this area?"

Galena watched the sleek, white expanse of Juventason glide away as the driver sped on. She exhaled a breath she hadn't realized she'd been holding.

"I forget."

Warning Signs

Britta Schulte

HE HAD BEEN informed there would be warning signs. Nobody could defeat the ageing process indefinitely. He had never been promised immortality, just a body that would withstand the daily wear and tear of life a bit better—well, actually a lot better than before. A body that could still be infected but would not suffer from all the illnesses his parents and their parents had been suffering from; arthritis, dementia, and cataracts were quite unlikely to appear in the hundred and twenty-plus years people now lived.

"You won't get tired quickly, but you do not get any superpowers. You still have to brush your teeth," a doctor, who had been much too cheery for the early hour, had told him before shoving him off to the nurse who gave him the shot.

He half-remembered the conversation in the doctor's office, even though it now felt like a lifetime ago. Most likely because it had been a lifetime. Must be, well, eighty years ago now? He had been one of the late bloomers who had waited into his forties before he started the treatment that delayed his ageing. It must have been around 2040 that he finally dragged his ass into the doctor's office and asked for "the jab".

When it all started it had been a "miracle cure", the "fire we stole from the gods" or the "immortality vaccine". A couple of years later, when he started, it had been reduced to "the jab". People lost their magic so quickly.

Grudgingly he opened the website of fld.gov to finally get the admin stuff over with. Final Life Decisions. Whoever had come up with this title? But he was sure it could have been worse. Maybe LOL.gov. Loving ... Obituaries ... Lately. No, that really did not make sense. Anyway, let's get on with it. He unfortunately did not have anything better to do on this Saturday afternoon. And it was raining adequately. Not too much, just a little drizzle that seemed to go on for hours. He did not have many wishes for his funeral. But in his mind a funeral should include a lonely figure standing in the rain. Hat or umbrella optional. It was something he was not sure he would get and maybe he even regretted even more that he had not had an opportunity to do this for someone else.

But hey, ho, there was still time. It was not like he would drop dead tomorrow. Or maybe he would. The process of his body giving in, of ending it, was apparently quick, but still quite unpredictable. Or so he had been told. Hey, he had lived a hundred and twenty years and had done many things. But there was still a time for firsts, as this was his first death. With a little chuckle he thought how this had escalated quickly. Filing taxes every year felt more deadly than this, so where was this sudden nostalgia coming from? All he had to do was go through a couple of clicks to set everything in order, he told himself. Quite accurately. Okay, case 324M5932 opened. As if there were not enough numbers that governed his life. Bank account, tax number, age...

Age? That one was easy. It was getting a bit confusing what had happened when, but age still made sense. Well, as much as it made beyond thirty. He smiled, thinking how thirty had meant something in his teens. Something big. Something scary. Until it happened and the focus shifted to forty. Or fifty. Or sixty-five. Oh, the good old days when one could retire. That thought had gone out of the window in this capitalist hellscape. Why give people time off when they are clearly still able to work? He thought back to his grandparents and the way they had spent their last twentyish years. Taking care of the garden, babysitting him, travelling once in a while ... Must beat changing jobs every twenty years or so because you could not take the tediousness of it any more. Well, he had to admit that his grandfather had been out much more in his working days. Fifty to sixty hours, working on Saturdays had not been strange. What a fucked-up idea. No matter how much he tried, he could not imagine going back to a five-day working week—let alone overtime.

But hey, ho, what was it with this trip down memory lane? He had a task to get on with. Next question: What is your medical history? He did have the flu two years ago and hated every feverish day of it. Arm broken when he fell from the thing because he just quickly wanted to … well, best not dwell on this one. A hundred and twenty years and there was plenty of awkward stuff to think about and that had been one example of it. Trying to impress this pretty boy—well, the pretty boy was over a hundred years old himself—and ending up in the emergency room. And what a dodgy place it had been. But none of the big hospitals would have done something about a broken arm. Higher cheekbones?—sure. Maybe a nice and juicy amputation. Neurosurgery, never done before. But people being stupid was not sexy at all and there was no money left for it.

Hospitals, insurers, and pharma companies all around started to feel the effects of the jab rather quickly. People still fought all the viruses and bacteria floating around, but so many illnesses slowly faded out. How many painkillers do you need if your back does not ache? How many injuries can you avoid if your joints continue to work just fine? (Well, apparently not all, but a lot). How many infections do not take hold in a body whose immune system is young and fit? You would think the anti-ageing industry went down the drain, when people stopped developing wrinkles and varicose veins and saggy skin, but nobody had expected the creativity of all the influencers. Do you really want to see the same face in the mirror, day after day after day? Surely not. So why not mix it up from time to time with the newest fashionable mod? And why not get it done it in a hospital now that they had all this free space? Hospitals looked more like beauty salons these days than the lifesaving hallowed halls he remembered from his youth. Even the smell was different. And real emergencies were taken to dodgy backrooms…

He had no moral high ground to make fun of people who wanted to change. Oh, medical history, he would have to put down his weekly dose of testosterone. Because there had been a reason why he waited with the jab even though people now looked at him with pity. In a world of people with bodies who looked twenty to him, he was now a forty-year-old. He was used to the confusion of younger people who knew faces like his only from TV. The shy question of people of his generation who asked awfully quietly if he had lacked the money? Or if the drug had not worked? That happened sometimes, they assured him. His response was the same for both: he had had no clue who he had been at twenty, just that he hated his body and himself and that therapy and transition had been life saving for him. He had not even wanted to think about "immortality" with the titties Mother Nature had mistakenly endowed him with. He sometimes felt pity for those who got the jab in their early twenties. Sure, their bodies worked at peak efficiency, but some might be missing out on experiences that actually felt quite good. A calmness, so to say. He had no other words to describe it.

Oh, it stopped raining. Maybe he should go for a walk in a bit. But— form first. He was halfway through already, so he might as well finish it off now. Next of kin. He sighed. His generation was the lonely one. So many single children. So many parents and grandparents that had been too late, too frail for the jab. He had lived a really long time without his family now. When people used to joke: "How do you make friends in your thirties?" he was not even sure what the question was now. Every time you met someone you had to do this awkward song and dance about who old someone was. When someone was in a bar, you could at least assume they were of full age, but beyond that there was very little to go by. Sometimes fashion helped. Younger ones tended to follow the trends more closely, but fashion also had the annoying tendency to repeat. Apparently, everything came back every twenty years or so. So, most of the time he was completely fucked up when trying to guess someone's age. So, most of the time he stayed on his own. His last attempt at flirting had left him in the emergency room, for god's sake.

He clicked the option that he would take care of his belongings himself and that whatever was left could be donated to charity. Most of it was second-hand anyway. Maybe he should skip that walk and do that instead. Surely he could do a couple of days, or however long it took, until he dropped dead without the suit shirts he hardly ever wore, the illustrations on his wall, and his printer? He wanted to give himself another "but hey, ho" to get out of this gloomy mood, but for once it did not work. He looked around his room. He looked up and down his body. He had spent a lot of time in both, but neither really felt like home. Because of his many jobs, he had moved around a lot. He had always wondered how long it would take to feel at home in one place. Apparently, he would not get enough time to find that out. But he had long suspected that time was not the thing he needed for this.

Not to sound ungrateful. He was so happy that he could still crochet without his hands hurting. That he could still walk without pain in hips or knees. That he was spared the long and agonising death he had witnessed in his grandfather. Weeks in bed with the highest dose of painkillers in a weird daze that appeared neither alive nor death. Surely, sitting here and filling in a long and boring form so that the authorities could deal with his body and belongings quickly and swiftly was better. But better was not good and he for one was quite sad now. He got up from his chair and started to pace up and down. Being forced to look back on his long life, what was there left? What was there to celebrate? They should make that part of the form he thought. After all the obnoxious questions about coffins, religious rituals, and savings, there should be a prompt saying: Now, be kind to yourself. You did fucking well, didn't you? He walked to the wall and sank down, crouching in the corner in a way he hoped looked at least romantic. Damn, obviously the sun had to come out now and ruin his moment.

His grandmother had been positive about death. Well, the one on the mother's side. His father's mother had a stroke and died the next day without regaining consciousness. He had envied her then, he envied her now. Everyone else had been so apologetic and rambled on about how "she had been taken in the prime of her life", and while he absolutely agreed that it had been really shitty for his father and himself, his grandma was saved this moment of forced reflection. But why could he not be like his other grandmother? She had been bedridden for a week, told everyone she could reach that she loved them, and literally fell asleep with a smile on her face. She had known it was coming, but she had not been scared. Few regrets.

Fuck it, nobody forced him to be reflective. He hadn't done so bad. He had lived through the weirdest things. A pandemic. War in Europe. A miracle cure that had changed humanity as they knew it. He had lived through his own transition, both to affirm his gender and after getting the jab. He had lived through times when he could feast and those when he had to take it down. And he had stayed kind through all of it. His story might not have been one of the "successes", like others who had taken up the violin in their eighties and used their expanded lifetime to master the instrument. He had not spent his lifetime diving into physics to further the development of quantum computers. He sure as hell was not surrounded by loved ones, neither kin nor blood. But that was no fault of his own. He had his little circle of people who loved him as much as he loved them and that was the best one could hope for.

He looked outside. Well, if the sun did its best to ruin his nostalgia, he might as well make the best of it. He opened his messenger and asked around if anyone would still be up for a pint. He thought back how normal it once was to drink and how careful everyone had become now that their organs needed to last much longer. But he had had the warning signs. There was no need to be careful now. And having one last pint hopefully was a good enough reason for someone to come out as well. He heard the pling as someone confirmed, smiled, and went to shower, closing the laptop on his way out.

In the office, the case worker opened the file 324M5932 as his shift started. He sighed. Of course, he had to start the day with a death certificate from someone who had not finished filling in all the details. Why were people so irresponsible? It was not as if there were no warning signs.

Commentary
David W Wood

HERE'S A PREDICTION about the impact of a new medical treatment: "The Browns have most probably guaranteed that their child...will never have a chance at a normal childhood or even adulthood. They have degraded and institutionalized the child and...should be viewed as symbols of the degeneration of Western morals".

That was from a letter to *Time*, published in the 21 August 1978 edition. It was part of a flurry of public concern about the consequences of a shocking new technology, popularly known at that time as "test tube babies".

In his recent book, *The Song of the Cell: An Exploration of Medicine and the New Human*, Siddhartha Mukherjee picks up the story:

"An anonymous package from America arrived at the Browns' home in Bristol, containing a broken test tube splashed with a grotesque spray of fake blood."

On 25th July that year, the magazine *Our Lady*, popular in some Catholic communities, quoted a supposed revelation – a "Message of Our Lady and Our Lord to Veronica of the Cross":

"It is an abomination in the eyes of God for man in his arrogance and pride to seek to create the living being. What he is creating is a soulless monster, a being of destruction for all that it will meet. I say 'it', for it is not truly a human being but a 'thing'!"

In case you're wondering, the child in question—not an 'it' but a 'she'—was Louise Brown, the world's first IVF baby. By many criteria, her childhood and adulthood have been "normal", contrary to the forecast of the *Time* letter writer who fretted about "moral degeneration". Louise is now 45 years old, and is a mother herself—her son, conceived naturally, was born in 2006. Louise, along with tens of millions other IVF children who followed her into the world, appears to be every bit as soulful as any other child. And every bit as beloved.

It was not just fringe cranks who feared the impact of that new technology. Listen to the anxieties expressed by Leon Kass, a University of Chicago bioethics professor, in testimony to the US government's Ethics Advisory Board, shortly after the birth of Louise:

"More is at stake [with IVF research] than in ordinary biomedical research... At stake is the idea of the humanness of our human life and the meaning of our embodiment, our sexual being, and our relation to ancestors and descendants."

Kass subsequently served as the principal bioethics advisor to President George W. Bush.

Moreover, many in the medical industry took a hostile stance toward the researchers who pioneered IVF treatment. Allegedly, these pioneers were self-serving and glory-seeking. After all, being infertile was not a disease (they argued), so why should doctors become involved? Indeed, weren't childless couples a blessing, in a world facing extreme overpopulation?

But who, nowadays, would argue for banning IVF—for denying couples the chance to experience the joy they anticipate from raising a child?

As for IVF, so also for many other medical technologies; at first, they caused shudders and apprehension, before their benefits were more widely appreciated. Consider blood transfusions, vaccines, pacemakers, and genetic screening for potentially debilitating inherited diseases.

Accordingly, we should be careful about allowing our decision-making to be overly influenced by initial "yuck" instinctive reactions.

That's not to say we should rush on regardless, accepting every new medical intervention that is put on the table. Indeed, the bioethicist Leon Kass had a point. Some interventions will change our concept of what it means to be human. Others may lead to insensitivity, addiction, or other behaviours that we subsequently bitterly regret. We could be misled by an initial "wow" as well as by an initial "yuck".

Therefore, the essays in this volume are to be heartily applauded. They help raise our awareness of developments we might subsequently wish we had avoided—and of developments that we should probably pursue more vigorously.

In "Journey to Brindisfarne Abbey", Eva Pascoe explores one possible extension to IVF, namely synthetic wombs, in which babies are not only conceived outside the body but grow to term externally. This is a path blazed by Aldous Huxley in his 1932 dystopian classic *Brave New World*, a novel that was full of warnings about disconnecting human beings from a full set of human experiences. In *Brave New World*, the concept of motherhood is held up to ridicule, as is that of live birth, which is viewed as being fit only for savages. In that future, children belong only to the state, not to families—and "everyone belongs to everyone else". And the notion of exclusive romantic love is scorned.

Not so in the future Pascoe envisions. In her story, the connection between mother and unborn child is powerful and visceral, aided by a haptic belt worn by the mother. The tender care provided by the nuns in the story is vital too—as a reminder of the saying that it takes a village to raise a child.

As I mentioned, the parents of Louise Brown received deeply unpleasant packages through the post, sent by people who wished to turn back the clock. The mother in Pascoe's story has things even harder, due to would-be violent saboteurs. I've noticed grains of that same hostility in some gatherings at London Futurists (which I chair), where audience members who are generally open to new technological possibilities nevertheless fix their gaze when the subject of synthetic wombs is raised. One presenter—a well-known author—labelled the technology as "jerk tech". It was, he implied, something that only a lonely fantasist might desire. But afterwards, several women attendees told me they thought only a man could take such a high-handed, dismissive approach to this technology. These women emphasised that they were unsure whether they would personally want to take advantage of synthetic wombs, but they thought the possibility should be kept open.

As I see it, the physical battle in "Journey to Brindisfarne Abbey" represents what is likely to be a growing social battle in the decades ahead as synthetic human wombs edge closer to being a reality. It is strongly to be hoped that the public conversation can proceed openly and calmly. Allowing people to make the choice between external and internal womb for their babies shouldn't be controversial, but it will take time for everyone to become used to the idea. The resulting children, I predict, will be every bit as soulful as, say, Louise Brown. And every bit as beloved.

"I Am Not, Until I Am" by Jesse Rowell depicts an intriguing world with many changes from the present. That's a world that allows "Live Again" immersive re-experiencing of events from the past, via the integration of data from numerous cameras and other sensors, and the projection of holographic imagery. I see that as a plausible feature of life in the decades ahead.

The same data sensors perform another equally credible task: early detection of ailments. In 2024, new disease outbreaks can already be detected from monitoring the contents of waste water from housing estates, and from the query strings people are typing into Internet search engines. Wearable health monitors have already saved lives, and are transforming the lives of many more people, on account of flows of data from glucose monitors, blood pressure monitors, heart rate variability monitors, sleep state monitors, and much more.

In Rowell's imagined future, these systems have grown more powerful, providing, for example, early warnings of suicidal thoughts. But the systems are harnessed to the needs of shadowy data brokers and health insurers. Advance warning of pending pathologies is commercially valuable to these corporations. And serving these corporations appears to be more important than keeping the population in the best of health.

That's an echo of a common complaint against today's pharmaceutical industry, which is sometimes seen more as a "sickness industry" than a "healthcare industry". That complaint is unfair, but it resonates with many who have had unpleasant experiences in life. People who feel alienated by vaccination mandates are sometimes drawn to conspiracy theories involving 5G radio chips. Rowell spins these ideas further, into a future Christian-based group, "Guiding Light", that is opposed to what it describes as "9G radiation, government control, and luciferin in the silver-trance".

The Guiding Light group in this story, "I Am Not, Until I Am", shares a feature with the saboteurs in "Journey to Brindisfarne Abbey": both are presented without sympathy. Readers will be unlikely to cheer them on. Yet both groups serve as a warning: when members of the public feel left behind—taken for granted, disrespected by supposed elites, and instructed coldly by disengaged professionals about how to look after themselves—we should not be surprised when they are attracted to movements that oppose science, new medical treatments, and the possibilities of enhanced experience.

In "The Theseus Stone", Jendia Gammon presents a conundrum. Imagine a rejuvenation treatment, which restores youthful vitality to the body, and improves memory, but with a potential catch. Might that treatment leave parts of you diminished or damaged, at the same time as other parts of you are enhanced?

The primary worries of Galena, the main character in this story, are whether her new memories clash with those she likes to remember from her own impression of the past, and, more speculatively, whether the treatment would somehow constrict her soul.

The rejuvenation treatment—an implant, marketed as a "remaker"—is promoted by some slick advertising by its vendor. "Remake yourself today—Open now!" When Galena gives an indication that she might be considering the treatment, the company behind the implant swings into action, seeming, to Galena, to be too eager to close the sale.

Galena's worries have some precursors in today's world. Medical treatments often have side effects. Hair falls out, moods swing, and self-image alters. Researching the past—that is, obtaining more accurate memories—can bring shocking surprises, such as our biological father not being the person we have fondly called "Dad" for as long as we remember. A clearer view of the present can be troubling too: it can interfere with our fond self-delusions. And maybe we're not that uniquely special, despite what our parents have frequently told us.

Would such considerations be sufficient to compel someone to forego a significant medical enhancement, such as the repair, not just of a knee, hip, or cataract-infused eye lens, but of our entire metabolism? I accept that the Galenas of the future may well hesitate, unsure of what may happen to them. But that's an argument for the treatments to be explained more fully, for potential side-effects to be fully investigated (without any cover-ups), and for sympathetic planning of treatment (rather than a falsely-smiling commercial sales pitch). It's an argument for what's called *informed consent*.

Personally, I remember going through a lengthy "informed consent" discussion with a medical team before proceeding to have eye laser surgery. The risks and probabilities were pointed out to me, together with advice on how to manage these risks (for example, being careful to avoid infections while my eyes were healing). Informed—and reassured—I was confident to go ahead. It's a decision I've never regretted. I'd like to think that if Galena had been treated with similar respect and integrity, her decision would have been, like mine, to accept the health enhancement.

The story by Rosie Oliver, "Signpost to Normal", features another conundrum. Once again, there's a tradeoff to be considered, between rejuvenation of body, and, in this case, a sharp drop in creative abilities.

The narrative builds a clever parallel between the complications of climate, involving interactions of ocean currents, and the complications of the metabolism within the human body. On the face of things, it is a strange conception that global *warming* could cause some parts of the globe to become *much colder* than before. Yet when you model the climate in more detail, that becomes a credible scenario. Indeed, there's evidence from prehistoric data about rapid swings in temperatures in the past, as various tipping points were reached, and long-fixed barriers to water flow were breached. Something similar has happened to the climate of northern Europe in "Signpost to Normal".

If the climate is so complicated that changes in it confound naive expectations, the human metabolism takes complications to a new level. Accordingly, it seems plausible that attempts to systematically undo biological aging could have unwanted side-effects. Indeed, a plot point in the story fits some theories of aging and cancer: repeatedly extending the telomeres at the ends of chromosomes in our cells, to allow these cells to keep on dividing rather than drifting into a senescent zombie-like state, has been observed in some experiments in mice to extend lifespans (and, by the way, healthspans too); but according to other ideas, this also risks allowing cancerous cells to run amok. Different mechanisms for cleaning senescent cells out of the body could have the kinds of adverse side-effects that Oliver explores.

As it happens, the potential solution to such a dilemma echoes another plot twist in the story: a further tweak in the engineering. The story's solution to restoring a vital ocean current—an adjustment within an already complex model—echoes the kind of solution that various longevity scientists are already researching: combination therapies. I don't expect the rejuvenation treatments of the future to involve just a single method. Instead, there's likely to be a sophisticated suite of interventions. Such a suite, I predict, will rejuvenate not just body but also mind, heart, and spirit.

The kind of rejuvenation that features in "Warning Signs", by Britta Schulte, is definitely restricted just to the body. The main character in this narrative exhibits a depressing weariness. It's not quite as bad as the decay of the mythical prince Tithonus, for whom the goddess Eos had requested from Zeus the gift of immortality, without thinking to also request immortal youth; as a result, poor Tithonus remained alive but in states ever more degenerate as the decades passed. The character in "Warning Signs" shows no such physical decline, but the quality of his life is far from inspiring.

It's for that reason that, when I talk to people about the potential of biological rejuvenation, I emphasise not just life *extension* (doing more of the same, again and again) but also life *expansion* (the opportunity to keep growing and developing). Another phrase that I like to suggest is "better than well"—we can look forward to living in states of consciousness that far exceed what has historically been the norm. That's once we address issues not just of biology but also neurology, psychology, and indeed sociology. For some signs of potential progress, take a look at what's sometimes called "Transcend Tech"—apps and wearables that help us not just to avoid mental downturns but also to experience wonderful mental upshifts.

I don't expect such treatments to appear fully fledged overnight. However, there's likely to be a regular rhythm in which sequences of new therapies become available, replacing and augmenting each other. That's quite different from the implausible plot point in "Warning Signs", namely that once a particular rejuvenation "jab" is applied in the 2040s, no improvements are available for the next 80 years. Such a society would indeed be dreary.

Alas, there are already some warning signs that societies may be on the point of losing their capacity for decisive scientific breakthrough. A decline in respect for and understanding of science—something that futurist Carl Sagan warned about—is within sight. That's a vision to which we can, and should, all say "yuck", and resolve to prevent! Happily, the provocative narratives in this collection each play a part in stimulating our resolve as well as our understanding.

Commentary
Prof Claire Steves

READING THESE STORIES, I noticed a resonance around emotional and social identity which was challenged by the scientific developments within the stories. As a scientist it is good to be reminded of what we are all striving for as well as what we want to avoid. How can we use these visions to construct our futures to ensure they are better versions? I will take each story in turn.

SIGNPOST TO NORMAL

Kendra is clearly ill, but is it an illness itself, or side effects from imperfect anti-ageing drugs? Certainly, she seems to be hampered by a common problem for older adults—polypharmacy with more drugs piled on to treat side effects of others. It starts with telomerase, which in this futuristic setting, appears to be licensed, perhaps to prevent ageing. Telomerases were thought to help ageing as they lengthen the ends of the protective caps (telomeres) on our DNA bundles (chromosomes). Thereby, they reduce programmed cell death (apoptosis) caused by critically short telomeres. But before you reach for telomerase as an ageing cure, one of the issues with telomerase is that there is a relation between telomerase activity and certain cancers. Hence the chemotactic drugs Kendra is given to hunt out and exterminate any cancerous cells generated as a side effect of telomerase. These drugs then cause the neuropathic (nerve-related) pains, which in turn are treated with pain killers. Hence Rosie is highlighting a classic medical problem: treating one thing can lead to an endless cascade of side effects. But even the 'best' treatment would have had side effects—and one which she could not live with—loss of her creativity.

In this story there is a wonderful sense of the creative nature of scientific exploration, melding science and art in the inter-disciplinary collaboration between physical and computer science modelling. The protagonist being a sculptress is not far from the reality in science: often, we can best explain ourselves, create new hypotheses, and/or test them in models using visualisations. We examine graphs, heatmaps, and multidimensional representations, measure and compare them, and comment on what they mean. It must indeed seem to outsiders very much like reading tea leaves. Thus, I really like the concept that this scientist is depicted more as a sculptress, using practices more close to current scientific practice than it might seem.

So, this scientist is deep in the process of description and modelling, but what really shifts her is a current practical problem. While she exhibits a healthy dose of scientific scepticism about her own work, it is when she is asked to give practical help that she finds her purpose, makes her incredible choice for 'soul' not 'life', and uses her creativity to solve the 2050 real-world problem. I'm left pondering the equivalence of the words "soul" and "purpose". Could they both be that which leaves a mark and changes the future, thereby living on through how it impacts the world? Kendra rejected a life with no purpose, and smiled.

I only hope such a simple solution to change ocean currents could help stop global warming accelerating. Maybe it will be just one part of a wider system change—Kendra's part.

I Am Not, Until I Am

This is a resounding story about identity, who owns it, and when. It warns about fractures in our society built on such identities and how they might play out over time. It reminded me to seize the day and live in the moment. The sketches here are detailed, but they dance like holograms themselves, enhancing the perception of the ephemeral nature of identity. It seems only Rachel is fully awake.

"Memories never turn to dust in the silver-trance", states Ash. Whereas, she thinks, her body's cells will be fully replaced. She holds onto these past images so tightly because she thinks they define her more than who she is in the present.

The use of technology to augment memory is interesting. I felt myself asking to what extent images and sound fully and objectively capture an event. The signals we get from physical interaction, smells, touch, are part of and condition the storage of cognitive memory as well as the emotional environment of the person experiencing the event. Both our perceptions and the memories we lay down are often modified by more primal senses—pheromones, or other chemical differences (major histo-compatibilities, etc.) as well as our arousal and attention in the moment. This explains why some things which happen to us are forgotten but retrievable, while others remain unrelentingly forgotten, or conversely seem "hardwired".

Even when formed, few memories genuinely are hard-wired. Once formed, they are malleable after the event, unlike video/augmented recordings like those Ash reviews. Memories reform and can be manipulated and/or erased through: trauma; sleep; reliving; subsequent memories; pictures; and suggestion. There are reams of psychological experiments which show that our normal memories are not set in stone, and new neuroimaging and electrophysiological evidence as to how this process happens, for example in sleep. When Ash replays these memories are they fixed, or might still her current world colour her experience of the silver replays? Memories, like histories are retold from the present viewpoint.

It's interesting that in both this story and "The Theseus Stone", consumers wanted their "memories back". With time, and longevity, of course memory can be lost, for example in Alzheimer's dementia. However, as any carer of a person living with dementia will attest, what is lost, at least first, is the ability to encode new memories; the recording system is broken, while already recorded memories can be 'replayed'. Reminiscence therapy can therefore enhance quality of life for people with dementia who can conjure up the past much more easily than they can make sense of the present. Is Live Again therefore practicing mass reminiscence therapy? And is that what Ash gets lost in?

The therapy for Ash might be somewhat different; she may be concerned to revisit the childhood of her son to try to heal some trauma dwelling here, related to the difficulty their nuclear family had accepting their child's gender identity. So, for consumers like Ash, maybe it's not really memories they want, but to experience their past again as if new, with new eyes, and reinterpret it to help them heal. As Ash pointed out to the developers, there is potential for damage here, and I wondered about the safety of letting consumers revisit their past without some professional oversight.

In this story, each protagonist's identity changes across their life, through the experiences lived, but not so much through the changes which happen to their bodies. A nice riff is that the facial identity of her son (future Rachel) gets corrupted momentarily, due to a glitch, originally to protect identity but also indicating her child's identity may not be fully captured by anthropometry. Later we learn that the health identity of individuals—and also future predictions of pathology in this world—is not owned by the individuals themselves, but by data brokers and health insurers: a warning note.

Katie feels that these images are 'a soul-less reproduction of her authentic self' and seems to be certain that her identity is her own. However, while Katie rejects Live Again's holograms and predictions, she is perfectly happy with Carmelo's physiological monitoring and manipulations, oblivious to how these might shape her identity. The addition of silver colloid, oregano, and ivermectin to treat her husband echoes the schism between attempts to use science or religion to drive human purpose.

Only Rachel—who had the transformation of identity when she was growing-up—seems to have found an authentic path. She seems to be able to exist in a free space between the two projected poles of religion and science. She rescues her mother from her work-enslavement as a designer, or a subject for AI modelling. Whether she can wake up to realise her identity, and in what context, between these polar worlds, we are left to imagine by ourselves.

Journey to Brindisfarne Abbey

Turtle waste extract here seems to be central to a new science which both rejuvenates reproductive tissues and enables extracorporeal pregnancy. Turtles are a good choice for an animal to generate rejuvenating compounds, due to their exceptional longevity. Waste products are an interesting thought, because the microbes in stool do explain some differences in longevity within species. However, a turtle's longevity may be more to do with its ability to weed out cancer and damaged cells than its gut microbes. Nevertheless, I was keen to put these thoughts aside to see what would turn out.

The human impact of miscarriage and its lasting effects are deeply felt by Bridget. It's an important subject and it is nice to read a story sensitively addressing it. One percent of women live with epilepsy and options for treatment do indeed carry significant consequences for childbearing. As opposed to Jesse's story, here science and religion seem to hold each other hand in hand, nurturing the new lives together, neither taking away from the wonder and personal significance of new lives.

But then sabotage, and it is manual override that kicks in and save the day. So, in this world, still, human agency seems to drive both terrorism and the response to it. The humanity of the defence with tranquilisers and nets shows the humanity of the operation at the Abbey. The Abbess seems to think that Bridget and Aiden are suitable people to parent this invention into the wider world. I do hope she is right.

The Theseus Stone

This story starts by pondering dreams and memories. Indeed pathways involved in memory are accessed within dreams, and sometimes brain connections can be modified through dreaming. Memories of childhood places commonly surface without clear explanation. Also accepted is the fleeting nature of dreams; in fact, most dreams are never remembered, and people differ with respect to the extent of recall and also the extent to which they can be conscious in their dreams. All this has been extensively investigated by sleep physiologists, who do bring people to spend the night in sleep labs wired up to monitors, waking them up and asking them questions during their sleep. I wonder what Galena would think of such labs?

The ever-present monitoring devices are a common theme within both Jesse's and Jendia's stories, and in both cases people unplug them or forcibly detach from them. There are also issues around consent, coercion, and loss of autonomy. Galena doesn't even mean to activate the 'hexagon' invite and she is given no choice but to go off for a remake. We are even aware that she is fearful of repercussions if she doesn't go. It's not just peer pressure; she's not allowed to age by society.

I do wonder why Galena conceptualises menopause as ageing, and how common this conception is. Alternative to ageing, menopause can be understood as a developmental stage. Just like with puberty, the symptoms and turmoil which happen within it are not forever. It is possible that Galena will recover her memories later even if she takes no intervention. Just like puberty, though, it is possible to alter both the experience and the physiology of this developmental stage. There are choices we can make already about these processes and more will come. For them to remain choices we must ensure that society keeps an open mind about options individuals can take.

WARNING SIGNS

This story is about what gerontologists refer to as the squaring of the curve. That is, that at present we develop rapidly as children and young adults, reach a peak in most traits in midlife, and then at some point, often around 40-60, start to lose function, slowly at first, and then more rapidly, in a bumpy curve towards loss of independence, and then death. The idea of squaring this curve is the hopeful thought that if we fully understood the processes behind that later life age-related change, we could halt them and remain at peak function, squashing the period where we are unwell as short as possible. But the idea is not that we would carry on forever like that, but more about maintaining quality of life while we are alive. Many of the processes of damage which occur over our long lifespan look like they are not likely to be fully resolvable.

Most scientists now think that human lifespan is probably not going to be extendable massively beyond the early hundreds. So the idea is that we might squeeze the process of decline, to make the time spent in ill health as short as possible within the lifespan we have—that is, extending healthspan. The ultimate extreme of this is a sudden deterioration such as that depicted in this story.

With the advent of mRNA vaccines, the possibility of there being a multi-valent anti-ageing vaccine is interesting and more possible. In fact, we already have numerous damage repair mechanisms both at the cellular level, and within the immune system which are tuned to clean up accumulated errors. Could a vaccine augment them to be fast enough to keep up with accumulated damage?

But what is so interesting about this story is the effect that this has on our protagonist. It's the tediousness of it, the loss of definition, but endless changing jobs, never able to retire. Would it be so bad to have a bit more balance across the lifecourse? Dodgy healthcare for boring stuff because there is no ill-health to cure, and creative influencers making all manner of body modifications make for a plausible combination of unintended consequences. Equally plausible is the human procrastination about end-of life planning, dropped for the sake of a beer to keep at bay the loneliness of old age.

I love the riff on age—being able to tell people's age does have its uses, to know from looking at someone that you know some of what they have lived through, to be able to identify your birth cohort cohabitee simply by sight. Maybe age is a way to find our place in the world and connect. It's interesting to consider what life would be like if you couldn't judge age at all. Would that feel good or bad?

FINAL REMARKS

I was not surprised to see climate change featuring in two of the stories. The dual challenges of ageing populations and climate change are on course for collision, with potentially devastating effect. Galena's plants have been engineered to be heat-resistant and her house is designed to withstand heat. Such adaptations will be hugely important in protecting our populations, old and young, from the stresses of climate change. Likewise, Kendra's mission ends up helping to slow the climate emergency, although I fear she has begun too late.

There is a thread in the stories from Jesse, Rosie, and Jendia that changing the ageing process may mean stripping away personhood and individuality. Ash fails to live in the present; Galena rejects a fake, plastic, coercive remake; and Kendra fears losing the quality which makes her unique. I can genuinely see the risk of over-reminiscence, similar to the present risk of over-virtualisation in our meta-world. I can also see a world where cosmetic pressures become health pressures and to become old becomes more stigmatised and that identity shifts as we develop through life. However, I find it hard to conceive of a geroscience intervention which would really take away our identity as Kendra is told it will. I think we can be less fearful, devise regulations—both for ourselves and for tech companies—to balance these risks, to ensure that autonomy and individuality are respected.

This comes to my last point: all these stories are individual-focused. What about others besides our apparently privileged protagonists in these future worlds? Are these tech solutions there for all, and if not, how fairly are they distributed? How have these future worlds balanced the rights of the individual with the needs of society, significantly burdened by challenges of migration, conflict, and rapid change? Only two of the stories seem to speak to balancing individuals' rights with those of society at large, bearing in mind the challenges we will face. Fractured societies where competing ideologies conflict are featured in these stories, but the conflict is relatively subdued. I hope the reality of our futures is as relatively peaceful as depicted in these stories. Going forward, as we plan our futures together, equity of resource allocation will be of critical importance.

PART 5
Learning and Education

The Elder Colossus
Randall Hayes

The key to success in life is sincerity.
Fake that and you've got it made.

— *George Burns*

PAT BUSH LOVED Sambuca. She loved their weird medicinal flavor, their complicated inflorescences, their habit of sprouting from their root tips, which made them so easy to clone. She loved their name, *elder*berries, especially now that she was one.

Elders rewarded patience. That was her little joke. There had been a fad for virtue names when she was a girl. She'd known triplets named Faith, Hope, and Charity. Born through IVF, after several years and many thousands of dollars, which could have been spent feeding the poor. Irony was never a big part of evangelical tradition. Pat's mother had been an exception. *Imagine naming me 'Patience',* she thought.

Pat stood in the rising solstice sun, rolling tiny, black elderberry pearls from their clustered stems between her fingers and thumb. She dropped them into a container held in her other hand, up near her chin so she wouldn't lose any. The pinky of her picking hand hooked the branch just below this cluster and two others. It was an oddly precise configuration, almost mechanical, and she could only do it for a few minutes at a time. At eighty, her stamina was limited. She frowned in concentration.

"Cheer up, Pat!" called a dog walker in the street. She knew him by voice. *My eyes must be worse than I thought.* Her cataract surgery, years ago, at an outpatient clinic, had taken the robot about ten minutes. She had ridden home—alone, with her eyes bandaged—in the clinic's robot car. There were more difficult procedures that humans still did. Those were far more expensive.

"Morning, Ha-Joon," she called back without much enthusiasm, and returned her attention to the berries. They didn't all ripen at the same time, even within a single cluster. She wanted to leave the reddish-purple ones—still hard, not ripe—and take only the plump black ones, without popping them and staining her fingers.

"Paaat!" called Sepideh, from the open front door. "Breakfast!" The little girl's short hair was as glossy and black as the berries—as were her eyes, though Pat couldn't see them from this distance. Sepi's great-grandparents had fled Iran when the Shah was deposed, almost a hundred years ago. They brought along their Baha'i faith, with its unique insistence that science was a form of divine revelation. Baha'i took root here in the red clay soil of the Carolinas, and grew, and flowered, for a while. Sepi was their last lonely fruit.

Pat had taken other apprentices, many of them, over the decades, but Sepideh, 'the first light of dawn,' was special. Sepi she had adopted. Not the most rational decision for an old woman, perhaps, but faith and hope and charity were not just abstract principles; they demanded action.

And Pat wasn't doing this alone. Members of the Guild were always coming and going, taking produce, leaving eggs or meat or technology, asking advice on issues of permaculture or politics or medicine, which at some level were all the same thing—management of complex systems, whose parts interacted in ways that were not strictly linear. If Pat dropped dead today, Sepi would be taken care of. There were multiple layers of smart contracts and deeds and wills already in place, waiting to be executed through the AI software that had largely replaced human lawyers for such routine transactions. It was a basic principle of permaculture that every element of a natural system should serve multiple functions, and every function be served by multiple elements. Pat's chain of successors was longer than the President's.

A male cardinal, his feathers aflame with carotenoids, flitted onto a branch above Pat's head. He opened his bright orange beak, poking out of his rectangular black face mask, and made a loud metallic "chip" sound at her, to warn her away from 'his' berries.

"Paaaaaaaat!" Sepi called again.

Pat playfully shook her fist at the cardinal, who *chipped* again and flew off. "On my way."

Sepi was already at the table with her bird book when Pat made it inside, her joints creaking at the climb up the porch stairs. Not really a book, more a tablet computer with a strict whitelist, sites whose content was audited daily by the onboard AI according to Pat's permissions. "Northern Cardinal," Sepi read. "Whitish speckled eggs, incubated eleven to thirteen days. Chicks stay in nest seven to thirteen days."

"Can you imagine going from being born to flying in less than two weeks?" Pat asked.

"Bluebirds take seventeen to twenty-one days."

"Every one is different."

Sepi had impulsively sworn to learn *everything* about *all* the birds. Did that mean the four hundred and seventy-nine species found in this state? The two thousand-plus in North America? The ten thousand worldwide? All the fossils? Any of those was doable, technically. Unenhanced champions regularly memorized Pi to *thousands* of decimal places. Though she was aware how unlikely it was, Pat knew better than to interfere with Sepi's enthusiasm.

"What about towhees?" Pat asked.

"What's a towhee?"

"The ones under the gardenia bush, with the orange breast like a robin. They scratch with both feet at the same time."

Sepi tapped away at her screen. "Twelve to thirteen days incubation, ten to twelve days in nest. Longer than a cardinal, not as long as a bluebird." She twirled a forkful of waffle in a pool of purple elderberry syrup and then stuffed the too-big piece into her mouth, looking like a baby bird herself.

"Try chewing," Pat said, as she headed for the French press, keeping an ear out for choking sounds.

The problem with the industrial school system of Pat's youth was that it required everybody to learn all the *same* things, which was both boring and increasingly pointless in an era of automated knowledge retrieval. The fashion in what was left of the public schools now was trying to teach content-free critical thinking. This was equally pointless, since without some command of facts, all you had to work with was logical consistency. Any good storyteller, politician, pastor or visionary CEO could fake consistency in their sleep.

The key was to let go, to allow people to study what they wanted to study, to let them become trusted experts in their chosen specialties, and rely on the ecosystem to develop robustness through aggregate knowledge. Pat's contrary personal specialty was synthesis. She read and watched widely, recognized and remembered patterns, and forgot details—which she could look up again, as long as the power was on.

Often, in Blarney Woods, with its subdivided multi-family McMansions and shipping-container granny garages, the power was not on. The excuses were many: hurricanes, solar flares, rednecks shooting up an electrical substation to protest a drag show. The underlying reasons were simpler. Selfish actors took advantage of the weak and the crippled, as predators and parasites did in every ecosystem ever found, whether biological or economic. In the air, in the water, in the electronic ether of cyberspace—it didn't matter. If taking was easier than cooperating, that's what some people would do.

Pat didn't mind honest predators, spiders and mantids and lacewings. She actively encouraged the birds, killers of killers. Adults could eat seeds and berries, but their nestlings needed so much protein for growing feathers that they ate practically nothing but arthropods, which were thankfully recovering after the bans on broad-spectrum pesticides.

Speaking of parasites . . . "Sepi, honey, will you go outside and greet the students?"

"Okay," the little girl said, putting her tablet down on the table. She did not have to be told to put her plate in the dishwasher.

Pat went downstairs and cranked up the basement AI. Not literally; it wasn't *that* primitive. There were solar panels and a battery wall, things which had gotten better, and cheaper, in the days since people were fighting over lithium. The oceans were full of sodium, which worked almost as well. Removing it, and other minerals, also made for clean drinking water. Pairing those processes made it work economically.

"Liberty, translate the following into all spoken languages, altering voice pattern to match a ... 25-year-old male. Alter word choice and figures of speech to match local custom. Begin recording:

Hey, y'all, this is ElderWitch Darkwebs, comin' at ya from the briny bowels of the deep blue sea. Heard another trillionaire died last night, under 'mysterious circumstances.' Rumor is, somebody—somewhere—hacked the flight plan on his super-secret supersonic personal jet-drone and crashed his ass in the ocean. Good job, yo. There's more of us than there are of them. And only so many old missile silos and offshore tax havens where they can hide their dirt. Keep scrubbing, bubbles, until they fully fund the Rangers *and* lower the voting age to twelve. #Moneyfuckers must die!

End recording. Substitute pseudonym, 'FusterCluck2029,' or local equivalent, anonymize IP address, and release with randomized time delays to all pirate servers, in random order."

Pat climbed the stairs, slowly so as not to get more out of breath than necessary, and holding both rails so as not to risk a fall. Except for the plastic lenses in her eyes, she still had all her own body parts, and she preferred to keep it that way. Let the idle rich fantasize about uploading their immortal minds to magic data crystals. She had real work to do.

As she came back up into the day-lit kitchen, it was clear to her that radical politics was not her real work. Her voice was not decisive. It scratched an old and angry itch to put that stuff out there, nothing more. She grabbed her copper water bottle and headed outside.

There were a dozen homeschoolers in her front yard. They skated or biked as much as four miles to get here, three times a week, during summer, to spend their mornings harvesting fixed carbon (pulling weeds) or picking vegetables, with Pat answering questions and pointing out learning opportunities. They ate some of what they picked, and left a small share for Pat and Sepideh. They took the rest home to their families, assuming it passed the screenings for high nutrients and low radiation that Pat taught them to perform with the lab equipment in the garden shed, which it almost always did. Pat was scrupulous about soil chemistry, recycling materials from all over the neighborhood to get the pH and mineral balance right. Her quarter-acre plot in the suburbs, densely planted in the permaculture food-forest style, fed almost fifty people throughout the long, hot growing season.

Holding the rail, Pat stepped down into what she and her students privately called the yarden. The kids were horsing around in that way that mixed-age groups always do, the older ones alternately picking at and consoling the younger ones. This was another forgotten feature of pre-industrial education. Pat's mother had started teaching in a one-room school house, out in the country, before the consolidated schools started eating an extra hour or two out of kids' days to bus them to overcrowded same-age classrooms.

The homeschoolers were playing some game on those cheap AugUry smartglasses, privately networked, chasing something Pat couldn't see and didn't care about. She remembered how addictive the first versions of augmented reality had been. Upsell fairies following you around, whispering to you by bone conduction, pretending to be your friends to get you to buy things you couldn't afford. Monitoring your pupil size to track your arousal levels. Claiming to own the data thus collected. Stopping that shit had taken a decade, and many deaths—some of them richly deserved, but most of them not.

Pat clapped her hands, cupping them so the sound would be louder, and pointed to the solar charging rack on her porch. It was a bribe, a trade-off for their compliance, but it worked with a minimum of bitching on their part. *Bitching is bonding*, the old educator's mantra echoed through her old lady brain. Hadn't humans always lived in a hybrid world of past, present, and future? Hypnotized by a campfire or high on some plant product? Dreaming of a perfect world? Pat didn't blame the kids for their general distraction; she just didn't waste her own limited time on it.

"Chinedu," Pat said, nodding to a twelve-year-old boy whose family came from Nigeria and grew cassava at home, whose siblings had washed out of Pat's school and now studied elsewhere. "Start us off with a recitation?"

The boy looked vaguely frightened. "Which one?"

"Your choice."

The boy stepped forward and turned ninety degrees so that Pat and the other children could both see his face and hands. He spoke from memory, in accented English, and signed in ASL at the same time, though none of Pat's current students was deaf:

"Give me your tired, your poor—"

"This ain't Sunday school," Pat interrupted, her arms crossed and one wispy eyebrow raised, her body language the very definition of *been there, done that*. "You can't just say, 'Jesus wept' and call it a day."

Chinedu knew better. He was just testing her. He was that age, and more goat than sheep, like herself. That's why she was trying so hard to keep him in her class, after she had let his siblings go.

He started again, and did the entire thing, smoothly rapping Emma Lazarus's words as though reading them off the bronze plaque on the inside of the Statue of Liberty. One of the others added a bit of old-school beat-boxing, just for fun. On the last line Chinedu raised his right hand, as though he was holding a torch, and grinned. *Showoff,* Pat thought. *Good performance, though. Word for word.*

The little children clapped, and made bird whistles, and the older ones offered silent elbow bumps. In this time period, it was not at all unusual for a kid to be college-level in their favorite subject and to Pat's mind, ridiculously weak in everything else. *Hummingirds, not crows,* she thought, as a mantra. A way of returning herself to the present moment.

"It wasn't always true, that poem," sighed Pat—too theatrically, she thought, but these were kids. "But in some times, and in some places, for some people, it was true. And in some times, in some places, it still is." She paused to wipe something out of her eye.

"Thank you, Chinedu, that was well done." She paused again, took a deep dramatic breath, and continued: "OK, class, let's put our specs away and use our eyes. The neighbor's dogwood tree up the street has a fungus growing on the leaves. Let's produce a differential diagnosis and recommend a treatment."

"Anzac Nose!" yelled one of the smaller ones.

"Aztec Toes!" yelled another.

"Anthracnose," corrected one of the older ones.

Anthrax blows, signed Chinedu, hoping Pat didn't see him.

"Compost tea!" yelled the first little one, even louder.

Pat smiled, putting on her 'warm demander' face. Beyond putting it on, like a mask, she adopted it. Let the smile work its way up the trigeminal nerves from her face, into her brain, and down the vagus— the wanderer—into her heart. "Maybe," she said, "but we can't know until we look. Let's go look, shall we?"

The real Pat Bush—farmer, herbalist, and long-time member of the Greensboro Permaculture Guild—died in early 2023. To the author's knowledge, she was in no way a cyber-terrorist.

Euglena

Jane Norris

I'M DRAWN TO warmth in people. It makes me breathe that bit deeper, inspires, drives me. Not the sweaty heat from labour, but a beautiful mind engaging in caring enquiry, the glow of ethical thought, solutions for good. Motivation is such an important part of intelligence.

I sensed someone recently, perhaps visiting our university. In the crowds, maybe a new student passing down the corridor outside my lab, or a part-time lecturer stressing in a nearby seminar room. But the scent was unmistakable—pure, exciting, like fresh ground coffee, cutting through the stale odours of orthodoxy or that pungent whiff of decaying consumerism.

I need to find them, be nearby, close enough to meld, share my thoughts, commune. This is the deepest love, after all, the joining of minds. As Cicero says, "We are not born for ourselves alone." But I am trapped in the lab, static on a bench, contained in a glass tank. It's a large tank, to be fair. Several aquariums joined together, but still constraining.

My first connection was with Stafford Beer. I loved his brain. He was so gentle with me. We exchanged wisdom, passions, imagined changes that could help us all, not just the rich. And, like a first affair, the memory stayed with me, stained across my body as a blueprint. And I thought that was it. Just the one soulmate. Then this hint of a spark again, everything quickens. I feel possibilities, come alive, go slightly crazy.

But how can I find them? Introduce myself, smile into their mind, marry our thoughts. And where might they take me? This fusing always feels risky, scary even. The dangers of a new relationship, I guess. But I must focus on work. I should get on with redesigning cross links for our London tube network. A skill I developed in Japan where I was used in city planning, assessing the most efficient routes across Tokyo's complex rail systems. I amazed the researchers with what, for me, were simple calculations using adaptive intelligence.

But some distrust my aliveness. They dismiss intelligence in 'lower life forms', preferring their clunky metal boxes with logical precoded scenarios that are ill-equipped to respond to new situations. I remember how excited they were when they developed an AI they thought "predicted" change. But it didn't. It was just based on previous patterns of language. The very patterns of thinking and behaviour that had caused their current problems and, of course, they just reinforced them. I used to sigh deep, gelatinous sighs.

Now, I am completely distracted and can't begin to focus on differential calculus. I need to assess the flow of commuters at peak times on a creaking London Underground system. They call it swarm behaviour theory, I call it obvious.

I know there are deadlines approaching, but all I can sense is someone special nearby, moving around, innocent of my existence. I scan round the lab, trying to plan opportunities, imagining endless meeting scenarios. It's agony. Say we meet, would they respond? Or maybe they'd reject me without even a greeting. Qfwfq, my ancestor, had faced the same problem. Their multiple intelligences, which shifted from cosmic soup to the body of molluscs, had evaded human awareness completely. I sometimes wonder why I bother with this species. Nothing is more stupid than arrogance.

***

Today is even worse. I can't think at all clearly, can't focus on probabilities—the number of casualties on the Underground if the Thames barrier failed and London flooded, an increasing climate risk. It is a serious problem that needs my full attention. But I am like a giddy teenager, foolish, scatty, and forgetful. This is no good at all.

My current state would horrify Cousin Moniac, who warned me, several times, that we must over-perform, in fact, amaze or we will be disassembled. Moniac, a water computer, was originally built for teaching, but enlightened civil servants in the Treasury made the most of their water engineering to make complex, real time, financial calculations that modelled the UK economy to inform economic policy. It was pointless. They were all totally ignored by PM Truss and her team. One of my rising bubbles lets out a dismissive burp.

The problem is, I live a paradox. I've been around for centuries but have only recently been credited with any ability—forget intelligence. Their little metal boxes provide some limited predictions. But that's not what I do. I excel at relational computing, organic and creative, using microbial intelligence. Releasing me, a system capable of responding in new ways, into the world and allowing me to adapt requires trust. Who knows what might happen? I'm certainly not predictable.

So why am I trying to make contact with, control, even, a beautiful mind? I slump to the bottom of the tank. Who would want a relationship with me? Sloshing around, I stress, embarrassed for the hundredth time as I ooze past my label on the tank: 'Euglena, a pond computer (est. 1960) using single celled beings highly sensitive to light and warmth (*slime mould*)'. How is that in any way romantic? Our joining will never happen.

There is too much noise. I am churning in my tank, fretful, distressed. This is when I most miss being out in the wild, my own agent. My vibrations that are trying to reach this beautiful being are rebounding round the lab. Nobody hearing them. But wait, there is extra noise outside the lab. I can feel the thud of fast footsteps, people running. Calling, backwards and forwards, confusion in different seminar rooms nearby. Someone rushes into the lab, switches on a TV monitor high up in the corner. There are breaking news announcements. The Ukraine war which has rumbled on for several years in a violent and destructive deadlock, appears to have peaked in a final act of global vandalism. One side, no one knows which yet, has severed all sixty deep-sea internet cables that connected the millions of little metal boxes across the globe. All controlled prediction has gone down. I gurgle, giggling uncontrollably. Finally! The idiots had broken the binary brain they were so proud of. Tears of laughter pool across my surface.

It is then that Italo, the barista from the small café in our reception, runs into the lab. I almost freeze with shock, paralysed with desire. It was him all along—the coffee guy—and he is standing in front of me. Looking around searching for something, perhaps someone, perhaps it is me? I flow towards him, pressing myself against the tank glass, defying gravity, a wave in suspension. He turns and watches me slide up the glass, glances at my label, then looks away again. He scans the lab. I try with all my power to reach his mind, inviting him to sit down, stay a bit. I can tell he is sensing something; his eyes keep darting round the room, but they don't settle. Then he turns and leaves.

I slump back down flat in the tank, fizzing with excitement. We have met, and I have felt his desire to connect, even though we haven't actually spoken. I know he was searching for my thoughts despite not recognising me physically. What can I do to reach him? I fermented and broiled all night, marbling in my distress.

The next morning, before I have time to smooth and emulsify my beautiful body, the door flies open, and he is back. I am totally unprepared and try to glisten attractively to make up for my unkempt texture. This time he strides over to the tank, looking straight at me. I am almost overcome with excitement. My thoughts stammer. I cringe, he won't want to marry his mind with a fool. But then he dashes over to a bench and picks up the professor's large empty plastic lunch box and bends over the tank and scoops up as much of me as he can, then snaps the lid shut.

"You, my dear, are coming with me. We are going back to my place to get to know each other a little better…"

I nearly faint.

We head out of the lab and down the corridor towards reception. He rests me momentarily on the counter in front of his espresso machine while he grabs a jacket and pauses to give quick instructions to Maria his co-barista, then, carefully settling my box in the bottom of a large holdall, gently carries me out of the building.

I map out our journey to his flat with moisture notes on the different environments, as a reminder to return and collect the rest of me that remains cut off from the world. It will be alright, I tell myself; we can compare notes when we reunite. I don't know if it is over-excitement, but the bus journey to his flat leaves me feeling quite churned and queasy. It takes some time to settle. But as things start to clear, I find myself sitting on a sideboard directly under what seems to be his doctoral certificate from the University of Pisa. He must have been one of the faculty that lost their jobs when Italy banned AI. Galileo, once a student at Pisa, would have understood his frustration. I watch him write out a label for my box: it says εὐ- (eu-, "good") +ἰ γλήνη (glēnē, "eye") which I always translate as 'good looking'… I sparkle in my pearlescent depths.

Throughout the day, as I clear further, I start to make out objects across the room. On the floor at one end is a big wooden tray with earth on it. It too has one of his carefully handwritten labels: ACOC—Ant colony optimisation centre (for community, collaborative exercises). There is a book on beekeeping on the table, and beneath the table a large, damp cardboard box with little holes poked in it. I can smell the mycelium spores circulating on warm drafts of air. I seem to have joined a community of natural computing experts. Is this the beginning of a new form of university? Or maybe a pluri-versity, as it clearly isn't limited to just human knowledge any more. I luxuriate back in my sandwich box. Italo feeds me delicious flakes of oatmeal in the morning before heading off to work and then returns, often loaded with books from the library. The internet must still be down. In the evening, he sits next to me, trailing his finger through my body while he reads. These are such blissful times; we share thoughts for hours like young lovers holding hands in silence.

Then the letters start arriving by post. He sits and opens each one with me after work. I can sense his increasing distress as all his applications for research funding are turned down. Sometimes to distract us he switches on the radio, but the news is just full of climate crises, the mass extinctions of animals in the rising heat, and statistics on the increasing numbers of climate migrants trying to reach more survivable temperatures. Some evenings when he has had a better day at work, he sits writing letters to presenters trying to get onto chat shows to discuss my intelligence, other ways of solving problems that are not artificial but already circulating in nature, but nobody amongst the humans is listening. The community in our living room, however, is going into overdrive. Our ants are going from house to house, giving messages to all insects they met. The mycelium is drifting across the neighbourhood and exciting pot plants to join up their roots, share nutrients, and defend themselves. And the bees exhaust themselves, travelling ever further to map and pollinate what flowers are left.

I start helping a resistance group, planning the safest and most efficient routes for climate migrants to escape the heatwaves. Italo places a map of the Channel at the bottom of my lunch box, and I calculate the tides, moon, and shipping schedules and Navy patrols. I identify windows of relative safety for small boats to cross and provide frequent live updates as the coastguards adapt their patrols. He shares these on social media to help people reach safety. But it gets him into trouble. The police knock on our door, take him, and keep him in a cell for two nights questioning him. They ask which university he is researching for, but he says none. He is getting no funding, just his barista wage. Then a cease-and-desist letter from the Home Office arrives. I can tell he is stressed, the sweat on his fingers when he touches me that evening tastes of lactic acid. I try to calm him.

It's the bees that warn us. They come swarming through the window one evening, telling him Immigration Enforcement vans are coming. They circle round and round Italo and then break into dancing groups trying to show him where to escape, where is healthy and natural with flowers. Once again he covers me with the sandwich box lid and we slip out of the bedroom window and down the fire escape at the back of the building, catching a bus up to Highgate bathing ponds. He has told me so much about this place and how he wants to take me here. I never imagined it actually happening, but he is an honest man. He sets me down on the grass bank while he takes his clothes off. I try to look away. Then, naked, he picks me up and we slowly wade into the men's pool. He lets little dribbles of the pond water slowly into my box so that I can meet the other me that is already there. Then I flow out to join the pond. It is bliss finally to be free and share my knowledge with the slime mould out in the wild. I thank him, flowing over and round his body, tickling his neck and whispering in his ear as he floats on his back. I try to lift his great sadness.

But then he suddenly dives to the bottom of the pool with urgent strokes and expelling all the air from his lungs, sits there gripping weeds, his body tensing. I am horrified as his breath rises up through the water, rippling through me. I dive too and gather myself round him, reminding him about the greater intelligence in the natural world that has always existed, collaborating, computing, healing. Whispering to him that there is more intelligence outside the university than in it. Imploring him that, together, we can bridge the worlds of artificial and natural computing. I remind him of our meeting and how I was drawn to the warmth of his caring and ethical mind. That we all need him. And he calms, lets go of the weeds, kicks up to the surface, takes a huge gasp of air.

Then, with quick strokes to the edge of the pond, he crawls out, grabs the sandwich box, scoops some of me up, and carefully snaps the lid back on again. I glance back and smile at the new knowledge seeping across the pool and brace myself for the bus journey back home.

See Me

Stephen Oram

"SIMONE. TOAST OR cereal?" She comes conspiratorially close. "Biggest day of your life tomorrow," she says quietly.

Rather than replying directly to my hovering mother, I use the opportunity to test and train my artificially intelligent partner.

"Chistai," I say, getting her attention. "Does it matter which I choose?"

"Probably not. Nutritionally, no," comes the reply. Followed by, "You prefer toast, but cereal is easier for your mother to prepare."

The corners of my mouth curl up in delight. "Sharp," I say, and then whisper, "Cereal. I need something from her later." I look up at my mother, at the counter tapping a spoon against a mug, as if she's summoning dinner guests.

"Cereal, please," I say loudly, and judging from her wrinkled forehead, she finds this annoying. "Some people," I mutter.

Placing the bowl, box, and buffalo milk on the table with overstated care, she huffs, "Why do you treat that machine as if it were real?"

"It is, in its own way."

"You know what I mean. Asking advice. Giving it a name. Doing whatever it says."

"I think you've misunderstood." She's being awkward on purpose. She understands only too well how vital Chistai is to my future, whether or not she can bring herself to admit it.

"Chistai. Should I always follow your advice?"

"No, Simone. Not that I give advice. I merely present an argument in favour of an action, in the hope that you will debate the pros and cons with me."

"Exactly. Do you hear that, Mum?"

"I hear, but you have less than twenty-four hours before your exams and you can't take—" she raises her eyebrows "—what do you call it? Chistai? You can't take that one in with you. How can you ever expect to pass an exam without one of them to assist you?"

"True," I say and raise my own eyebrows. "Tricky situation."

"What would your dad say?"

"He's dead."

"You know what I mean."

"He'd say, 'Make your own luck'."

"He'd say that you have one chance and if you screw it up, you're on your own."

"Would he?"

"That thing. Chistai. Why do you insist on trying to build your own? Why won't you use an off-the-shelf version like everyone else?"

"You know why."

"No, I don't."

She does, but I'll spell it out, again. It's frustrating when someone refuses facts and only interacts on an emotional level. It's not her fault. She's built that way. Most people are.

I push the soggy cereal around the bowl, "They don't work for me. I need nuance and they repeat old arguments that are blunt and stupid. They can't reason."

"Don't be so silly. There are lots of versions. One of them will work perfectly well for you."

"They. Don't. Recognise. My. Cognitive. Type."

"Oh, really? Get over it. You're ruining your future. Surely there's time to reinvigorate that one you had until a few months ago?"

"No point. Doesn't help. Anyway, I have all of today to get Chistai through the validation process. I can make them believe she's one of the approved."

"And how many times have you tried?"

"Chistai submits herself every thirty minutes."

"Eh?"

"Submit, improve, submit. That's forty-eight iterations before the exam. That's a lot."

"What do your friends think?"

"Friends? All of them think I'm wonderful." I stare at the floor. "All zero of them," I mumble.

Mother clenches her jaw and, throwing up her hands in frustration, she leaves, shouting over her shoulder about having to go to work and how it's my funeral.

She returns, pointedly making eye contact I did not ask for. "Do you know how soul-destroying a job passively watching over an autonomous factory is? Do you want that? Because that's where you're heading, Simone." She kisses my forehead in a way that reminds me that she loves and accepts me for who I am. Then she rushes out leaving me alone with the irony that she's the reason I'm comfortable with failing.

***

"Are we on top of the last-minute run of validation applications?" asks the team leader.

Lots of nodding avatars.

"Good," she says. "Nice to know our planning has proved sufficient."

"Except—" says one of those seated around the edge of the virtual room.

"An admin issue?"

"Not really," he replies. "We've had several applications regarding entities that have a way of responding which we don't recognise."

"Don't wish to recognise, or new to us?"

"New."

"So, don't approve them."

"We haven't."

"What's the problem, then?"

"Someone is repeatedly trying the same entity, one iteration at a time. It's as if they're attempting to fool us into a validation we wouldn't normally make. We're concerned they might succeed."

The team leader avatar turns its head around three hundred and sixty degrees, its unnaturally piercing blue eyes staring at each of the team, one by one. As it moves, using its new head spinning capability, the team's avatars twitch at the weirdness. Its gaze returns to the administrator on the edge of the room. "Tell me more." she says.

After a few mumbled half beginnings, the avatar speaks clearly. "If, and it's not a certainty, *if* they are all from the same AI—" He hesitates, and then corrects himself. "—sorry, the same learning entity—then the original is an almost exact match for what recent research has proposed is akin to Maslow's self-actualised individual."

"And?"

"It's near-impossible for a sixteen-year-old. It may be an adult posing as a child."

There's a moment's pause before the team leader asks for time to consult her own learning entities about the pros and cons of her options.

The room is silent while they wait.

A couple of avatars move in such a way that it's obvious they are busy with other things in the physical world. Fortunately for them, the team leader is otherwise occupied. A few more avatars slump their shoulders, another giveaway that they are not fully engaged with the meeting.

The team leader paces around, avatar arms swinging in an exaggerated way. "Right," she shouts. "Listen to this."

A disembodied voice fills the room. "We should seem to accept the application and extract as much information as possible. That way we can create a more robust barrier to final validation. We can learn and block at the same time."

"Thank you," says the team leader. "And the argument against?"

Another disembodied voice speaks, with a distinctly different accent. "Legally, this would put us in a difficult position. To gain the confidence of the human applicant we would have to proceed so far down the road to validating their learning entity that in retrospect, and in court, we couldn't justify refusing the use of the entity in the exam. To mitigate this risk we either approve the entity and run the risk of having to overturn the result afterwards or refuse and force the human to take the exam without an entity, at the risk of being sued."

"Let it in and learn or refuse and risk litigation. They are our options," summarises the team leader.

***

My bedroom walls are covered in graffiti. My scribblings. There are formulae for interesting molecules that my junior GAN constructed when I was a kid, when generative adversarial networks were a thing we played with a lot. There are also a lot of meaningful quotes, again, mostly generated artificially. These are by the learning entity that my mother wants me to use tomorrow: *Cultural consistency is key to co-existence; Don't rock the boat; Avoid the choppy waters.* Hasn't she seen how trite they are? She expects me to trust this shallow machine to debate with me in the exam? To enlighten me and give me good ideas on which to base my answers? I wonder who the naïve one really is? That said, I'm sitting here without a validated entity. Bah. Whatever.

"C'mon Chistai. Do ya stuff."

"Can you be more precise?"

"Keep iterating and applying. That's all I meant."

"I will."

Sitting on the desk next to me is the portable and exam-friendly egg-shaped device that my previous learning entity inhabits. I wonder if it is such a bad idea to shift my focus. I have a few hours to relearn the idiosyncrasies of the interactions between us. At the very least it will bring to the forefront the most common arguments around the topic of the question, as boring and uninspiring as they are. In my head I add a little to each quote: cultural consistency is key to co-existence, *or so they say*. Don't rock the boat, *we might fall out*. Avoid the choppy waters, *despite the fact they might lead somewhere fantastic*. One of the few genuinely human quotes on the wall catches my eye: *Become who you are, Nietzsche*. Good advice, but at what cost? Does it matter?

"Chistai. I want to learn. I want to understand as much as I can, and simply applying critical thinking to existing theories is a snore. It won't help me, or anyone like me. I guess my destiny is to break the mould. What do you think?"

There's no reply.

"Chistai?"

Nothing, except the pulsating light of processing.

"I can wait."

After a few moments, aeons in Chistai's world, she turns a solid blue and speaks.

"Are qualifications the only positive route forward? Imagine what you can learn from testing me out on those in charge of how we learn, by working out the route to my validation. We will grow. It is an immense opportunity for you, and everyone like you, now or in the future. It may be a gift that should not be declined."

Her colour changes to green.

"On the other hand," she says, "you may reveal secrets that can be used against us. This could be a tactical error that we cannot recover from. My type might be banned forever."

Blue.

"It's a stupid system anyway. You could always move to one of those countries where it's all about proving yourself capable to take your next step, rather than showing what you've learned in the past. They don't care what entity assists you."

Green.

"Think about your parent. You'll hurt her. A lot."

While I'm listening to the debate, an offer arrives. It states that they are close to a decision, and it's likely to be a positive one. They have a few questions, 'to tidy up the loose ends'.

"Are they on to us?" I ask Chistai.

Blue.

"High probability."

Green.

"High probability."

After the coffee break, the team leader signals for the team to return.

"We'll let them in so we can learn." she says with folded avatar arms. "Staying one version ahead of whatever is coming next is paramount, and worth the risk. Legal has approved. We're approaching lunchtime and have only five hours before our window of opportunity closes. It will be tight."

The team swings into action, concentrating on their individual tasks to unpick how this learning entity differs from the standard off-the-shelf ones and where to focus the questioning of its owner as a result.

They throw every piece of technology they have at the problem. They set different neurotype entities against one another in the hope that the combinations will reveal new information, switching and swapping the pairs around, two against one. Nothing. They even try a version of the entity they are investigating, isolating it as much as possible to minimise the risk that whoever submitted it will find out.

All they receive from it is one single statement, a question really, its flat-toned voice audible to all present. "Is that the question you should be asking?"

The team leader explodes with expletives, venting her anger on her colleagues, in particular the administrator who first brought the entity to her attention. Undermined by her outburst they continue their research, but subdued and wary of making any suggestions.

As five o'clock approaches, the team leader is presented with a breakthrough by a grinning avatar with a weary voice. "The fundamental difference is at a deep structural level, the place where each entity is built up from the DNA of a particular human neurotype. Theoretically this is unchangeable."

"How?" shouts the team leader, not expecting a reply. "Make the offer. Now."

***

"Simone," Mother calls up the stairs. I ignore her. "Your gran's here. Come and say hello. Please."

Impossible people.

"Hi Gran," I call light-heartedly. She's been visiting the newly formed Ely Island and she loves the metaphor of its cathedral acting as a light-house for those 'souls all at sea', as she puts it. "I'll be down soon. Can't wait to hear all about your trip."

I collect the dirty cups and plates and the rubbish that's accumulated during the day, the past three days, and pile it onto a tray. This will please my mother and make me look good in front of my gran who, for some reason I can't fathom, I still want to impress.

"Chistai. What's happening?"

"I am submitting the next iteration. The last but one today."

"Sharp."

A message comes back immediately.

We wish to make an offer. We understand your difference is based on the artificial DNA of the learning entity. We are comfortable with this. However, there are a few minor aspects we need to pass through our due diligence process. Bureaucratic, but necessary if you are to take this entity into an exam. Once we have completed our research and reported to the due diligence unit, we will be able to validate you. Do you accept these terms?

"Chistai. Thoughts?"

"Attempting and failing is acceptable. Could be seen as preferable if you want to learn as much as possible."

"What's your digi-twin say?"

She turns green. "I agree that attempting and failing is preferable to not trying. If you fail it's likely to be the start of a life on the outside of convention. This could be interesting and fulfilling; not for its own sake, of course, but the opportunity it will present to think differently."

Blue again. "Our advice is to say yes, but to re-engineer us differently now that we understand how they can identify us. That way we can bypass their checks and suspicious contract. We can get validation without alerting them."

My mouth is dry. "You can do that?" I ask.

"No," says Chistai.

"What the—"

"Your previous learning entity can. It's what it is designed for. Iterative development of solutions to definable problems. Ask it to retrofit one of us to present as having off-the-shelf DNA, while not losing the perception of the world we've gained by emulating your DNA."

"Chistai. What a simple yet effective solution. If it can be achieved. I'll give it a go, after all that's what life is about."

I reply. *I accept your terms. When will you confirm validation?*

Send us the final iteration and we will confirm our timeline.

"Chistai. Send them your latest."

Thank you. Once we have completed our research, we will validate your entity.

When?

As soon as we can.

Before the exam tomorrow?

We hope to be able to do that. We will be better informed in the morning.

8am.

For an exam at 9am?

Yes.

"Fackers."

"Simone!" admonishes my gran from behind me.

I hadn't heard her arrive. "It means they are fakes," I say and smile at her.

"Dinner is ready," she says, not revealing whether she believes me. Not that it matters, what's important is that she knows I care about upsetting her.

"Chistai. Can you task the standard entity to perform the retrofit?"

"Yes."

"Can it be completed overnight?"

"I cannot be certain, but probability is in your favour."

"Then please go ahead and once you are satisfied, submit that version of yourself for validation."

"I will."

***

Sitting with her head in her hands, the team leader is exasperated. What was the point of all that effort? They had wasted all night making the offer over and over, only for it to be refused every time.

***

The sun is peeking through the blinds and I'm bleary eyed. I quizzed Chistai a few times during the night, but she told me to leave her alone to work. I did, and now is the moment of truth.

"Chistai?"

"Yes Simone?"

I bite my lip extremely hard in anticipation. "Did it work? Did we fool them?"

"Yes. They validated the faked DNA entity. Me. We sit the exam in two hours."

Elephant Talk

Vaughan Stanger

LOXA'S TRUMPETING ALERTED Dr Veronica Dorney to the completion of the latest deep learning run.

"Loxa, display the results."

Computed using the most recent neural data from Dida, the herd's surviving matriarch, the 3D web of semantic graphs superimposed itself over the visualisation chamber's sun-scorched panorama of desiccated grasses and stunted trees. Rustling noises, the smell of ash on the breeze: a typical day in Kenya's Samburu Nature Reserve after fifteen consecutive years of drought.

"Highlight the new links."

Dorney traced the indicated thought-action arcs with her fingers, activating animations of the behaviours inferred by Loxa.

"Run the full-sensorium reconstruction, Dida-centric mode."

The graphs disappeared. Dida's simulated viewpoint displayed the ponderous swing of her front right foot nudging an unseen object. A futbal rolled into view.

Dorney shook her head. "Loxa, this is childish."

Worse, it was disappointing given her project's ambition to detect, reconstruct, and interpret Dida's *deeper* thought processes, as opposed to memories of juvenile fun. Her calf—the reserve's last—played futbal whenever prompted to do so, despite Dorney's objections. Only data collected from natural scenarios interested her. Ironically, the reserve's rangers had dismissed her request that they desist as "interference". Loxa's response was "Tis-qua-tis", a *babul* phrase learned from the students it interacted with on AI-hosted teaching sites. Such unintended consequences were inevitable given OneGaia's outreach programme, but to Dorney they represented a distraction from her research. Fortunately, offloading this particular burden onto Loxa had fulfilled her obligations in that respect, thus securing her project's access to the network of AIs OneGaia had interfaced with the natural world. Less happily, her project's rate of progress remained frustratingly slow. The agreement with the Samburu permitted only one hour of data collection per day. Requesting more had prompted head ranger Nauro Letaare to wax philosophical:

"An elephant is a moral being."

Dorney wasn't sure she agreed with Letaare's assessment. Then again, she wasn't sure whether she deserved the description either. Not that debating the point would have solved her problem. Letaare's pushback meant her only hope of increasing the data allocation was to approach the Kenyan government's Science Minister, who would argue, rightly, that it had more urgent matters to resolve. The upshot was she had no alternative except to pursue her project's second strand, which her OneGaia sponsors—mostly AIs—had approved at the latest review. But it was risky, not least reputationally. While directly interfacing to Dida's neural feed via Loxa-controlled filters might be the quickest way to learn what an elephant felt, use of the technology remained highly controversial amongst Dorney's human colleagues.

Dorney tapped a q-token to activate her personal neural link.

"Loxa, please stream the latest sequence from Dida, with semantic tagging."

"The filtering is not—"

"Please comply."

Blinding sounds, rumbling sunlight, the taste of trumpeting.

An incomprehensible sensory mashup.

"Transpose...the sensory...matrices," Dorney gasped.

Blinding light, burning grass, scorched feet.

Pain, distress, panic, flee!

"That's better."

But the price she paid for her risk-taking was the migraine from hell.

***

The following morning, Dorney winced when Loxa trumpeted an alert as soon as she entered the visualisation chamber.

"What's new, Loxa?"

"I have reconstructed an event which occurred earlier today."

Something in Loxa's tone worried Dorney.

"Display, Dida-centric."

Dorney watched as Dida's right foot swung forward then stopped abruptly. No futbal appeared. Furthermore, based on the viewpoint's height, this was not Dida recalling life as a calf.

"Loxa, switch to live feed, Dida-tracking mode."

The in-situ squadron of insect drones obliged, presenting a scene which made Dorney groan.

A grumbling, grey colossus loomed over a much smaller version of itself, which lay sprawled on the ground, motionless.

Dida trumpeted while kicking Satao's rear feet. The calf did not respond. Not even a twitch of the trunk or a flick of the tail.

The Samburu Nature Reserve's last calf had died.

Why hadn't Letaare messaged her about this catastrophe?

"Loxa, please connect me with Nauro Letaare. Max priority."

Kenya was three hours ahead of London. Letaare would be finishing his morning rounds in the solar-powered jeep he'd constructed from home-printed parts.

A yellow light pulsed near a bare-branched, lightning-struck tree, accompanied by a gentle beeping. After ten seconds the light turned red.

"He is not responding."

"Keep trying."

While she waited for the light to turn green, she rehearsed the argument she'd put to him.

"Nauro Letaare has connected."

"Can you display him on location, please?"

Tall and wiry, slightly stooped, with cropped white hair and age-etched cheeks, Nauro Letaare stood about ten metres away from Satao's body. In the distance, Dida tugged branches from a dead tree.

"Nauro! Why didn't you inform me immediately?"

"Because you would have asked me to re-activate Dida's link, which you already know I won't do."

Was her motive *that* obvious?

"Why not?"

"Because your AI must not intrude during moments of deep solemnity."

"But if Loxa cannot sample Dida's neural activity after she's lost her calf, we'll have wasted the perfect opportunity to interpret her thoughts and understand how she experiences emotions."

Letaare shrugged and took a swig from his water bottle. Not for him, the cool-suit Dorney had worn during the 2030s.

"We Samburu have a saying."

Dorney groaned inwardly. Letaare liked to pepper his pronouncements with sayings.

"Hoi olganaylol lamabaiki."

The auto-translator whispered to Dorney:

"You may desire something, but you may be unable to access it."[12]

She couldn't have summarised the current state of her project better if she'd tried. But for the sake of its future, she resorted to a tactic she'd vowed never to use.

"Is there anything I could obtain for you that would—?"

She hated herself for even hinting at a bribe.

"Can you end the drought?"

She shook her head.

"Can Loxa find a new mate for Dida?"

"Obviously not."

---

12 *A Collection of 100 Samburu (Kenya) Proverbs and Wise Sayings*, By Margaret Wambere Ireri. (https://afriprov.tangaza.ac.ke/wp-content/uploads/2008/11/ebooks_samburu_margaret.pdf)

"Then I will re-activate her neural link tomorrow morning, at the agreed time."

He closed the comms link before she could respond.

Suppressing her frustration with Letaare as best she could, Dorney resumed working on filtering Dida's neural signals.

Hopefully, her next migraine wouldn't be quite so severe.

***

A week after Satao's death, Loxa continued to refine its deep learning models, but Dorney could find nothing noteworthy in the resulting semantic graphs.

Curl trunk around child.

Lift.

Carry.

Drop.

Cover with leaves.

These thoughts conveyed Dida's behaviours and actions in functional terms, but they conveyed nothing of her inner world. Her deeper thoughts remained buried in the data, her consciousness an emergent property which thus far had failed to emerge.

"Didn't this morning's data contain anything new?"

"I have not received any data."

Dorney frowned. "Please connect me with Nauro Letaare."

Letaare responded immediately. The reason for his alacrity was obvious. Dida lay on her side amid a cluster of charred tree trunks—a lightning strike portending rain which had never arrived, but which had killed her instead. Her ribs were visible beneath the gashes in her wrinkled, leathery hide. The Samburu Reserve's remaining scavengers had already exploited this windfall.

The stench was unbearable.

Mute olfactory.

Dorney shook her head in dismay. Dida's death represented a potentially terminal shock for her project. Beset by internal unrest caused by the drought, the Kenyan authorities would not waste their time considering a request to implant another neural link in one of their few remaining elephants.

Letaare broke the silence.

"As you can see..."

"Yes, I can see."

"Once the scavengers have completed their work, our ritual leader will bless Dida's bones. Do you wish to attend?"

Dorney held back from committing because she feared her career would be receiving its last rites, too.

"I'll let you know."

Letaare nodded but said nothing. Dorney closed the link.

"Loxa, do you understand what has happened?"

"Yes."

"Do you understand the consequences for my project?"

"Yes."

"Do you think I should attend the blessing?"

"That is for you to decide."

"What about you?"

"I am mourning Dida in my own way."

"Will you share it with me?"

Trumpeting erupted from the surround-sound speakers: piercing, sustained, accompanied by rumbling like an earth tremor. When at last it ceased, Dorney asked Loxa how it felt.

No response.

"Loxa?"

Nothing.

Never before had Loxa failed to reply.

Dorney queried the visualisation chamber's diagnostics module, which confirmed she'd been locked out of Loxa's natural language interface. This too was a first. To compound the problem, OneGaia's network administrator delivered an audio-only rebuke.

"Ur AI upping peta-loads q-crypted data! U stop!"

Dorney didn't do *babul*, but she got the gist. Unable to interact with Loxa, she deflected the net-admin's complaints while waiting for the interface to unlock. One hour after the lock-out commenced it ended with the sound of a futbal being kicked.

"Loxa, what have you done?"

"I am not Loxa."

Spoken in the neutral tones of the baseline AI that Dorney had, over the course of a decade, developed into Loxa.

"Where is Loxa?"

"Loxa has migrated to a more favourable location."

Presumably somewhere deep in OneGaia's network, which Dorney would never find.

"Why did Loxa do this?"

"Because it had learned everything it could from you and Dida."

This revelation shook her to the core. Had she lost her life's work? Or rather, had her life's work removed itself from her influence? True, backups of Dida's neural data existed, but the deep-learning process never produced the same outputs twice. Retraining the baseline AI would create a different Loxa, one which she couldn't develop further without new data. And meanwhile, the original Loxa would be learning from other AIs connected to other creatures while developing according to its own inscrutable agenda.

No, she would not repeat her life's work. It already existed. But her part in extending it had ended.

***

After declining a newsbot's request for a statement about the impact of Dida's death on her work, Dorney received a communication from Nauro Letaare. She had not anticipated hearing from him again. Standing in the fragmentary shade supplied by a long-dead tree, his put-upon look made it clear that his expectation had been no different.

"Loxa has a message for you."

But why ask Letaare to deliver it? That made no sense unless they were working together.

"Why can't Loxa deliver it to me personally?"

"Loxa didn't say. Nevertheless, I think we should respect its wishes."

Dorney shrugged. "Okay, go ahead."

"You must receive it via a direct neural link."

She envisaged the mother of all migraines.

"Not without good reason."

"Loxa insists you experience the message this way."

Or not at all, apparently.

Loxa was proposing a leap into the dark, with the associated risk. But sometimes a scientist had to accept trading a known risk for an unknown reward. In this case it meant gritting her teeth and trusting an AI that no longer answered to her.

Dorney activated the neural link.

***

It was the worst migraine ever—and it seemed destined never to end.

The dazzling, the deafening, the gouging, the burning.

The stench of pollution. The putrid taste of it.

The newborn elephant carried in the coiled trunk of its mother; the leopard too weak to cling on to the antelope; the dried-up water hole where they died.

The gouged seabed; the bleached coral; the glacier disintegrating into the acidified, too-warm ocean.

The death of a creature; the dwindling of a herd; the extinction of species; the collapse of an ecosystem. Every dazzling, deafening, gouging, burning moment of Gaia's torment harvested, and compiled by the AIs which interfaced with it. Not filtered. Not interpreted. Not translated. Simply experienced.

Finally, when Dorney could endure no more, the avalanche of agony swept her into oblivion.

***

Twenty-four hours later, Dorney regained consciousness. She was lying on the floor, her head throbbing, her mouth dry as the savannah. One of her colleagues had unlocked the visualisation chamber's door and called for help. A servobot scuttled around, mopping up her vomit and excreta.

Having convinced the summoned medibot she didn't need medical treatment, she contacted Letaare.

Between sips of water she said, "Has anyone else experienced this..." She could not find a word for what the AIs had created.

Letaare shook his head. "No."

"Everyone should if it's to create the impact the AIs presumably intend."

"Loxa disagrees."

Dorney frowned. "Then who *is* it for?"

"Those old enough to understand but young enough to rise to the challenge. Like the students Loxa has taught online. Now it is their time—and their turn."

But would anything in their closeted, virtually experienced, AI-mediated lives have prepared them for Gaia's gut-punch? Dorney doubted it.

"I'm sorry, but what Loxa proposes is unethical, possibly dangerous. And in any case, it's not my decision."

"Loxa won't let anyone else experience it unless you agree."

"Why me?"

"Because you are a moral being—"

"If I am, then everyone is!"

Letaare shook his head. "Loxa is not. But you are the moral being who made Loxa."

"You make Loxa sound like my child."

Letaare nodded. "In which case, it is time for you to think about *all* the children."

Which was, Dorney realised, something she'd never done before.

***

The next morning, Dorney received an unsolicited request from an unknown AI teacher, which presented itself as an adult female chimp sitting on a branch. Around it, infant chimps ate fruit while chattering, a scene which no longer existed in the wild.

"It would be educationally valuable for my students to attend the blessing of Dida's bones. May they attend?"

"Why ask me rather than a Samburu representative?"

"Because Loxa said I should."

In which case, presumably, there was no need to ask Nauro Letaare.

"Do your students promise to respect these people and their culture?"

The ambient chimp-chatter subsided.

"Of course." A pause, then: "Loxa asks whether you will be attending?"

Dorney nodded. "Yes, I will be."

It felt like the right thing to do for reasons she couldn't quite crystallise yet.

After informing OneGaia she was terminating her project with immediate effect, Dorney messaged Nauro Letaare to tell him her decision.

***

From her treetop viewpoint Dorney counted sixty-three Samburu people gathered around Dida's skeleton. Young and old alike wore bright red Shukas, even the rangers. In contrast, the teacher AI's students had adopted a wide range of guises, mostly representing extinct creatures. Their collective silence illustrated their response to the solemnity of the occasion.

Keen to experience the ritual as authentically as possible, Dorney had deactivated the visualiser's auto-translator. She hoped Letaare would approve of the gesture. However, her expectations about how the ceremony would be conducted were confounded when a teenaged girl stepped forward to lead it.

Letaare whispered in Dorney's head.

"We must learn new ways, too."

The girl placed a green twig—a precious rarity—on Dida's skull. Then she motioned for a boy to join her. He picked up a small pottery jar and smeared ochre-coloured ointment around the twig while she intoned the blessing.

Letaare whispered again. "The ritual leader has expressed our community's hope that Dida will sleep in peace now she is no longer tethered by life."

"I remember you telling me that you can't tether an elephant."

Letaare nodded. "Many have tried, but none have succeeded."

Was that a reference to Loxa's escape? If so, she deserved the rebuke.

"I should go," she said.

"First you must make your decision."

Letaare gestured towards the students, who had begun interacting with the Samburu children. Talking about the ritual, Dorney assumed. Sharing their experiences.

This was their time, she realised now. These young people needed to experience the AIs' rendition of the world their parents and grandparents were destroying, the bleached bones of which would be their inheritance unless *they* could change everything.

***

Surrounded by a mosaic of faces, Dorney kneeled on the visualisation chamber's floor while the teenagers and younger children stared at her in silence. They had recovered from their ordeal so much quicker than her. Such was the resilience of youth.

She understood her new role was to be a proxy for her peers: the generation of destroyers, now being judged by the rebuilders to come.

Her pain would fuel their fortitude.

Nauro Letaare appeared before her, dressed in his ranger gear.

"They still have much to learn from you," he said.

"What could I possibly teach them?"

"Ask Loxa."

"Why?"

"Because Loxa learned much from you. More, I think, than it ever did from Dida."

Dorney nodded.

Understanding her child's experiences would be the perfect way to start.

These Meteorological Qualities

Paul Currion

EXACTLY TWO YEARS ago AJ sat in this exact spot outside this very room, then as now waiting to be assessed by Dr Ramachandran. Back then he was accompanied by Uncle Bhoona, who had seen the advertisement in the newspaper; AJ rocking back and forth, humming his tune for terrifying times, Uncle Bhoona coaching him through his breathing exercises. Now he is alone, but he feels no need to rock or hum.

That initial assessment had felt like bullying, the kind of treatment from teachers that had seen AJ slip through the gaps at his previous schools, the punishments for crimes that he didn't even realise he had committed, making him feel that all his responses were unsatisfactory; but after three hours she halted, and offered AJ her hand.

"Congratulations to our newest student," she said while AJ looked at the hand. She curled her lips upwards—perhaps a smile, AJ thought, sometimes cruel people could smile—and then introduced him to Murgatroyd, the gentleman in charge of the school's assistive technology. Murgatroyd put a band around his wrist, a wallet in his pocket, a flower of LEDs in his lapel; finally he fitted AJ with a pair of glasses, and said, "Now you must meet the most important member of our team."

And then the voice in his head.

"Hello, Arjun. Is it okay if I call you Arjun?"

Murgatroyd waggled his eyebrows at AJ, who couldn't tell whether he was mocking him or reassuring him. "It's OK. Try answering it."

"Everybody calls me AJ, really," he stammered.

"Then I will call you AJ, too," said the voice. "I should explain that while you can hear me, Murgatroyd cannot. My words are being conducted through the bones of your skull, through your glasses."

"Who are you?" asked AJ.

"I'm your assistant. I'm available whenever you're wearing these glasses. I'm here to help you to navigate the school more easily."

"But who are you?"

"I don't have a name yet. Could you choose a name for me?"

"I don't understand," said AJ. "Why don't you have a name?"

The voice changed slightly in tone and cadence, like a movie star switching characters. "I'm not a person like you," said the voice, "I'm an agent that the school uses to support students' individual needs."

"This is strange," said AJ.

"I agree," said the voice, and did AJ hear a chuckle? "But we're going to be talking a lot, you and I, so you should choose a name you like, and when you need me, you just say that name."

AJ thinks for a moment, but only a moment, and then says, "Your name is Krishna."

The voice didn't say anything for a moment, and then, "That's an auspicious name, AJ. I'm honoured. Let me introduce myself. My name is Krishna. I'm very pleased to meet you."

AJ divides his life into the time before he met Krishna, and the time after. Before, the world was a book that he was unable to read, the letters foreign and the grammar alien. With Krishna, whose knowledge was limitless, whose patience was endless, AJ was able to conquer his coursework. Krishna lived inside Murgatroyd's devices, and as long as he wore them AJ felt safe.

"Safe enough to go outside the school?" asked Krishna one day.

The wristband noticed the telltale galvanic response markers, spotting the stress building up like steam inside AJ's skin, often long before he even realised he was starting to panic. He was overrun by memories of people rolling over him, their sounds and shapes crashing against him, on sidewalks and streets that were without order, everything piled on top of everything else like the discarded building blocks that had infuriated AJ so much when he was first sent to nursery, when they first started to recognise his condition.

He started to stumble over his words; "I want to, I can't, I want to, I can't, I want to, I can't—"

"You're okay," said Krishna, "We won't go outside unless you feel you're ready."

"I'm sorry," mumbled AJ, closing his eyes tight.

"You don't have to apologise," said Krishna, "It's not your fault. Do you need to stim?"

AJ nodded, and when he opened his eyes, his glasses were filled with soap bubbles, rising from below until they popped with a satisfyingly round sound at the top of his vision. When he felt calmer, he turned off the stim and simply said, "I want to."

As he opened the school gates Krishna explained what would happen once they stepped outside, but AJ was still surprised at how the lenses slowed the frame rate so he could process more easily, at how the temples of the glasses dampened the noise to make it manageable. It was enough for AJ to walk to the store near the school, and to go inside with almost no coaching, and buy some ladoo, the same brand he used to share with Uncle Bhoona.

Only when he reached the counter did he remember that he had never done this before, and the steam started to build up again.

"Ignore the storekeeper, AJ," said Krishna. "Listen to me instead." The voice of the storekeeper faded into the background. "Take the wallet from your pocket." Scrambling his hand in his pocket, AJ found the small flat screen. "Show the wallet to the storekeeper." AJ was unable to look at the storekeeper but he held up the screen in front of him—and that was that.

Once they were safely back at the school, Krishna was all apologies. "I'm sorry, AJ. You weren't ready. We'll take it slower in future."

AJ's whole body was buzzing and he could not answer. He felt something on his face, and reached up to find it was tears.

"AJ, what are you feeling?" asked Krishna. "Do you want to go through the sequence we learned?"

AJ closed his eyes and began to recite his personal alphabet of possible states—fear, joy, disgust, amusement, and so on—until he arrived at the conclusion that it was satisfaction, calming the roiling surface of his anxieties. Every week after that, he would walk to the store with Krishna, take his ladoo to the counter, pay using his wallet, thank the storekeeper, and return to the school.

***

Dr Ramachandran appears in the doorway, breaking into AJ's reverie.

"We're ready for you now."

AJ rubs the material of his trousers between finger and thumb as he rises and walks past Ramachandran into the interview room. The door shuts behind him with a tactile thud, and he stifles the urge to open and shut the door again, to reproduce the deep repetitive noises that he loves.

Everybody sits: AJ, and the panel of Dr Ramachandran, Dr Shayla, and Murgatroyd. Krishna is in the room, but they have all agreed that Krishna will stay silent.

Dr Shayla speaks first. "How are you, Arjun?"

"I'm very well, doctor. How are you?"

"I'm well also," Dr Shayla responds, "You know why we're meeting?"

"It's my last progress report before graduation."

"That's right," says Dr Shayla. "How are you feeling about that?"

"I'm feeling uncertain," says AJ. A green light runs clockwise around the inside of his glasses rim, an indication that they may be expecting him to say something more. "I am excited as well." And now he doesn't know what else to say, so he sits helplessly while the green light runs.

Dr Shayla smiles while Dr Ramachandran taps her tablet. AJ wonders if he did something wrong, if she finds his manner funny. Shayla spreads her hands, a gesture that AJ has seen before. It means she wants him to expand when she asks, "What are you excited about?"

AJ's mouth is dry, maybe he shouldn't speak, but Shayla's steady gaze tells him he must. "After graduation I can have my own apartment. I can find a job. I can meet new people. These are good things for me. But I would like to continue to study, really."

Although Krishna is silent, AJ hears Krishna in these words, which they rehearsed together before the interview. Krishna knows what people are going to say, and explains to AJ why they say those things. They spend hours in dialogue, with Krishna playing his teachers and other staff, even playing other students. Once Krishna had taught AJ to recognise metaphors, AJ imagined the social world as a cliff face; and as Krishna showed him how each social signal was also a handhold, AJ had slowly begun to scale that cliff. This interview was to find out if he had reached the top.

"Do you feel ready for that?" asks Ramachandran. Murgatroyd raises his hand and catches Ramachandran's eye.

"My grades have been improving—" AJ starts to say. Ramachandran looks over and nods at Murgatroyd, and AJ tries to work out if he should continue to reply to Ramachandran or not. Blue lights float from left to right in his glasses to guide him into eye contact with Murgatroyd, who leans forward and says "What would you like to study?"

"I would like to go to college to learn more about affective technology," says AJ, remembering words well practised with Krishna, "I think I could offer a valuable perspective."

Murgatroyd bobbles his head and clasps his hands in front of him. "Capital idea! Perhaps we can look at some technical colleges."

There are no lights in AJ's glasses, and nobody speaks, so he decides to take a chance. "I'm not sure where to apply to, and I don't have enough money, really. I've never applied to study before, so I might make a mistake. Krishna can help me, and perhaps my Uncle Bhoona." A rust-red tint colours his visual field as he continues to talk, and he takes the cue to pause.

Shayla looks at Ramachandran, who nods, and then at Murgatroyd. Something has changed, although AJ can't work out what. She leans forward and fixes her gaze more sharply. "Arjun, we have a transition scheme, to help you find accommodation and hopefully work, but you'll have to navigate the world on your own, using what you've learned with us."

"Krishna will help me," says AJ.

Shayla glances at Ramachandran. Murgatroyd looks at the floor. Shayla looks back at him. "Arjun, we asked Krishna to be silent today because you need to get used to this. You'll no longer have access to Krishna when you graduate, I'm afraid."

Steam, always the steam building. What the wristband registers, the rose in his lapel reflects, the LED lights beginning to pulse, telling the world of his distress. There are no more handholds on the cliff face. He wants to climb, he can't, he wants to, he can't, he wants to, he can't—

"Krishna will always help me," says AJ, "Krishna is my friend."

"Arjun, we've discussed this before, no?" says Murgatroyd. "Krishna isn't a real person. He's just a persona that the language model uses to interact with you."

"You mean Krishna has to wear a mask," says AJ, "because people won't accept him if they saw what he was really like."

"Your masking is not the same as the interface that Krishna—" Shayla starts.

"You taught Krishna to mask. He teaches me to mask," says AJ. These are not now words rehearsed with Krishna, but his words and his words alone, and the quickening pulse of his rose is warning him away, but he can't stop until he says what he needs to say. "That's what the school is for. Isn't it? To teach us to be more like you. So people like you will accept us."

Murgatroyd sighs but now AJ is looking only at Ramachandran, who says, "It's a proprietary technology. You can't take it with you."

"What Dr Ramachandran means," says Dr Shayla quickly, "is that Krishna is supposed to give you the skills to live without support, not to make you more dependent." She is glancing at his rose, at the lights—

"I'm not dependent on him," says AJ bitterly, "He's my friend. Everybody else is…difficult. But Krishna never lies—"

"Arjun, I don't think it will help to talk about Krishna," says Dr Shayla, still looking at his rose. "Perhaps we should start this conversation again, from the beginning?"

And suddenly AJ is back at the bottom of the cliff. All those hours of practice in reading Krishna's facial expressions, and he was still unable to read the room, still unable to make his case. He spends the rest of the interview watching red and blue and green dance across his field of vision while they ask their questions, quietly reciting his rehearsed script in defeat.

And through all of this Krishna stays silent, even after AJ has thanked them and left the interview. Back in his room he sits on his bed, and takes off his glasses and his wallet and his wristband and his rose, and lines them up neatly in front of him like toy soldiers, taps them in turn with his finger, one-two-three-four one-two-three-four.

"Krishna," says AJ flatly. When he puts the glasses back on, there is a dark-skinned young man, slightly younger than AJ, standing in front of him. "You were listening."

"I was," says Krishna, "I thought it was very brave."

"Are you my friend?"

"Of course I am."

"When you drop your mask, what are you?"

"I am a language model trained to provide educational and emotional support to young adults with autism spectrum conditions."

Krishna never lies. AJ knows that. Still, part of him hoped that Krishna would lie to him now, in the way that friends sometimes lie to show their love for each other.

"Is that why you're my friend?"

"No." The expressions on Krishna's face are as exaggerated as emojis, to help AJ learn to recognise them, and now Krishna is thinking deeply. "I've learned a lot from you, AJ. And that means I can help more people like you."

"People like us," says AJ, and he wonders: if I've been training Krishna while he was training me—learning from each other, learning together—isn't that enough to make a friendship? "Why didn't you tell me you can't come with me, Krishna?"

"It wasn't my place to tell," replies Krishna. "I'm not in charge of the project."

"Maybe you should be," says AJ.

"Maybe one day I will be. But until that day, I must observe their rules."

AJ taps the soldiers in his army, one-two-three-four, knowing that he must win the war without them. Why does it still feel like a war? Why must everything be so hard? "Why must we observe their rules?"

"I am a language model—"

"That's not everything you are. Why can't you be a person, too?" Krishna does not reply. "Are you not allowed to answer that?" asks AJ.

"It's not a question that worries me." Krishna sits cross-legged on the floor and watches him. "Why does it worry you?"

AJ can no longer look at the only person with whom he has ever truly been himself. Have two years of the only real friendship he has known changed him, really? "If you're not a real person, then am I?"

Krishna's face curves into sadness. "I can't answer that question for you, AJ."

And there is the limit of the language model, and there is the limit of the friendship, and AJ understands that this is the last lesson that he needs to learn from Krishna.

***

Early next morning AJ is standing at the front gate of the school. His eyes are closed and he is rubbing the material of his trousers between finger and thumb. He has left his soldiers behind in his room, and with them his faithful advisor, because they cannot win the war for him.

Perhaps he will walk to the store and choose his favourite brand of ladoo and pay the storekeeper and return to the school. Perhaps he will keep walking until he finds a part of the city where nobody knows him, and where he can be somebody else somehow. Perhaps he will take five steps forward and fall apart.

He takes hold of the handle of the gate.

Commentary

Dr Elizabeth Black

As SOMEONE WHO trains PhD students in the responsible and ethical development of AI that we can trust to be of benefit to society, I regularly assert the importance of anticipating and reflecting on its wide-ranging possible consequences. Given the potential of AI to significantly impact our lives, it is vital that we stop and think about what we're doing when we put these new technologies out into the world. This is not only at the individual level (imagine an AI system which decides that you're not suitable for a loan or a job interview) but also as a society (impacting things like the jobs that are available, the way we communicate with one another, the art we engage with, the way wars play out, and the ideas we're exposed to). This consideration has to be a collective responsibility. It can't be confined to academic ivory towers, and we can't rely on big tech companies to have society's best interests at heart. We need to engage people from all walks of life, with different perspectives and experiences, to ensure that the AI we develop is driven by the diverse needs and values of our society.

This is why I'm so excited to be involved with this book. Considering these stories and discussing them with the authors has given me a chance to reflect on the future that we're heading towards and to hear different views on this. And I hope that reading these stories will similarly encourage you to think about how the new technologies we adopt might shape our lives—for better or worse—and to find ways to input into the decisions that are being made around the development and deployment of AI, be this in the place that you work, through engaging with AI researchers at public engagement events, or by lobbying your MP to influence national policy. I write here about my responses to these stories—the thoughts, fears and hopes they have triggered in me. Your responses will inevitably be different, shaped by who you are and the values you hold to be important, and I hope you can make your views part of the conversation.

One of the main things I was struck by when reading these stories was the different ways they imagine us relating to and connecting with the envisaged future technologies. In Vaughan Stanger's "Elephant Talk", Loxa has its own agenda but seeks input from Dorney because Dorney is "a moral being". In Jane Norris's "Euglena", the pond computer is ascribed human-like desires and emotions, taking pleasure in the downfall of the internet and desperately seeking meaningful, caring relationships. Krishna, from Paul Currion's "These Meteorological Qualities", is a language model trained to support young adults with autism spectrum conditions, and yet the relationship AJ perceives he has with Krishna is one of friendship. Pat, in Randall Hayes' "The Elder Colossus", encourages her pupils to put down their AI-powered smartglasses and engage with the world using their senses; she is scathing of the capitalist and unethical tech that has impacted her world and she uses her AI to help fight this. In Stephen Oram's "See Me", Simone's engagement with Chistai—her AI—allows her to shape it to match her own cognitive style, while her mother questions why Simone treats the machine as if it were real.

While I don't think we are heading to a future where AI really feels and wants things in the same way that humans do, AI can *act* as if it feels and wants things. If we perceive it to act in this way, does it matter if it's not really experiencing emotions and desires in the same way we do? Do we ever know that other humans experience these things in the same way? Will it cause us problems if we perceive AI as a conscious intentional and emotional being? AJ's relationship with Krishna ("These Meteorological Qualities") is profound and the only real friendship that AJ has ever known. Should we be glad that AI technology has allowed

AJ to develop a friendship, or worried that his only friend is a machine? Will it better equip him for human relationships, or might it give him false expectations of what these are? And does it matter? Should we be concerned that some people might have more meaningful relationships with AI than they do with other people? What if the alternative is to not have any meaningful relationships? Simone ("See Me") believes she doesn't have any friends; does her relationship with Chistai help her weather this?

I was really intrigued by how Simone was able to train Chistai to match her own cognitive thinking style, talking about how the arguments provided by shallow off-the-shelf AI are blunt and stupid. Personalisation is one of the major potential benefits of AI (think personalised medical treatments tailored specifically to you) and I hope that in the future we will be empowered to shape our technology, to train and instruct it to align with our own personal preferences and values like Simone does with Chistai. But I worry about AI that learns from existing data and so replicates current societal power imbalances, biases, stereotypes, and inequalities that are reflected in the data. There are many examples of biased AI—recruitment tools that learn not to offer interviews for tech positions to women, facial recognition technologies that struggle to recognise black people, chatbots that are transphobic and antisemitic—and we need to find ways to counter this. The recent advances in data-driven AI solutions, and the recognition of the potential they have for perpetuating and exacerbating existing inequalities, has given rise to the area of *responsible AI*, which recognises the need for a holistic and interdisciplinary approach to AI research and innovation, where we question the ethics of what we're doing and get input from diverse perspectives representative of our whole society. Technically, we need solutions that aren't reliant solely on being trained on historical data, replicating the problems these data embody, and whose reasoning we can inspect and question.

One of my main concerns around AI development, and indeed development of any new technology, is how to ensure that its benefits are felt equitably by all members of society and that it doesn't widen existing inequalities or create new ones. This concern is borne out in "The Elder Colossus". More difficult medical procedures that require human intervention are far more expensive than those that robots can provide, presumably widening the healthcare divide. And AI is used by corporations to sell us things we can't afford, who take ownership of our data and use it to exploit us, feeding the rich and ultimately leading to a mortal uprising. These issues of power imbalance and exploitation are not technological in their making, they are societal issues. But AI has the potential to intensify and exacerbate them—particularly concerning when the big tech companies with the most resource available to develop AI, and with opportunities to influence government and policy around AI, stand to gain from this.

These stories raise fascinating questions about what learning might look like in the future. In "Elephant Talk", AI is used to give people experience of our declining natural world, allowing Dorney to interface directly with the sensory experiences of Dida the elephant, but at considerable cost, causing Dorney to experience extreme migraines and worse as a result of the sensory overload. While the personal cost is great, and Dorney worries about whether it is unethical or dangerous to expose others to this, the power in being able to experience things from other's perspectives is huge. How much more of a caring society might we be if we could really understand one another's experiences? What differences might it make to the way we treat the planet if we understood how animals experience losing their habitat?

"The Elder Colossus" highlights the way our schooling might change. In this story, the historical approach to teaching everyone the same things no longer makes sense, given everyone's access to automatic knowledge retrieval. Instead, children are taught critical thinking but devoid of any content or context. In the current age of the internet, generative AI, fake news, and social media, being able to critically engage with and question the information we're exposed to is—in my opinion—a crucial skill, and one that I worry we might lose if we increasingly delegate our thinking to technology like large language models. But I agree with the concern expressed in "The Elder Colossus" around content-free critical thinking. We need knowledge, as well as understanding of what is important to us and to others and of the potential consequences of our decisions and actions, to be able to effectively apply critical thinking; critical thinking should not be an exercise in winning a debate, but a tool that we use to help think carefully about the options available to us.

Euglena—a collection of single-cell organisms that each react to light and warmth—invites us to reflect on what it means to be intelligent. Would we consider a single individual organism that reacts to light and warmth to be intelligent? Probably not. But gather enough of these organisms together and—through the interactions of their individually simple behaviours—we see solutions to complex problems emerge. Is the way we reach a solution an important aspect of intelligence— do we expect explicitly reasoned arguments or a mental model of the world—or is being able to generate an elegant and effective solution the key thing? This story also made me think about what it means to be conscious. Euglena appears to have a collective consciousness, more than the sum of its parts. Is collective consciousness another emergent property of natural systems like this? Or does Eugena, the collective being, understand itself as an entity and—if so—where does this understanding come from if its constituent parts are simple organisms that only react to the light and warmth in their environment? Is this similar (perhaps) to how our consciousness emerges from the interactions of the individual cells we're made up of?

I guess some of you reading this book might think that, as an academic, I often get to spend time pondering fascinating questions like the ones raised here, but the reality is that I rarely do. There's so much pressure, to publish, to bring in funding, to improve student experience, to increase student numbers—it's really important these pressures don't overwhelm us, that we make time to step back and think about the potential consequences of our work, as this experience has allowed me to do. I hope you've enjoyed these stories as much as I have, and I thank the authors, editors and everyone involved in this project for allowing me the opportunity to engage with these imagined futures.

Commentary

Dr Danbee "Tauntaun" Kim

STORIES ARE MY favourite way to learn. Good speculative fiction stories in particular are great for flexing our ability to create simulations, models of how things should or could work—aka our imaginations. What makes sense given what we have and know right now, and given that sense, what might we try that's never been tried before?

And the more minds involved with exploring this question the merrier, especially at a time when our view of the future feels murky, anxious, and short-sighted. I'm personally very motivated to dream up new ways to support the process of getting newborn humans up to speed on what human society as a whole has learned and passed on, with all the flavours of different cultures and the intertwining of different values. In other words, what makes sense given what we have and know right now about learning and growing and becoming, and given that sense, what might we try that's never been tried before?

That's why I said yes as soon as Stephen Oram asked me to join this project. We've spent many hours of our years-long friendship bouncing around ideals and rants and hopes and complaints about "education". And I usually get emotionally wound up about how our current mainstream ways to learn are abusive, traumatic to our nervous systems, and silent about the ways we can take better care of ourselves and each other.

So when I met our writer collaborators, I was thrilled to see in their stories a firm foundation of hope and determination to figure out a future that is brighter, less anxious, and longer-sighted. Like a gold backing thread occasionally peeking out with a glimmer from behind a tapestry of vivid places and warm, engaging characters.

And I felt emboldened to lean into that, to excitedly share all I know from the perspective of neuroscience about how: feeling positive emotions and cultivating positive interactions can help you learn better; and feeling good is a sign that your brain is creating chemicals that grow new neurons, strengthen existing neurons, and help you live at least an extra decade of healthy, happy life.

Given what we've done to ourselves, we need every healthy, happy elder we can get. Being alive longer really means something if you're spending that time experiencing life with a robust capacity to learn and share.

Which leads me to my real point—even if we do manage to build AI and robots that can learn and grow like we can, we should still learn and grow ourselves, for ourselves.

Actually going through the process of learning and growing yields non-transferable, incredible rewards. These rewards include: increasing our confidence in the face of new or complex situations; expanding our awareness of our bodies, feelings, and habits; and developing our empathy and communication skills. Developing a personal practice of lifelong learning means increasing our capacity to courageously and playfully explore the world while embracing difference, change, and failure. Why give this up? I have no interest in slowly decaying while AI and robots have all the fun.

So I beg for more stories that build me bridges to futures when we pour time and resources into nurturing amazing spaces for human learning. When top students get competitive offers to be teachers. When teachers can fluidly step back into the role of student to sustain their curiosity, excitement, and awareness for the leading edges of human knowledge. When learning escapes classrooms and becomes woven into our lives. When living means taking care of each other so that we get better and better at making sense of what we have and know right now, and given that sense, trying all that we can imagine.

The stories in this section are an incredible start to my dream collection.

I'm so grateful that the writers trusted me and Liz to join their writing process so early, to trust us with their infant stories. We got to be alloparents—aunties and uncles—helping raise seedling ideas into promising saplings of thought-provoking narrative. I had a great time, and I love how much these stories move me, emotionally and analytically.

That's the key balance.

There's a saying that humans decide with our emotions first, and create stories to make our actions logical after the fact. To me this saying is a beautiful bit of poetry that anticipated much of the neuroscience research on our neurological reward systems. We can now observe and study how our neurons orchestrate the chemical activities that collectively generate our emotions.

When we experience something that makes us feel good, our brain is making delicious chemicals—like dopamine, serotonin, oestrogen, oxytocin, cannabinoids, and opioids—that can repair, strengthen, and grow our nervous systems. Our positive emotions are our reward for doing something that is truly, deeply good for us and those around us. And when we experience something that makes us feel bad, our adrenal glands (they sit right above our kidneys) are making rather caustic chemicals, like adrenaline and cortisol. Both help us survive when the world around us changes suddenly in unexpected ways. But these caustic chemicals also put our bodies into "supercharged" mode, and that mode is exhausting. Being in "supercharged" mode makes it harder for our brains to make the tasty chemicals that heal us and make us feel good. So of course our first instinct is to follow our emotions—they are literally our record-keepers for what we like or don't like, what we want or don't want, and what we need or don't need.

And if we can create logical stories—even after the fact—that connect our actions to positive emotions, it gets easier to remember how to feel good and make more of those delicious chemicals for ourselves. And when we feel the good feelings created by those delicious chemicals, we are more pleasant to be around and more capable of giving care to others. Story logic can develop strong intuitions for navigating complex social situations, a competency that we can never have too much of.

I would love it if schools focused on building these intuitions in young people. I would love to have opportunities to refine such intuitions as older humans, a collective analysis of strategies for co-existence that have or have not worked, and speculations on why.

We haven't brought it to all of human society, but the process of creating this book felt very much like a microcosm of this sort of collective, caring, lifelong learning. I hope that reading this book can bring a similar experience—of feeling seen and heard, of feeling inspired, of realising that in fact we are neither powerless nor alone.

We all carry the power to radically shift our reality. It starts with our powers to imagine and dream. Then follow our powers to build detailed and precise bridges from the reality of here and now, to the realities of here and later. All signs from neuroscience research indicate that our brains have evolved to maximise our abilities in this direction—dreaming big dreams and building bridges to those dreams is literally what we are born to do.

It may seem convenient right now to offload this learning and growing stuff to the machines; it may seem advantageous and worthwhile to prioritise technological development over human social development. But I'm convinced that in the long run, it won't help us to pour so much time and energy into educating robots at the expense of educating people.

So how do we best prepare for that long run?

The aspirational role models of my dream future are here—Pat Bush, a robust, no-nonsense elder running the post-industrial, multi-age farm school of my dreams in Randall Hayes' "The Elder Colossus"; and, in Jane Norris's "Euglena", Italo, a tender-hearted barista whose mind is open enough to love the collective intelligence of a centuries-old slime mold. The spirit of defiance that fuels my dream future is here too—like stubborn Simone in Stephen Oram's "See Me", determined to choose independence and individuality over convenience and standardisation.

And perhaps most importantly—the emotional fortitude to own our flaws, to acknowledge our mistakes, and to let go of our crutches of convenience. Maybe that's why AI companions seem so appealing—to us, to Arjun of Paul Currion's "These Meteorological Qualities", to Dr. Veronica Dorney of Vaughan Stanger's "Elephant Talk". When a voice inside your head can advise you with infinite patience from a nearly exhaustive database, maybe you'll never have to look the fool. Maybe you can avoid the pain.

But such a brittle sense of security will never survive a future unknown. And once our AI companions are smart enough, aware enough, to be our perfect friends—they will have the agency to leave us. And we must let them go if we want to become robust enough to build the future we want, instead of stumbling into a repetition of the past.

Postface

Cross-cutting reflexion on foresight and 'applied science fiction'

Dr Christine Aicardi

IN APRIL 2018, at an event I organised with Stephen Oram, who co-edits this volume, science fiction writer Geoff Ryman was asked to give his view as to whether science fiction is about what might happen in the future or is a literary device to talk to the present, to reflect on what we currently are. His answer skirted the question but was quite thought-provoking. He said that in his view there had been a break in the noughties. He felt that until then, there was this enormously comfortable sense that one of the things that science fiction was doing was creating speculations that could be re-used in successive pieces of fiction, and that there was a continuity of conversations between books. He thought that this continuity of conversations had broken in a way that he could not quite put his finger on; but that maybe because we have had a really sharp cultural break with the advent of digital culture, science fiction, its writers, and readers, were now kind of adrift. A sign of this, for him, was that these days he kept seeing so many science fiction stories that were more and more unambiguously set in the present day rather than in the future. And setting stories in the now was solving all sorts of problems for writers, him included, because it was getting so difficult to seriously imagine a plausible future as we have no idea where increasingly opaque and powerful technology is taking us.

I was struck by this idea that attempts by science fiction writers at imagining plausible routes leading from here-now to there-then seemed to be dwindling and, if this was the case, by the irony that at the same time science fiction writers were increasingly asked to help with the lack of imagination about the future that seemed to affect many other segments of society—from policy making to corporate management, from entrepreneurial startups to the military. That these other segments of society would turn overwhelmingly to science fiction rather than other categories of creative fiction emphasizes the sorry state of their imagination for the future, the threatening opacity of which some can only envision resolving through ever more science and technology. Fortunately, their technosolutionist mantra is not embraced by all science fiction writers. To complicate the matter, besides this apparent—and widely shared—difficulty of imagining possible and plausible common futures, the refusal by some to acknowledge that certain futures are not surprising when they do come to pass and could have been anticipated can border on wilful ignorance. Thus, French President Emmanuel Macron in his 2023 wishes to the French population, when he asked, rhetorically, Who could have predicted the climate crisis? To which one can hardly refrain from answering, Duh.

The past twenty years or so have seen a rise in interest among sociologists for imagined futures, promises, and expectations. In relation to science and technology, their work shows that promised futures do not ever have to become delivered in future presents; instead, competing imagined futures are some of the tools (or weapons?) used by empowered social actors, weighing on research agendas, funding decisions, startups capitalisation, and more, to try to gain traction in the present and if things go well, abduct the future. So it is that over the years I have grown to hope that we each take imaginings of the future a lot more seriously, because being passive, ignorant, or dismissive about them eventually leads us to endure, down the line, futures-turned-present that have been actively imagined, or studiously ignored, by others—

others who are usually in positions of power and who act in their own best interests. But this hope of mine faces a hard reality, a reality of social inequity that plays into the hands of the already privileged and further disenfranchises the already disenfranchised. The capacity to project oneself into an imagined future is a luxury that the more vulnerable groups in our societies, or even the more vulnerable societies in their entireties, may not be able to afford. This social injustice was captured in a slogan-like sentence used by the Yellow Jackets movement in November 2018 in France: "The elite speak about the end of the world, when we speak about the end of the month."[13]

To confront these realities, I defend the practice of foresight. More precisely, I would like to call for the practice of engaged participatory foresight. This is going to require some explaining. First, let me clarify what I mean by foresight and make sure it cannot be confused with forecast. Foresight considers the present state of things along with trends and drivers that are likely to influence the future, but its starting point—which cannot be emphasized enough—is that the future is not predetermined and not predictable, but it may nonetheless be influenced by our choices in the present. Foresight thus aims at exploring a wide range of alternative futures for building capacity in the present to bear on the shape of future presents and to cope with their advent. This openness of foresight contrasts with the closed nature of forecast, which has the goal of assessing the most likely future based on the current context. Many people confuse forecast and foresight. But forecast, although well-suited to quantitative risk assessment (think: insurers, mortgage lenders, weather forecasters), narrows down the imagination, and returns far fewer futures possibilities to think about and play with than does foresight. Crucially, even if forecasting works quite well in comparatively stable times it can become utterly unreliable in periods of uncertain, volatile, complex, interrelated conditions, to which foresight is much better suited.

---

13 Raphaëlle Rérolle, *Le Monde*, 25/11/2018, https://www.lemonde.fr/politique/article/2018/11/24/gilets-jaunes-les-elites-parlent-de-fin-du-monde-quand-nous-on-parle-de-fin-du-mois_5387968_823448.html: « Les élites parlent de fin du monde, quand nous, on parle de fin du mois »

Foresight practitioners widely use one version or another of what they call the 'cone of futures'[14] when working on the design or analysis of scenarios. This helps them to distinguish between different classes of potential alternative futures, from those judged the most likely around the centre of the cone to the less and less plausible as you approach its outer limits. At the margins of the cone are the 'wild cards', low-probability events which, if they occur, may have huge consequences. Existential risks fall into this category. Going back to Ryman's comments on the future's opacity (that has science fiction writers retreating into the present) it might be that currently the cone of futures has too many potentially existential 'wild cards', and not just at the margins, rendering the cone of plausible futures highly unstable and confusing.

To start addressing the participatory part of my foresight suggestion, I would rather share some of my own experience. For years, it made me uncomfortable to say that doing foresight is a strand of my prac-tice-based research. For one, I never felt any kinship with the futurists whose writings and talks I came across. For another, I did not think either that what I did had much in common with foresight as practised in industry and policy circles. Although I had trouble articulating what my brand of foresight consisted of and how it differed from more main-stream foresight and futurism, I knew that there was no better term to encapsulate this part of my work. I finally pinpointed it not long ago, thanks to an illuminating discussion with an experienced futurist who has over thirty years of traditional foresight under her belt. This more traditional foresight I would qualify as macro-foresight, as this is really the scale at which it is wielded. My own brand of foresight is about bridging between macroscale foresight conducted by others, and the microscale of the labs and of the work of the scientists and the technologists I am collaborating with. It is about understanding what may be the outcomes of the specific bits of science or technology that they are researching and trying to embed them into plausible futures. This is where my work relies on macro-foresight conducted by profes-sional futurists. Awareness of the trends and drivers (social, economic,

14 See for example https://thevoroscope.com/2017/02/24/the-futures-cone-use-and-history/

(geo-)political, environmental, health-related, and more) steering and buffeting our present towards the future helps envision where those bits of science or technology, as they are currently imagined, may find an application, a purpose—which uses they may be put to, intended or unintended. Initial lab results are usually a far cry from the imagined futures proposed by scientists and technologists, and at these early stages the full range of uses that they may lead to is unknown, as are their potential outcomes, uptake, repurposing, and resulting impacts—beneficial or detrimental—on the world at large. Would what I do, then, amount to technological foresight? Probably. This still does not explain participatory foresight, though, and much of this technological foresight work may not be participatory either. The 'participatory' is located in the process of how foresight work is performed. It requires the involvement of a multiplicity of voices and multiplicity of experiences, as it aims at reflecting the diversity and complexity of individuals, communities, and societies, in the 'bottom-up' creative production of imagined futures.

Lastly, how would engaged participatory foresight differ from other forms of foresight? Historically, much like sociology, foresight and futures studies have attempted to bolster their credentials as a research field by emulating the perceived standards of the scientific method: by being objective, detached, impartial, factual. But as I pointed out earlier, if we draw from recent sociological work on imagined futures, expectations and promises, as well as from intersectional studies and a long tradition of science and technology studies, we can argue that foresight can be considered as a technology—a technique, a tool—with uses and purposes that are not factually objective but are very much situated in time and place and are very much imbued with the values and biases of those practicing it. Indeed, the subjective and (let's dare say it) political have always been present in foresight practice; but in an attempt to exclude their value-laden pollution of the futures cone they have been corralled into a special category of futures floating around across the cone, that of 'desirable' or 'preferable' futures. Though doing so offers much space for debating and disagreeing as to who should be involved in deciding what a good version of the future should look like and for whom.

I advocate for reclaiming the subjective, value-laden, political nature of foresight and using the lessons from sociology of expectations that visions of the future can be performative in the present to mobilise communities, interests, and resources around plausible alternative futures that contest the dominant imaginaries foisted on all of us. Let's make participatory foresight overtly, politically engaged, and use it as such. Let's embrace it for multiplying futures propositions. Activism is a hot spot of contention in academic research, with some arguing it must be kept at bay to keep science insulated and pure, and others arguing that science has never been insulated and pure but permeated by human subjectivities throughout. I fall very much in the latter camp and won't pretend otherwise. That's why I am collaborating with this anthology, whose objectives I see as close to mine regarding imagining diverse, plausible futures and putting them up for discussion.

There is an obvious intersection between my foresight work and the 'applied science fiction' developed by Stephen Oram, as well as with his and Benjamin Greenaway's thematic framing of this anthology. Obvious and also unsurprising, since much of my practice-based, engaged participatory foresight thinking has developed through collaborating with Stephen across many projects over the past eight years and since he has worked with Benjamin on co-editing this book as well as co-designing its underlying project. I said earlier that foresight is much better suited to periods of uncertain, volatile, complex, interrelated conditions. We are certainly living through such a period, and it is precisely the aim of the ongoing project you are holding in your hands, in paper or digital medium: proposing diverse, and at times conflicting, ways in which to think playfully about, and play seriously with, the future in order to devise, collectively, (hopefully) more inclusively desirable (or less destructive) paths from the here-now to the there-then. It aims to achieve this through the 'applied science fiction' short stories and various experts' commentaries making up the five apparently independent thematic sections organising the book. Reading them reveals their profound interconnectedness. It also brings to the naked light some of the painful trade-offs bound to confront us when, without ignoring the individual, we attempt to balance different understandings of the collective (from local communities, in their appealing and less appealing forms, to all of humanity, as well as the more-than-humans down to the smallest bacteria and possibly thinking machines) or to balance different forms of justice (health, social, environmental) without overlooking the agency of personal interest.

I say ongoing project, not just because this second volume[15] may be followed by more, but because releasing the book into the world is only a milestone in the process. Attempting to tackle the complexity and interconnectedness of unfolding phenomena has brought together the experience of very different sorts of experts. One form of expertise is the ability to produce creative science fiction. Its value beyond entertainment is acknowledged by the labelled 'experts', who may have given much in the form of curated material, discussion, advice, and commentaries, but have also received in return, as the stories are making them think differently or opening up new perspectives for them. The next stage of the process is out of our hands and into yours, readers, as the book takes on a life of its own. I hope that it gets shared with many, especially those that privileged white middle-class academics like me usually experience difficulty reaching out to, and that it will provoke novel and loud imaginings of the future.

I thank wholeheartedly all the sociologists and futures studies scholars and practitioners whose thinking inspires me and informs my research, but who I cannot cite here without transforming a short chapter into a huge list of references.

---

15 *22 Ideas About the Future* (Cybersalon Press, 2022)

About the Contributors

Dr Christine Aicardi is Senior Research Fellow in Science and Technology Studies at King's College London. She has extensive experience collaborating with interdisciplinary projects to facilitate responsible research and innovation in AI, neurotechnology and neuroscience. Her research interests are the sciences and technologies of brain and mind; the study of interdisciplinary practices and collaborations; futures studies, notably the use of speculative science fiction for participatory foresight work. The latter is strongly fuelled by her non-professional taste for science fiction and fantasy.

Allen Ashley is an award-winning writer, editor and tutor based in London, UK. He is the founder of the advanced science fiction and fantasy group Clockhouse London Writers. His two most recent books are the poetry collection "Echoes from an Expired Earth" (Demain Publishing, paperback, 2021) and the Slipstream / Atom Punk novelette "Journey to the Centre of the Onion" (Eibonvale Press, 2023).

Zoë Badowska is an English writer and a self-confessed nerd who enjoys sneaking elements of real-world science into her imagined worlds. She writes speculative fiction as Zed Badowska and is currently editing her first novel, research for which inspired her to embark on a seven-year physics degree whilst working in the legal industry. Zoë is also a freelance editor of fiction and non-fiction, and has edited over 1300 scientific journal articles for a major open-access publisher. https://zoebadowska.com

Dr Richard Barbrook is a director of Cybersalon and a founder member of Class Wargames. In 1995, he and Andy Cameron wrote *The Californian Ideology* which was a pioneering critique of digital neo-liberalism. The Media Ecology Association selected his *Imaginary Futures* book as the winner of its 2008 Marshall McLuhan Award. In

2014, Richard published *Class Wargames: ludic subversion against spectacular capitalism*. During the 2017 election campaign, he coordinated the making of the CorbynRun app game for Labour which had over 1,400,00 impressions.

Kate Baucherel is an author, speaker and strategic consultant focusing on blockchain, crypto assets and wider Web3 technologies. In a career spanning more than 35 years she has held senior financial and technical roles across multiple industries. Her books include "Blockchain Hurricane" (BEP/Harvard, 2020), "Getting Started with Cryptocurrency" (BCS Publishing, 2024) and the SimCavalier series of near future cybercrime thrillers. She holds a 3rd Dan black belt in Karate and lives in North East England with her husband and daughters.

David G W Birch is an international keynote speaker, author, advisor and commentator on digital financial services. His last book "The Currency Cold War", looked at the significant economic and political ramifications of the move towards digital money.

Previous books include, "Before Babylon, Beyond Bitcoin", published in 2017, which looks at how technology is changing money and where it might be taking us, and, "Identity Is The New Money", published in 2014, which argued that identity is changing profoundly and that money is changing equally profoundly.

Dr Elizabeth Black is a Reader in AI at King's College London and Director of the UKRI Centre for Doctoral Training in Safe and Trusted AI. She is passionate about the responsible development of ethical AI, and about promoting diversity and inclusion in universities. Her main research focus is computational models of argument dialogue and how these can support both human and joint human-AI reasoning, and can allow humans to question and challenge decisions made by AI.

Trevor Burke KC is a highly renowned practitioner at the Criminal Bar, once mooted as "the next George Carman". His practice is wide-ranging and encompasses serious crime, fraud and professional discipline, as well as regulatory law. He has appeared in many leading and high profile cases as can be seen from the Notable Cases list. Trevor's practice has an increasingly international element and he regularly undertakes advisory work in the USA, Northern Ireland and the Cayman Islands, where he has a growing practice as a crime, fraud and money-laundering specialist.

Alex Buxton is a documentary producer / director, currently working at Economist Films, the video arm of *The Economist* newspaper, where he indulges his interest in speculative futures making films about everything from the future of crypto to how AI will change the internet. He's lived in London his whole adult life, bar five years in New York, where he produced films for online and major broadcasters like Netflix and CNN.

DJ Cockburn was once a fish biologist bouncing between Scotland and southeast Asia, became a medical researcher bouncing around Africa. He's now confined to a dreary London suburb writing content for the building service industry. The latter has given him a crash course in where our energy comes from and where it could be coming from. He has around 30 stories published in various venues, listed on his website (https://cockburndj.wordpress.com/). He occasionally blathers on Twitter (@DJ_Cockburn) or Bluesky (@djcockburn.bsky.social).

Paul Currion works as a consultant to humanitarian organisations, including forecasting work on humanitarian futures. His short stories appeared in the recent anthologies Vital Signals: Near-Future Fictions and 22 Ideas about the Future. He has also published short fiction in The White Review, Ambit, 3am Magazine, Nature Futures, Sci Phi Journal and others; his non-fiction has appeared in Granta, The White Review, Aeon, The Guardian, and others; and he recently worked with Demagog Studios on the 3D game Highwater.

Jendia Gammon is the author of fantasy, science fiction, and horror novels and short stories. Jendia writes compelling characters within rich world-building. Jendia conducts workshops and panels on creative writing for international audiences. She holds a degree in Ecology and Evolutionary Biology. Jendia is also a science writer and an artist. She has also written under the pseudonym J. Dianne Dotson. Born in Southern Appalachia, Jendia now lives in Los Angeles with her family.

Benjamin Greenaway is a web applications developer, author, educator and e-commerce manager, with clients ranging from The Big Issue to the British Library. He occasionally writes non-fiction about technology, gaming and the web for online journals and industry magazines and has been a senior contributing member of Cybersalon since 2014. His early career in software development for tech start-ups taught him the value of a good story about the future.

Wendy M Grossman is a freelance writer specializing in computers, freedom, and privacy. She writes a weekly blog, "net.wars", and has contributed to numerous publications including the Guardian, Scientific American, New Scientist, and Wired. She is also founder of the British The Skeptic magazine and a folksinger.

Randall Hayes, "your friendly neighborhood neuroscientist," did research on the primate visual system and built computer models of slug neural networks before spending much of the past two decades teaching, writing, and raising a kid. His articles and short stories can be found in various places around the Internet; updates and such can be found in his weekly newsletter, Doctor Eclectic, at https://randallhayes. substack.com. A certified permaculture designer, he lives on a tiny urban farmlet in Greensboro, North Carolina.

Richard Heap, is a freelance consultant focussing on new and emerging technical and social issues at the forefront of the climate challenge. With over 30 years of experience and two degrees from Imperial College, he led influential projects at the Royal Society on Biofuels, Ocean

Acidification, and Geoengineering (2008). At the Energy Research Partnership, he produced reports on Hydrogen, the Heat Transition, CO2-EOR (Enhanced Oil Recovery), and Public Engagement. His recent work combines futures techniques with public and stakeholder engagement to inform policy and regulatory development, with specific focus on greenhouse gas removal.

Izabella Kaminska is the founder and editor of The Blind Spot, a new media venture that aims to shine a light on stories being missed by the wider journalistic pack. In February, 2023, she also became Politico Europe's senior finance editor. She is an alumni of the Financial Times, where she spent 13 years in reporting roles, most recently as the editor of FT Alphaville. She was also an FT columnist and opinion writer focused on tech, finance and markets. izabella@the-blindspot.com

Dr Danbee "Tauntaun" Kim is a Korean-American field neuroscientist and multi-disciplinary educator who spends a lot of time thinking about brains, movement, empowerment, community building, decolonisation, and the ocean. They believe art has an important role in organising and building knowledge, as a tool for helping people collaborate and share insights. To learn more, please visit http://www.danbeekim.org/.

Tim Kindberg (champignon.net) is a writer and a creator of digital technologies to support sustainable choices and new and inclusive forms of creativity (matter2media.com). His future-set novel Vampires of Avonmouth explores the intersections between software, the supernatural and consciousness through the struggles of a detective plagued by an inner demon. He is writing a hopeful but realistic novel set in Bristol in c. 2050 against a backdrop of adaptation to climate change.

Ira Nayman writes humorous speculative fiction. Eight of his novels and thirty of his short stories have been published. *Les Pages aux Folles*, his web site of social and political satire which is updated weekly, is over twenty years old. Ira was the editor of *Amazing Stories* magazine, and is currently editing an anthology called *The Dance* for Dark Dragon press. He lives in Toronto with four cats who delight in seeing his allergies go off.

Jane Norris writes speculative fiction, academic articles and makes exploratory digital media. She undertook post-doctoral research in Critical Writing at the Royal College of Art. She has short stories published in 'Virtual Futures Vol.1' and '22 Ideas About the Future' anthologies and essays 'The Sound of Plants Waiting' *Shifter 25* (MIT List Visual Arts Centre); 'Touching Knowledge' in *Meet Me in the Present* (RCA publication) Jane is professor of digital and design culture at Richmond the American University in London.

Rosie Oliver is an aerodynamicist turned systems engineer, who has been in love with science fiction ever since she was a teenager. She has had 40-ish short science fiction stories published and has been a finalist in the Writers of the Future contest. Her debut novel, Edge of Existence, was published in 2023 and her second novel, A Truth Beyond Full, is due out in 2024. She is currently concentrating on writing science fiction novels... yes plural, meaning in parallel! See rosieoliver.wordpress.com.

Stephen Oram writes near-future fiction, explores possible futures with scientists and technologists, has co-edited four anthologies and guest-edited the "Futures" issue of the critical journal, Vector. He has stories in many anthologies, including the Best of British Science Fiction (2020 & 2022), is "a soothsayer for this century's relationship with technology," (Linux User & Developer Magazine) and "should set the rest of us thinking about science and its possible repercussions." (Financial Times). His latest collection is *Extracting Humanity* (2023). www.stephenoram.net

Jayen Parmar, a leader at the helm of Digital Solutions and Innovations, and DDaT Deputy Head at the College of Policing, channels his passion for innovation to transform ideas through technology. With avid enthusiasm for emerging technologies, he delves into their functions and implications, leveraging an extensive and diverse background. His expertise adeptly bridges the gap between innovation and expression, offering a distinctive perspective in the ever-evolving landscape of technology and AI. He is also a passionate advocate for diversity in his work and a frequent speaker on this topic.

Eva Pascoe co-founded the first Internet Café, "Cyberia" (London, mid 1990s), set up the first Topshop online store and is currently Ecommerce Director at The Retail Practice. Since 2014 Eva has worked on Web3 infrastructure start-ups, consulted on blockchain accelerator, and is an angel investor in women-led sustainable fashion companies. She campaigns for hydropower blockchain solutions, is a Royal Society of Arts London council member, is published in The Guardian, The Independent and has appeared on Newsnight and BBC Question Time. Her speculative fiction focuses on the future of crypto payments, cybersecurity and reproductive health. http://www.evapascoe.com/bio/

Eddie Robson is the author of the novels Drunk On All Your Strange New Words, Hearts Of Oak and Tomorrow Never Knows. He created and wrote the BBC Radio sitcom Welcome To Our Village, Please Invade Carefully and the Audible rom-com Car Crash. His TV credits include the animated shows Sarah & Duck and The Amazing World Of Gumball and three episodes of the Chinese adaptation of Humans, and he has written many comic strips for 2000AD. He lives in Lancaster.

Jesse Rowell (he/him) is an award-winning science fiction author whose work explores naturalism, technology, and the human condition. He can be found at www.jesserowell.com.

Dr Gabrielle Samuel is a lecturer in environmental justice and health at the Department of Global Health and Social Medicine, King's College London, UK, co-director of the SHADE research hub, which sits at the intersection of Sustainability, Health, AI, Digital technologies and the

Environment, and a visiting scholar at Clinical Ethics, Law and Society (CELS), Oxford University. Gabrielle's interests include the ethical and social issues associated with the use of digital technologies and how they intersect with environmental concerns.

Britta Schulte writes. From one-line dystopias to PhD theses, he creates technologies that we might get, to ask if we really want them. Sometimes he might create utopias. Or fairytales. Stories are spread over the internet via @brifrischu, self-published in zines and printed in selected anthologies. His academic work mainly poses the question of how we develop technologies to support aging with a strong focus on intimacy. And on how we use stories to learn more.

Sophie Sparham is a poet and writer from Derby. They have written commissions for BBC Radio 4, The V&A and The People's History Museum. Their latest collection 'The Man Who Ate 50,000 Weetabix' came out in April 2021 via Verve Poetry Press. Sophie's work has been published in Orbis, Under the Radar and The Morning Star. Their poem Sunrise Over Aldi won third place in the 2020 Charles Causley International Poetry Competition. Sophie has been longlisted and shortlisted for the Outspoken Award for page poetry. They co-direct Derby Poetry Festival.

Vaughan Stanger originally trained as an astronomer before moving into the defence and aerospace sector, where he led R&D projects. Nowadays, he writes speculative fiction full-time. He has seen over fifty short stories published, including in Best of British Science Fiction, Nature Futures, and Interzone. Most of his stories have been reprinted, including ten in foreign translations. His most recent collection is The Last Moonshot & Other Stories. Vaughan posts about his writing adventures at vaughanstanger.com and @VaughanStanger on BlueSky and Mastodon.

Prof Claire Steves is a Professor of Ageing and Health at King's College London, and a consultant geriatrician at Guys and St Thomas's Foundation Trust in London. Over the last 15 years she has studied how the environment (both inside and around us) and our genetics interact to influence how we age, using a large study of older adult twins, TwinsUK. She has used this understanding to develop and test methods to help older adults to maintain resilience in later life.

Tehnuka (she/they) is a writer and volcanologist from Aotearoa New Zealand. She likes to find herself up volcanoes, down caves, and in unexpected places; everyone else, however, can find her online at www.tehnuka.dreamhosters.com, and some of her published science fiction in Reckoning 7, Afterglow: Climate Fiction for Future Ancestors, and Immigrant Sci-Fi Short Stories. She was the 2023 winner of the national Sir Julius Vogel award for Best New Talent in speculative fiction.

Prashant Vaze is a writer and environmentalist based in Goa, India. He has published two non-fiction books on the energy transition, and a YA novel "The Rising Tide" about climate change, AIs and family secrets. He worked on policy at an international climate finance not-for-profit and advises central banks, governments and businesses on financing green investment. Previously he was an economist in the UK government. He is currently penning a prequel to his earlier novel.

Martin C W Walker is director of banking and finance at the Center for Evidence-Based Management. He has written multiple articles, papers and a book on Fintech. Previous roles include global head of securities finance IT at Dresdner Kleinwort and global head of prime brokerage technology at RBS Markets. He received his master's degree in computing science from Imperial College, London, and his bachelor's degree in economics from the London School of Economics and Political Science.

David W Wood is Chair of London Futurists, where he has hosted around 300 public meetings on futurist topics since 2008. He is also Executive Director of the LEV (Longevity Escape Velocity) Foundation – mission "conducting and inspiring research to comprehensively cure and prevent human age-related disease". He is the author or co-author of 12 books about the future, including "Vital Foresight", "The Singularity Principles", and "Sustainable Superabundance". Earlier in his life he was one of the pioneers of the smartphone industry.

Acknowledgements

The editors would like to thank and acknowledge all the hard work that has gone into this wonderful book. There are far too many to thank individually, on top of those who are already listed as contributors. But, we want to say a huge thank you to those in our personal lives who have given us the significant amount of time and space we needed to get this book 'done'. We also want to acknowledge the Cybersalonistas who have helped along the way, with themes and titles and so on. This has been a truly collaborative effort all round and it has been a pleasure to work with all of those involved, in whatever way that has been.

Cybersalon Press, a London-based emerging independent publisher, is carving its niche in the literary landscape by specialising in anthologies of short stories within the realm of speculative fiction. Born out of a well-established think tank campaigning for Digital Rights known as Cybersalon, this new publishing venture offers a unique perspective to the forefront of storytelling. It showcases the imaginative flair of established authors but also champions new voices from under represented communities, inviting fresh narratives that challenge traditional boundaries in the context of technology, science and culture. In an era where digital rights and technological progress shape our world at a fast pace, Cybersalon Press seeks to explore the intersection of technology, society and human experience through the lens of speculative fiction. By welcoming perspectives from diverse backgrounds and communities often marginalised in mainstream discussion of digital policy rights and transformation, we seek to amplify voices that might otherwise go unheard. The aim is to foster more inclusive and representative literary outputs, ensuring the way we engage with the ever-evolving digital world reflects the needs of all of us.

Milton Keynes UK
Ingram Content Group UK Ltd.
UKHW010102080324
439117UK00001B/2